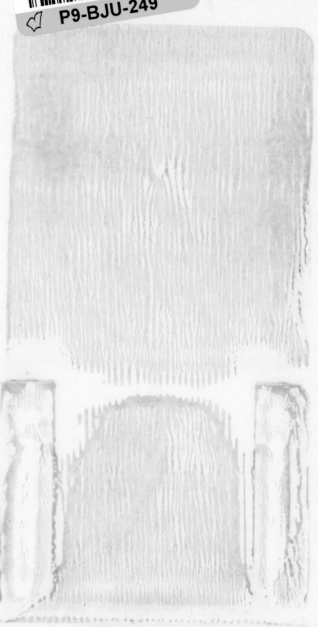

THE MOVIES AS MEDIUM

By Lewis Jacobs

The Movies as Medium
The Emergence of Film Art
Introduction to the Art of the Movies
The Rise of the American Film

THE MOVIES
AS MEDIUM

Selected, arranged and introduced by

LEWIS JACOBS

OCTAGON BOOKS

A DIVISION OF
FARRAR, STRAUS AND GIROUX
NEW YORK 1973

Reprinted 1973

OCTAGON BOOKS
A division of Farrar, Straus and Giroux
19 Union Square West
New York 10003

Library of Congress catalog card number: 72-12837

ISBN 0-374-94139-4

For Ellen and Stuart, Carol and Paul

Preface

THERE IS AN URGENCY today to learn more about the fundamentals of motion-picture expression. Critics and filmmakers are questioning old conclusions and attempting to arrive at a deeper understanding of film art—an awareness comparable to that already achieved for painting, writing, and music. The rich outpouring of distinctive pictures, the flood of serious writing about film in books and periodicals, the upsurge of film courses across the nation in colleges and high schools and now even in the elementary lower grades, clearly demonstrate the new and more intense involvement of audiences and practitioners—particularly of the current "under-thirty" generation—with the creative values of film expression. This book undertakes to investigate the nature of the movies as a medium, to help those film enthusiasts who recognize the cogency of cinematic art and craft and are determined to understand it.

The essays collected here scrutinize the fundamental resources and processes of film expression. It is hoped that by presenting them in this particular interlocking order, we will enable the reader to discover for himself the correlation between means and end. A second intention is to provide a storehouse of ideas about film technique and form which can furnish a framework for evaluating what one receives from different kinds of film. An additional objective is to stimulate thoughts and observations about film art, not based solely upon individual taste, contemporary fashion, or content, but fortified by comparisons and distinctions of a more definitive plastic nature. To throw further light on the recurring question of criteria and to make the reader aware of the multiple aspects of film art, the book starts with personal statements by a variety of directors expressing divergent views and styles.

The following pages will reveal, more than any formal acknowl-edgment, my indebtedness to those filmmakers, scholars, theorists, and critics whose essays help make up this book. To others whom I have been unable to include but whose works have influenced and helped shape my ideas, I declare my indebtedness by includ-ing them in the bibliography at the end of the text, and urge the reader to follow them up on his own.

I wish to thank Jay Chapman, who was kind enough to read cer-tain sections of this volume and to give me excellent criticism.

One debt that can never be sufficiently repaid is that which I owe my wife for her continuous helpfulness and guidance in every aspect of this work.

LEWIS JACOBS

Acknowledgments

I wish to thank the following authors, representatives, and publishers for their courtesy in granting me permission to reprint the selections included in this anthology:

Arthur Goldsmith, "The Ambiguity of the Photographic Image." Reprinted from *Infinity*, March 1964, by permission of the author.

Nicola Chiaromonte, "On Image and Word." Reprinted from *Encounter*, January 1963, by permission of the author.

Herbert A. Lightman, "The Subjective Camera." Reprinted from *American Cinematographer*, February 1946, by permission of the author and the American Society of Cinematographers Editorial Board.

Gregg Toland, "Composition of the Moving Image." From *The Complete Photographer*, No. 16, © Copyright 1942 by National Educational Alliance, Inc. Reprinted with the permission of the publisher and the Greystone Press.

Ezra Goodman, "Movement in Movies." Reprinted from *American Cinematographer*, June 1945, by permission of the author.

Hilary Harris, "Thoughts on Movement." Reprinted from *Vision*, No. 5, Spring 1962, by permission of the author.

Stanley J. Solomon, "Modern Uses of the Moving Camera." Reprinted from *Film Heritage*, Winter 1965–66, by permission of the author and the publishers.

Irving Pichel, "Change of Camera Viewpoint (Seeing with the Camera)." Reprinted from *Hollywood Quarterly* (now *Film Quarterly*), I, 138–145, by permission of The Regents. © 1946 by The Regents of the University of California.

Robert Gessner, "The Faces of Time." Reprinted from *Theatre Arts*, July 1962, by permission of the author.

Maya Deren, "Tempo and Tension." Reprinted from *Movie Makers*, May 1947, by permission of Mrs. M. Deren.

John Howard Lawson, "Time and Space." From *Film: The Creative Process* by John Howard Lawson. Copyright © 1964 by John Howard Lawson. Reprinted by permission of Hill & Wang, Inc.

Ivor Montagu, "Rhythm." Reprinted from *Film World* by Ivor Montagu, by permission of the author and the publishers, Penguin Books Ltd. © 1964 by Ivor Montagu.

Carl Dreyer, "Color and Color Films." Reprinted from *Films in Review*, April 1955, by permission of the publishers.

Sergei Eisenstein, "One Path to Color." Reprinted from *Literaturnaya Gazeta*, July 1960, by permission of Jay Leyda (translator) and *Sight and Sound*.

William Johnson, "Coming to Terms with Color." © 1966 by the Regents of the University of California. Reprinted from *Film Quarterly*, Vol. XX, No. 1, by permission of the Regents, and the author.

Bela Belazs, "The Acoustic World." Reprinted from *Theory of Film*, by permission of the publishers, Dobson Books Ltd. © 1953 by Dobson Books Ltd.

Henwar Rodakiewicz, "Treatment of Sound in *The City*." Printed by permission of the author.

Kurt Weill, "Music in the Movies." Reprinted from *Harper's Bazaar*, September 1946, by permission of the publishers and the Estate of Kurt Weill.

Alexander Bakshy, "Dynamic Composition." Reprinted from *Experimental Cinema*, No. 1, 1931, by permission of the publishers.

Arthur Lennig, "The Sense of Form in Cinema." Reprinted and revised from *Film Notes*, 1960, by permission of the author.

Jonas Mekas, "The Other Direction." Reprinted from *New Cinema Review*, September 1969, by permission of the author and the publishers.

For the privilege of reproducing brief statements from interviews and articles by writers and directors, I am grateful to those persons and publications listed under each quotation.

Photos courtesy of Arnold Eagle, Saul Bass Associates, Cinerama Inc., Columbia Pictures, Lewis Jacobs Collection, Janus Films, Museum of Modern Art Film Library, Paramount Pictures, Francis Thompson, Twentieth Century–Fox, United Artists, and Slavko Vorkapitch.

Contents

NOTES ON THE CONTRIBUTORS

PART ONE

Aims and Attitudes

"Creation must take place between the pen and the paper, not before in a thought or afterwards in a recasting."

GERTRUDE STEIN

Directors Speak:

"*I*t is under the director's guidance that the film is created, transformed from the inadequately expressed idea of the script to a living sequence of sound and images. And for the appearance of every image he is dependent on the cameraman. It would be simpler if we could regard the cameraman as a 'technician' merely who complies with the director's demands; but, to demand specific effects, a director must be a cameraman himself, which is rare. It is not perhaps generally appreciated that composition, lighting and movement are very often the cameraman's responsibility, and yet these are among the chief means of expression in the cinema."

Lindsay Anderson

From "Creative Elements" by Lindsay Anderson, *Sequence*, Fall 1948

"It is the story which fascinates me most. The images are the medium through which a story can be understood. To be a lover of form for me means being a lover of substance. I am very susceptible to landscape. When I am shooting a film, I always try to establish a rapport between characters and landscape."

Michelangelo Antonioni

From "There Must Be a Reason for Every Film" by Michelangelo Antonioni, *Film and Filming*, April 1959

3

"To make a film is for me a very personal experience. It is a driving force like hunger and thirst. Some people express themselves by writing books, painting pictures, climbing mountains, beating their children or dancing the samba. I express myself by making films."

Ingmar Bergman

Quoted in "Notes on the Films of Ingmar Bergman" by Ian Jarvie, *Film Journal*, November 1959

"The ultimate spell is created out of that moment in the approach to the work of art where the intellect is ultimately baffled and the spell reverberates back in time over all the moments of the approach. I see the intellect as always in charge of and charged by feeling."

Stan Brakhage

From "Notes" by Stan Brakhage, *Film Culture*, No. 25, Summer 1962

"I strive for a cinema that will give me an integral vision of reality; it will increase my knowledge of things and beings, and will open to me the marvelous world of the unknown, which I can neither read about in the daily press nor find in the street."

Luis Buñuel

From "Cinema: An Instrument of Poetry" by Luis Buñuel, *Theatre Arts*, July 1962

"Whenever I am making a film, I find myself in a dream-like trance. The outside world completely disappears and the dream life of the studio fills my whole existence."

Jean Cocteau

Interviewed by Francis Koval, *Sight and Sound*, August 1950

"We have to wrench the film out of the embrace of naturalism. We have to tell ourselves it is a waste of time to copy reality. We must use the camera to create a new language of style, a new artistic form."

Carl Dreyer

From "Thoughts on My Craft" by Carl Dreyer, *Sight and Sound*, Winter 1955–56

"What I am interested in is showing the things behind the things, not just to make statements on what can be seen. I'm often criticized for this—people say that I see reality fantastically deformed. But that is a superficial comment. I think everyone sees life around him in a more-than-superficial manner. What's the sense of being 'objective' in film? I don't even think it's physically possible."

Federico Fellini

From an interview by Gideon Bachman in *Mademoiselle*, November 1964

"You don't compose a film on the set. You put a pre-designed composition on film. It is wrong to liken a director to an author. He is more like an architect, if he is creative. An architect conceives his plans from given premises—the purpose of the building, its size, its terrain. If he is clever, he can do something within these limitations."

John Ford

From an interview by Jean Mitry in *Films in Review*, August-September 1955

"If to direct is a glance, to edit is a beating of the heart. To anticipate is the characteristic of both. But what one seeks to foresee in space, the other seeks in time."

Jean-Luc Godard

From "Montage, Mon Beau" by Jean-Luc Godard, *Cahiers du Cinema*, No. 3, 1966

"Sometimes I plan as many as six hundred camera set-ups before I begin to shoot. If I ever tried to improvise . . . on the set, I couldn't get the effects or reactions I want to get . . . My interest is in how to pluck the emotion from people . . . by juxtaposition of images on the screen."

Alfred Hitchcock

Quoted in "Pete Martin Calls on Hitchcock" *Saturday Evening Post*, July 27, 1957

"The most important element to me is always the idea that I'm trying to express, and everything technical is only a method to make the idea into clear form. I'm always working on the idea whether I am writing, directing, choosing music, or cutting."

John Huston

From an interview with Gideon Bachman in *Film Quarterly*, Fall 1965

"I am trying in all the films I do either to eliminate as much dialogue as I can or to make it an embroidery on the outskirts of action. Part of the behavior is what they say, but not the essential part of it, and in that sense I think my work is getting more cinematic."

Elia Kazan

From "On the Young Agony" by Elia Kazan, *Films and Filming*, March 1962

"The important thing is not to start thinking of the camera too soon, because then you stop concentrating on what's happening and start worrying about how somebody will get from one place to another and what will happen then. There's a way to shoot any scene. So you work first on the content of the scene, then on how you'll shoot it."

Stanley Kubrick

From "How I Learned to Stop Worrying and Love the Cinema" by Stanley Kubrick, *Films and Filming*, June 1963

"In motion pictures both image and sound must be treated with special care. In my view, a motion picture stands or falls on the effective combination of these two factors. Truly cinematic sound is neither merely accompanying sound (easy and explanatory) nor the natural sounds captured at the time of simultaneous recording. In other words, cinematic sound is that which does not simply add to, but multiplies, two or three times, the effect of the image."

Akiro Kurosawa

From "On Image and Sound" by Akiro Kurosawa, *Cinema*, August 1963

"I believe in artistic rebellion. I think new approaches, new forms are needed to reflect the changed world we live in."

Fritz Lang

From *Happily Ever After* by Fritz Lang (Penguin Books, 1948)

"I never use a script with any camera directions, simply because I never know what I want until I get on the set. I feel that what one gets on film is only the raw material. I believe that my greatest value to a production comes after the shooting. I work on every phase of the cutting, mixing, looping, titling."

Richard Lester

From an interview in *Saturday Review*, December 25, 1965

"The only thing that is an absolute for any art that deserves the name is point of view (i.e., content). No point of view is sterility. Sterility, no matter how it's dressed up, is the death of theatre and films."

Joseph Losey

From "Mirror to Life" by Joseph Losey, *Films and Filming*, June 1959

"I'm always amused by avant-garde critics who'll probably sit
down and say about this film, 'Well, the two-frame cuts came
from *Last Year at Marienbad*, and this came from . . .'—which is
nonsense. There's one general premise: almost anything that any
of us has done you can find in a John Ford film."

Sidney Lumet

From "Keep Them on the Hook" by Sidney Lumet, *Films and
Filming*, October 1964

"I am totally involved with the sensory business about motion
without any intellectual story, or anything else other than just motion."

Len Lye

Quoted in "Len Lye Speaks at the Film Makers' Cinematheque"
Film Culture, Spring 1967

"There is an area in the human mind (or heart) which can be
reached only through cinema, through that cinema which is always
awake, always changing. Only such cinema can reveal, describe,
make us conscious, hint at what we really are or what we aren't, or
sing the true and changing beauty of the world around us."

Jonas Mekas

From "Notes on the New American Cinema" by Jonas Mekas,
Film Culture, Spring 1962

"In exterior settings the details, the light bring essential cinematic
ideas. One is in contact with life, which one is not, on the stage or
studio. The people and the landscape dictate to you elements
which have nothing to do with theories, be they even of Eisenstein."

Satyajit Ray

From "Film to Film" by Satyajit Ray, *Cahiers du Cinema*, No. 3,
1966

"If the purpose is to make the audience laugh, cry, be excited or frightened, then the greatest quality a film can have is the sense of the precise rightness in the means used to that end."

Sir Carol Reed

Quoted by Harvey Breit in "I Give the Public What I Like," *The New York Times*, January 15, 1950

"All technical refinements discourage me. Perfect photography, larger screens, hi-fi sounds, all make it possible for mediocrities slavishly to reproduce nature; and this reproduction bores me. What interests me is the interpretation of life by an artist. The personality of a filmmaker interests me more than the copy of an object."

Jean Renoir

Quoted in *Film: Book One*, 1959

"For me film is an attempt, still very crude and primitive, to approach the complexity of thought and its mechanism. But I stress the fact that this is only a tiny step forward by comparison with what we should be able to do someday . . . I find that as soon as we delve into the unconscious, an emotion may be born . . . I believe that, in life, we don't think chronologically, that our decisions never correspond to an ordered logic . . . I am interested in exploring that universe, from the point of view of truth, if not of morality."

Alain Resnais

From an interview by R. M. Franchi in *New York Film Bulletin*, March 1962

"A director, I believe, has only one responsibility always. That is to say as clearly, fully and passionately as he is able to. This is the task of every artist, and he can only hope that if he is himself articulate enough he will speak to other people. The more the better. But he must never try to think of his material in audience terms, or he is likely to fall between every stool."

Tony Richardson

From "The Man Behind an Angry Young Man" by Tony Richardson, *Films and Filming*, January 1959

"The cinema is a work of art when motion conforms to a perceptible rhythm with pause and pace and where all aspects of the continuous image relate to the whole."

Josef von Sternberg

Quoted in "Josef von Sternberg" by Herman Weinberg, *Film Heritage,* Winter 1965–66

"I'm one of those who feels everything—everything—that goes
into a picture affects the viewer, although the viewer doesn't realize the impact of tiny, minor things being built up for him. This
working upon the subconscious has a great effect, greater than
most moviegoers or movie makers realize."

George Stevens

Quoted in "Wrinkles and Realism" by Jack Goodman, *The New York Times,* September 9, 1951

"Aesthetic considerations are what concern me most. I believe, for
instance, that there are two kinds of cinema, one stemming from
Lumière and the other from Delluc. Lumière invented the cinema
to film nature or action. Delluc, who was a novelist and critic,
thought that one could use this invention to film ideas or action
which have a meaning other than the obvious one, and so, closer
to the other arts . . ."

François Truffaut

From an interview by Louis Marcorelles in *Sight and Sound,* Winter 1961–62

"Let us agree once more; the eye and the ear. The eye peeks; the
ear eavesdrops. Distribution of functions: Radio—ear-edited,
"hear!" Cinema—eye-edited, *"see!"*

Dziga Vertov

From "The Writings of Dziga Vertov" *Film Culture,* Summer
1962

"Pictures can't be assembled like an automobile, or some other factory product, and still be artistic. A film has to represent the slant of the person who makes it, and that can only be achieved by permitting the maker complete freedom."

King Vidor

From "Vidor's Individualist Manifesto" by Bosley Crowther, *The New York Times*, November 13, 1938

"I think that color on the screen must be applied in psychological doses, not mechanically. That is why we do not 'observe' color; it means little to us and we are not conscious of it. After some time the viewer does not look at a color film any differently than at a black and white film. Color is a factor in art, and must be used where it has a function to fulfill."

Andrezej Wajda

From "Destroying the Commonplace" by Andrezej Wajda, *Films and Filming*, November 1961

"Cinema as a medium of expression fascinates me, of course, but ever so often—when directing—I ask myself whether we really know what we are doing and whether there is any reasonable proportion between the thousands of man-hours spent on the director's job and the final result."

Orson Welles

Interviewed by Francis Koval in *Sight and Sound*, December 1950

"I hate to have people face each other and talk-talk-talk-talk, even if they are in a moving taxicab. I make *moving pictures*. On the other hand you will not find in my pictures any phony camera moves or fancy set-ups to prove that I am a moving-picture director."

Billy Wilder

Interviewed by *Playboy*, June 1963

"Gregg Toland's remarkable facility for handling background and foreground action has enabled me to develop a better technique of staging my scenes. I can have action and reaction in the same shot, without having to cut back and forth from individual cuts of the characters. This makes for smooth continuity and an almost effortless flow of the scene, for more interesting composition in each shot, and lets the spectator look from one to the other character at his own will, do his own cutting."

William Wyler

From "No Magic Wand" by William Wyler, *The Screen Writer*, February 1947

"The greatest influence on my style, if there is such a thing, I would say was Flaherty, with whom I worked for a while. I can't say that I tried to imitate his style, but I did become deeply influenced by his point of view on picture making and life in general. In a sense some of the methods I use stem from Bob's point of view of picture making. As you probably remember, he liked to spend a long time with the subjects of the film he was about to make . . . In a sense I try to do the same thing."

Fred Zinnemann

From "A Conflict of Conscience" by Fred Zinnemann, *Films and Filming*, December 1959

PART TWO

The Nature of Film Expression

"The desire to build up a world apart and self-
contained, existing in its own right . . . represents humanization in the deepest, certainly the
most enigmatic, sense of the word."

ANDRÉ MALRAUX

The Raw Material

LEWIS JACOBS

Whatever else can be said about motion pictures, there is no denying that they are a form of creative expression. There is also no denying that filmmakers, like artists in other media, are endeavoring to communicate a private vision whose distinction resides in the way a selected subject is scrutinized, developed, and given form and meaning through the use of the medium's unique means of expression. For an artist to control and utilize his medium, he must be aware of the raw materials, resources, and methods of composition generic to his chosen medium. The painter seeks to express his world, attitude, and point of view through the means of color and form. The structural elements of his composition—line, light, space, mass, volume, texture, pattern—are directed toward an organization built of color. Color functions as the core, the raw material of the painter's art. The musical composer works in the same fashion with sound. Through the succession and relationships of sounds, he builds an aural composition. Sound is the raw material of his medium. Language is the means whereby the writer expresses himself. His raw material is words. Through the selection and arrangement of special words in a special order he is able to communicate facts, feelings, ideas.

At first glance, one might assume that the motion-picture medium is merely a combination of these and other, older arts and therefore that its raw materials and method of composition are a conglomerate of these. But one needs only to view films to realize that while the motion picture does utilize aspects of other media, something new, special, and peculiar has been evoked which sets the screen medium apart from other forms of expression and endows it with a character and identity of its own. This is apparent whether the film is a drama, documentary, educational or spectacle, fantasy or newsreel, biography or cine-poem. Every film, whether its subject is factual or imaginary, confronts the viewer with a special kind of experience, a cinematic experience, which involves a confluence of senses—visual, aural, kinesthetic, spacial, temporal—that is different from that of any other medium.

To probe this difference, to arrive at an understanding of its nature, requires some comprehension of the medium's technological base. The advent of the movies waited upon the invention of a special kind of camera, a special type of celluloid film stock, and a particular kind of projector which could present hundreds of individual photographs in a continuous flow on a large screen. The sequential order of these photographs—shifting from the representation of one person to another, one place to another, one event to another, and one duration of time to another—and the speed of these changes, produced an illusion of movement that evoked a meaning beyond that contained in any single photograph of the assemblage.

The combination of "shooting" the individual photographs, assembling them into a particular order, and projecting them at a certain rate of speed provided the new medium both with a means of expression and with a mode of composition inherent in its technique. In actual practice, the making of a motion picture begins with the recording of subject matter into pictures and sounds on individual strips of film, called shots. The ability to shape the shots is what enables the filmmaker to express his thoughts and feelings. The shot, then, is the movie's primary means of expression. As such, it can be regarded as the medium's fundamental raw material, out of which is constructed the entire film.

Although technically a shot is defined by a change in camera position—on the screen it may last as briefly as $\frac{1}{24}$ of a second or as long as ten minutes—structurally the shot is the smallest component of film expression, the indivisible unit of composition from which the larger structures are composed and into which they can be divided. Thematically, the shot contains an incomplete fragment of meaning and depends upon the succession and sequence of other shots for complete significance.

Two or more shots with the same locale make a larger division of composition, called a scene. Its unity is determined by a singleness of objective and the completion of a segment of meaning. A single shot can also be a scene, when its photographic content has a completed unity of meaning.

Two or more scenes, connected, form a larger division, called a sequence. The contents of a sequence have a completed unity of action and meaning similar to that of a chapter in a book or an episode in a story. A number of sequences, combined, make up what is technically called the continuity. The completed motion picture is therefore a complex organization of pictures and sounds derived from the choice and order of shots.

If shots are to serve the creative impulse of the filmmaker in the same way that color serves the painter, sound serves the composer, and words serve the writer, then they must be viewed as the basic means of his medium, the essential building units of his film organization. The more integral their role and the greater their interaction, the more meaningful becomes their content and the more energetic the film structure. Considered in this way, the shot's value consists of more than the photographic representation of its subject (which is usually taken for the whole of it). How much more depends on an awareness of the aggregate factors and relationships embodied in the context of the shot's visual and aural organization and of its relation to the scene, sequence, and continuity as a whole.

Everything that is essential for a film structure must first be expressed in shots. Shots are not invariable in their properties, but mutable. Subject matter can be made to take on different appearances, viewpoints, aspects of motion, tone, color, speed, and sound, depending upon the way it is photographed. Shots need not be a literal representation of matter, any more than color for the painter need be a literal rendering of color in nature. Shots can provide subject matter with an actuality that is explicit and recognizable and also with associations and connotations of meaning, implications, overtones, feelings, thoughts. In addition, shots can suggest degrees of fantasy, imagination, stylization. A shot derives its fullest meaning from the manner in which its components are selected, arranged, and finally related to other shots in succession.

In this regard, the filmmaker has at his disposal certain variable plastic elements which can be molded to give his content cohesion, individuality, and value. These are: image, movement, time, space, color, and sound. For the filmmaker these six elements constitute the primary substances from which a shot is composed. They provide the shot with definition, impact, and style. How significantly a shot functions depends first upon how eloquently the plastic elements are used, and then upon how they interact with other plastic elements in a meaningful series of shots.

To understand the particular nature of the plastic elements, their expressive possibilities, and how they function within and between shots, it is helpful to isolate and study each element separately. However, this analytical method necessarily breaks up into parts what is essentially a unity. The plastic elements never exist singly but always in combination, a combination in which one or more may dominate—imagery here, movement there, sound or color in a third. Their separation here is wholly arbitrary, a kind of vivisection for study purposes.

In this connection it is important to bear in mind that there is a danger of becoming too preoccupied with the means of expression, so that what is expressed—the *matter*—is neglected. What is of first importance, as in any art, is the subject and the artist's attitude toward life. Film technique, like technique in all arts, is only a means toward an end. The deployment of the plastic elements and the style of expression are of value only insofar as these forces serve the subject and theme, or provide a breakthrough, a new approach to the medium itself. In the final analysis, the determining factor of a movie's significance is something more than the sum of its technique and form. Nevertheless, it must not be assumed that what a film reveals about man's concern with being alive, or his involvement with a medium, can be conveyed without communicating the medium's own being in terms of individuality and imagination.

It is also important to recognize that, as in every medium, one overriding condition exists that defies the very act of analysis, and that is the always unique ingredient, the individual artist himself. It is his abilities, his decisions, his choices, his acts that create the work. The final distinction, what makes one film stand out from another, remains indefinable as the individual's personal vision.

PART THREE

The Plastic Elements

"This is what makes the cinema an art: it creates a reality with forms. It is in its forms that we must look for its true content."

ALAIN ROBBE-GRILLET

I. IMAGE

The Meaningful Image

LEWIS JACOBS

*P*erhaps the most obvious plastic element of a motion picture is the screen image—the essential factor upon which filmic expression depends for its existence, the core component to which all the other plastic elements are related. Although the subject matter may have attracted the viewer to a film, it is the images which first capture his attention and, when caught, then control and direct his interest. They enable him to pause for a studied examination of a detail, direct his survey to a panoramic view, or carry him along with a speeding vehicle. Every image, therefore, even if on the screen for a brief instant, is of importance if it is to convey subject matter clearly and meaningfully, and sustain the viewer's concern.

It is composition which gives the screen image its precision and determines the degree of its effectiveness. There are five factors which govern the composition of an image: the way a subject is lit; the subject's relation to the screen frame; the distance between the camera and the subject; the angle of vision from which the subject is seen; the visual interaction between two or more images in succession.

The factor in composition which first strikes the viewer's attention is light. Without illumination of some sort, the motion-picture camera could not reproduce the subject's image onto film. It is light which enables the camera lens to transmit an image of what is before it into a photographic reproduction. Thus light and visual composition are interlocked.

In nature, light is more often a conglomeration of tones, lights and shadows, highlights and reflections, so that objects and forms stand out, merge into the background, or are lost in deep shadows without any organizing relationship. The variations of light and shade in real life are so complex that confusion can result when they are reproduced representationally. Sometimes this is the effect desired and the confusion is designed purposefully. But usually the control and arrangement of light become mandatory in creating order from disorder.

By composing the qualities of light and its complement, shadow, the director can render his subject matter in the way he wishes it to be seen. Skillfully used, light and shade—through designed chiaroscuro and the degrees of brightness, darkness, diffusion, and intensity of illumination—are an effective means for evoking atmosphere, form, mood, and emotion, endowing the pictorial image with clarity, vigor, and design.

Light also helps create the conditions for the composition of images in succession. When other visual determinants of the image, such as shape, size, and angle, are artfully arranged in the interplay of light and shade, illumination can serve to unite one image with another through contrasts and similarities of pattern, tone, texture, scale, and area. Here the infinite number of ways of varying the contrast between light and dark not only affords the possibility of evoking a vast number of different sensations from individual images but becomes an expressive means for creating a sense of movement to lead the eye purposefully from image to image and give the pictorial progression itself a distinction it might otherwise not have.

Since every image in a motion picture is generally seen within the rectangular frame of the screen, there is at once a second discipline of composition to be taken into consideration: shape. The borders of the screen establish both a fixed surface that has to be filled and a specific shape in which the subject matter has to be composed. Within these enclosing conditions, the subject's physical arrangement, its lights and darks, its lines and masses, balance and proportions, when contained in a way that is ordered and functional with regard to individual images and the ordered succession of these images, contributes further to the effectiveness of screen imagery.

The rectangular shape of the screen can be altered in a number of ways to give the composition variety and make the image more apt. The use of spot-lighting effects and such camera devices as masks, irises, distortion prisms, split and multiple screens allow for a diversity of shapes that destroy the screen's rectangular proportions and provide opportunities for "dramatic" framing of images. By breaking with the familiar format of the screen, the filmmaker can endow the pictorial image with freshness, vitality, and activity, adding movement and tension to its sequential order.

The most impressive examples of the manipulation of the screen's shape occur in Griffith's *Intolerance* (1916). With daring originality, he cuts into the then square shape of the screen, sometimes to block out entire sections, at other times to open the entire screen frame gradually from a minute area. He contrasts the format and size of shapes so that the viewer's eye is kept moving from image to image. The screen is sliced down the center to reveal an elongated image, or the screen is cut diagonally to emphasize an oblique image or a detail in a way that adds a feeling of variety and dynamism to the flow of images.

Like shape, size too can be manipulated. The distance of camera to subject sets up a dimensional proportion in relation to the size of the screen. If the camera is close to the subject, details are enlarged, what is seen takes on a special import. With the camera at a greater distance, the broader aspects of the subject are highlighted. From such visual appearances came the technical concepts of close-up, medium shot, full shot, and long shot, each designating camera proximity to the subject.

On the screen, size has a qualitative as well as a quantitative aspect. The size of an object affects our feelings as well as our recognition and understanding of it. "Big" and "little" particularize and generalize. The close-up focuses attention on what is important through magnification of relevant details and exclusion of unwanted portions of a subject. The full shot encompasses all of a subject and facilitates recognition. A constant change in subject size defines salient features, clarifies them, or intensifies the viewer's awareness of them.

The ordered succession of changes in the size of the subject—

whether regular, irregular, or random—can be a means of forcing the viewer to experience a consciousness of movement in time. The different impressions he receives from successive enlargements and reductions of proportions, measurements, and dimensions of the subject direct his eyes to move quickly over some images, slower over others, compel him to make an abrupt stop or cause him to continue, and in this way evoke a sense of motion. Even though the subject itself may be stationary, the visual stimulus is mobile. The directional force provided by the variations in size thus adds a further dynamism to the screen's images.

Subject size is closely related to another important aspect of image composition: camera viewpoint or angle. As size relates to the distance of subject to camera, so angle relates to the view from which the camera sees the subject—above, below, straight on, or oblique. The camera angle can force the viewer to observe a subject from a particular point of view, concentrate his attention on some aspect or characteristic of the subject, shift his attention, suggest a relationship between separate images, or justify some logic of film structure.

For example, the filmmaker may wish to minimize the subject. A high angle can make an object appear small and insignificant. A high angle may also make the patterns of a subject's movement— if taken from the proper distance—more clearly discernible. A low angle, on the other hand, exaggerates height; it can endow an object with unexpected dominating force. The manipulation of camera angles can be equally significant in distorting and accenting content by changing the customary way of seeing things, thereby adding dramatic, comic, or psychological import not inherent in the material, and so become a means to fresh vision and insight.

The camera angle is important not only to composition but also to the clarity of the film's continuity. Angle may serve as an index of the camera's (and the spectator's) point of view. Are the pictorial images being seen through the eyes of the director, from the viewpoint of a detached observer or of an involved participant, or perhaps from the subjective viewpoint of one of the characters in the film? Being able to distinguish and make clear first-person, third-person, or multiple viewpoints becomes a matter of compelling significance. Each point of view is potentially a different aspect of the same material seen through diverse angles of vision.

Each must therefore be conveyed in a different way if the viewer is to know from which point the action of the film is being shown.

Through light and shade, shape, size, and angle, the filmmaker can synchronize detail and assign a purpose and cohesion to the screen image. But the film image, no matter how well composed and pleasing to the eye, is not meant to be an isolated thing or self-sufficient as is a painting or photograph. Its sole justification is its contribution to other images that precede and follow it. As such, it only comes into full meaning when joined with others in a continuity of time. This affects the choices and decisions as to how images are to be shaped, molded, and composed, for they must be considered not just individually but in association, in sequence. Thus the designed and arranged interplay of compositional devices becomes the means of pointing up such relationships and uniting the images in a continuous flow. Because of this, movement is a vital factor in image composition. But since, in addition to adding visual flow to pictorial compositions, movement raises problems, it is discussed at length, as a separate plastic element, in a later section.

From the earliest days of movies there have been films whose major strength and effectiveness come from an intense pictorial flair. Often these movies are imbued with a visual imagery that overcomes other weaknesses and achieves a specific personal style. At the height of the silent era, such studio productions as *The Cabinet of Dr. Caligari* (1919), *Siegfried* (1923), *Metropolis* (1925), *The Last Laugh* (1925), *Variety* (1925), and *Sunrise* (1927), among others, stood out for individualized lighting, composition, and camera angles.

Stemming from different artistic doctrines, the Soviet pictures of the same period—*Potemkin* (1925), *Ten Days That Shook the World* (1927), *Storm Over Asia* (1928), *Soil* (1928)—showed another kind of fresh pictorial vigor and high visual imagination. Soviet filmmakers turned their cameras away from studio sets to shoot in real forests, city streets, mountains, vast farms, palaces, fortresses, factories, and peasant homes, and imbued their imagery with an intense reality and pictorial dynamism that dazzled the senses.

With the coming of sound, films which displayed a pronounced bent for rich chiaroscuro (*Blonde Venus*, 1942), sensuous pictorial elegance (*Song of Songs*, 1933), and strikingly dramatic visual compositions (*Thunder Over Mexico*, 1933) were lifted to prominence primarily because of their pictorial effects.

In recent years the films of Orson Welles, Akiro Kurosawa, Michelangelo Antonioni, Ingmar Bergman, Alain Resnais, and Federico Fellini, among others, have contained some of the most sensitive and complex imagery the screen has ever seen. Fashioned with subtle artistry and a richness of meaning, distinguished by visual beauty, these films continue to demonstrate how screen imagery can transform subject matter and endow film with distinction and style.

The Ambiguity of the Photographic Image

ARTHUR GOLDSMITH

Despite the realism of photography—its powers of detailed, even literal description—
the photographic image can be ambiguous in its parts or in its total effect. In fact, ambiguity, achieved by design or accident, seems
to me to be of greater importance in contemporary photography
than is usually recognized.

By ambiguity I do not mean the word only in its narrower dictionary sense—an expression (visual expression in this case) that is
"doubtful or uncertain; esp. from obscurity or indistinctness; also
inexplicable." I mean it in an extended sense, too, as used by the
British poet and critic William Empson in *Seven Types of Ambiguity*.

To quote Empson, an ambiguity is "any verbal nuance, however
slight, that gives room for alternate reactions to the same piece of
language." In analyzing the effects of verbal nuances and the interaction of the alternate responses they produce, Empson touched
on one of the deep roots of poetry. But it is not only verse that
can evoke meanings or emotions that echo, clash, and mingle in
rich complexity. A photograph, too, can generate power by a similar effect, and ambiguity is an aspect of the poetry of vision as well
as of the poetry of verse.

This is not to say that ambiguity has virtue as a device for its
own sake. Many photographs are ambiguous by mistake, because

of faulty seeing or technique, or because the photographer was not clear in his own mind or heart what he wanted to communicate. Others are obscure by design, but boring or meaningless in their obscurity. Ambiguity only adds richness and heightens the effect of a photograph when it serves to express a complex emotion or state of mind.

THE ENIGMATIC DETAIL

To begin with, consider the simplest and most obvious kind of photographic ambiguity—a detail in a picture (or cluster of related details) that is so blurred, badly lighted, or tightly cropped that we can't readily tell what it represents. If identifying this enigmatic detail is important to the purpose of the picture (as in recognizing a tool in a how-to photograph), obviously the ambiguity is a flaw. The picture doesn't "read"; its intended meaning is garbled.

But even if the enigmatic detail is unimportant it may weaken the picture because it is distracting. Its obscurity creates a visual riddle. We look at a snapshot and wonder: what is that pale blob that seems to be resting on Uncle Harry's shoulder—a basketball? a dinner plate? a Stilton cheese? The closer we come to identifying an obscure object in a picture, without doing so surely, the more insistent and annoying it tends to become.

On the other hand, an enigmatic detail, seen in context, sometimes may suggest an idea that reinforces the photograph's meaning or emotional impact. A curious example of this kind of ambiguity occurs in Edward Steichen's portrait of John Pierpont Morgan. Steichen, in his memoirs, recalls that many people have asked him how he induced Morgan to pose with a dagger in his hand. Actually, no such prop was used. The odd, triangular highlight under Morgan's left hand is not reflected from a knife blade but from a portion of a chair. However, Steichen's Morgan is Morgan the Corsair—a fierce and imposing figure. Even a viewer not familiar with the more ruthless aspects of Morgan's career might well jump to the conclusion that he is holding a dagger. And even if one recognizes the chair as a chair, the idea of a dagger, with its associations of potency and violence, also may arise in the mind, adding to the portrait's power.

THE VISUAL PUN

Another type of photographic ambiguity is the visual pun, or play on images, created by relating two or more objects in space with comic or dramatic effect, or by pointing out a visual similarity between dissimilar things.

Visual puns can be created in the camera by choosing a viewpoint that makes the image of a foreground object touch, overlap, or merge with the image of something in the background—for example, a man apparently supporting an automobile in the palm of his hand.

One typical comic visual pun that has retained its freshness and humor more than most is Robert Doisneau's photograph of a policeman at the entrance to a fun house—an entrance shaped like gaping jaws with teeth. Taken in a literal sense, there's nothing very funny about the picture. Here is a cop standing in front of a trick doorway. But the photographer's choice of angle forces us to see an alternate, metaphorical meaning: the policeman is about to be devoured by a gigantic ogre—the jaws are ready to close on him. The man's look of bland unconcern in the presence of this horrible danger, and our awareness of the absurdity of this figurative interpretation, give the picture its comic bite.

Visual puns can be used for more serious ends, too. The double meaning of juxtaposed images can be employed for satirical effects, to suggest surrealistic relationships, or to strike a dissonant note that expresses the absurdity or disorder a photographer senses in a situation. One frequently finds a caustic, sophisticated use of visual puns in the work of Elliott Erwitt, to name just one contemporary photographer who employs this type of ambiguity in his work. A photograph from his Bahia set (reproduced in the September 1963 *Infinity*) comes to mind: the rear end of a donkey weirdly jutting out from a tree trunk, so that seemingly only half the animal is there.

Another type of visual pun is achieved by pointing up visual similarities between dissimilar things. The intended effect might be humor, as in showing a bald-headed man studying one of Buckminster Fuller's geodesic domes. Or it might take the form of showing an inanimate object in such a way that it suggests a human being or animal, with ironic consequences. A brilliant example of this kind of double meaning is Robert Frank's photograph of a new Cadillac shrouded in a winding cloth like a gigantic mummy—a corpse lying in state—awaiting its resurrection by a Los Angeles car dealer.

Visual puns of an even more complex type can be produced by putting multiple exposures on the same piece of film, or superimposing images on one sheet of printing paper. If this is done crudely, the effect is painfully gauche, but when it is handled with taste and subtlety the effect can be a lovely blending of the real and the surreal, a dream-like fusion of memories and associations, as in the photographic montages of David Attie. The danger of a visual pun is that if it is too pat, too obvious, it quickly loses its novelty. But when used to make a significant comment rather than merely as a gimmick, it can be a valuable application of ambiguity in photography.

THE AMBIGUITY OF HUMAN EXPRESSIONS

We grin, smile, laugh, frown, sneer, leer, snarl, grimace, glower, purse our lips, wrinkle our brows, narrow our eyes, and otherwise express our feelings by the contraction of certain facial muscles. However, the way we experience an expression when we encounter it "live" and the way we encounter it at second hand, immobilized in a static, photographic image, are two quite different things.

Face to face with a person, we usually know what causes a particular expression or at least can draw upon a number of cues, conscious and subliminal, to give us a fairly accurate insight. However, removed from context of time, place, and circumstances, many human expressions are ambiguous. Is a man glowering because he has a bad temper or because his shoes are too tight? Is that bemused, slack-jawed expression the effect of love, a subnormal IQ, or direct contact with the infinite? As has been said of the Mona Lisa, one may wonder whether a girl's complacent smile is due to the fact she has just learned she's pregnant, or just learned she isn't. The truth is, we often need some explanation from an outside source to know what actually caused a particular expression.

Sometimes, as in the case of personal acquaintances and public

figures, we see what we expect to see, ignoring possible alternatives. Karsh's famous wartime portrait of Winston Churchill is a
case in point. To many viewers, it seems to capture the essence of
the man's defiant spirit—one practically can hear the resounding
words, "We shall never surrender," echo off the walls. However,
according to Karsh's account of the sitting, the expression was induced by removing Churchill's freshly lighted cigar from his
mouth. It is perhaps irritation, rather than defiance, showing on
the great man's face.

However, I doubt if it's necessary or even desirable for us to
know the exact meaning of an expression in a portrait. In fact, a
degree of ambiguity may contribute to the portrait's richness and
power. An expression that is too explicit quickly becomes tiresome,
but one that only hints at the emotion and personality within is
intriguing. It invites us to participate as interpreter, to seek and
weigh alternatives.

I think of the complex blend of sorrow, pity, gentleness, and
childlike pathos in Philippe Halsman's Einstein, or the shocking
directness of the Mexican peon's gaze in one of Cartier-Bresson's
early pictures—a glance combining entreaty and menace. (I do not
know whether he wants my friendship or my heart's blood.) Irving
Penn's superb portrait of Colette has been on my wall for some
time, yet I feel far from certain about how I read those wrinkled,
powder-white features, except to feel the exhalation of a very ancient and cynical wisdom. We all have our favorite portraits like
these, which have an enigmatic presence whose fascination is never
exhausted.

THE AMBIGUITY OF THE EXTRACTED MOMENT

If one imagines time as being linear and directional, a still photograph represents a point somewhere along that line. In looking
at the photograph we see rigid, crystallized present removed from
the flow of time—a present whose past and future we can only sur-
mise and whose circumstances we must try to construct from limited evidence. Thus the very act of tripping a shutter isolates the
subject and contributes a degree of ambiguity to the image.

This ambiguity of the extracted moment is common to most
photographs of happenings taken at snapshot shutter speeds and is

the reason why pictures usually need captions in order to communicate on a photo-journalistic level. The image itself is likely to raise questions and suggest multiple meanings—or at least leave room for more than one interpretation. Who are the people in the picture, where are they in time and space, and what are they doing? The function of words in a good caption is to fill in these gaps, adding the information which isn't self-evident.

The fundamentally ambiguous quality of the image itself can be demonstrated by almost any of the so-called funny picture books that have appeared on American newsstands in recent years. A photograph of Khrushchev that went out over the UPI wire means one thing when it appears in a newspaper with an explanatory caption. The same picture has quite a different meaning when reproduced in one of these books with a caption that gives it a comic twist. But it is not just the absurdity of the caption that causes a laugh; it also is the aptness of the new meaning, which must fit as a possible—if farfetched—interpretation of the situation and expression. The possibility of a double meaning must exist in the picture, and the words merely exploit this ambiguity.

Of course, the photo-journalistic level is not the only one on which a photograph can reach us. It may have a universal appeal beyond time and place. If a picture touches us more than superficially, ambiguity may be one of its chief sources of poetry and power—the device that saves it from the calendar-art literalness which some critics from the art world attribute to all photography. The mystery of time frozen into a pattern is as profound as it is obvious—a key to what fascinates us in the work of so many photographers of the passing moment.

When we look at a snapshot (in the broadest sense of the word), it seems to me that what often happens is something like this: we experience a swift, intuitive response to the photograph as a whole—an emotional reaction that cannot precisely be verbalized —resulting from the interplay of shapes, forms, textures, lights, and darks. More or less simultaneously we try to find a rational meaning to the event or situation portrayed. Why is the photographer showing us this particular fragment of time and space? What meaning, if any, did it have for him and may it have for us? In a photograph with an ambiguous quality, we must work from subtle, equivocal clues, filling in the blanks and devising solutions. In this mental play, and in reconciling emotional and rational responses, the viewer participates in the creative act.

To demonstrate this playful use of ambiguous visual elements in provoking the viewer, I can remember no more intriguing example than a picture Henri Cartier-Bresson made in Madrid in 1933, of a fat man in a black hat walking through a playground. One might guess the location is Spain from the faces of the children. However, the geography of the picture is not important—it is a scene out of a timeless dreamscape with the burning sunlight and razor-edged shadows of high noon and a mixture of weird and banal details. What is the white wall that looms in the background with its random geometry of tiny windows? Are the bars to keep the inhabitants in or intruders out? What games are the children playing? The figures are so positioned and the picture so cropped we can't be certain. Who is the fat man and what brings him here? If you look closely, you see that he, too, is a curiously ambiguous figure—his eyes are hidden by the black shadow from his black hat.

In itself each of these ambiguities is capable of a rational, commonplace explanation. But their total impact takes us beyond the commonplace aspects of the scene, leading us to imagine that something strange is happening. It is the ambiguity of the image —the many questions raised but not explicitly answered that give the picture its charm and power to fascinate.

THE PERILS AND REWARDS OF AMBIGUITY

If in the preceding comments I have given the impression that I think ambiguity is a Good Thing, I'd like to add a strong qualification. I do not believe that fruitful double or multiple meanings are achieved very often by trying hard. One does not usually say: "I will make a frightfully ambiguous but meaningful picture," and then go out and do it. Nor is making a self-conscious cult of obscurity likely to lead to much except boring, sterile pictures. Ambiguities that have the power to stimulate us, to ring chimes or discords in our subconscious, are ones that occur spontaneously out of the photographer's response to what he sees.

Empson's warning about verbal ambiguities serves equally well with visual ones. He said: "An ambiguity is not satisfying in itself, nor is it, considered as a device of its own, a thing to be attempted; it must in each case arise from, and be justified by, the peculiar requirements of the situation."

What are the "peculiar requirements" that justify the use of ambiguity? They are to be found not only in the nature of the subject being photographed but also in the photographer's attitude toward the subject. To modern man, in a chronic metaphysical quandary, life often seems complex, equivocal, and contradictory. A photographic art that expresses this consciousness of life must be capable of complex and many-layered statement. In the poetry of vision as well as the poetry of words, ambiguity is one means that can give the statement its necessary richness.

Infinity, March 1964

On Image and Word

NICOLA CHIAROMONTE

A footprint on the sand is the *sign* of a man's passage. The cross is the *symbol* of Christianity. Tears are signs of emotion; words are symbols of thoughts.

A word is a sign only when it is used in a strictly utilitarian way —to indicate or command. In other cases words, even though they have a precise meaning, change with their context. Only in zoology does "horse" signify *equus caballus*. In general discourse it can mean the beast that draws the peasant's cart; the fantastic quadrupeds yoked to Phaëthon's chariot; the animals on which Murat's squadrons rode forth; the heroic creature of equestrian monuments; or all these things. The meaning of a word lies not only in its dictionary definitions but in the host of associations that they evoke. It is not just context that defines and enhances the significance of a word, but syntax and order as well. In the most primitive communication among people, words are merely indicative or instrumental.

Between a sign and the thing it signifies there is the fixed, determined relationship of cause and effect. We see this in the case of the footprint on the sand, the tear on the eyelash, or the trademark of a commercial product. But no matter how closely tied a symbol is to the thing symbolized, the relation is variable, flexible, and free. It is in poetry, however, that the symbolic value of words reaches its apex. The cross has become the symbol of Christianity not because of its form but because the Christians, following St. Paul, at a definite moment in their history decided to adopt the instrument of Christ's torture as their emblem. Similarly, the relation between a word and its meaning depends on its origin, its history, and its usage. Naturally, for a non-Christian or an indifferent Christian the cross is merely a sign; but for a true believer it evokes the fundamental tenet of his faith: the sacrifice of God-Man. Of course, a word can also be used as a label or as a signal of command. But not by lovers and poets and those who wish truly to commune with others.

A word, then, can be a symbol. A photograph, however, can only be a sign, an unequivocal sign of the passage of a material object before the camera eye. Similarly, the traces left on a movie film by a motion or a series of motions are also signs. But if a coherent discourse can be considered the "trace" of anything at all, it is the trace of meanings that a human mind in its experience of reality has apprehended and wants to communicate.

To identify a word without penetrating its meaning is utterly useless, and in order to penetrate its meaning, we have to repeat in some way the experience of its discovery. Ortega y Gasset justly observed that understanding a discourse involves our comprehending not only *what is* expressed in it but also what is left *unexpressed,* and what cannot be expressed. Ineffability is an intrinsic condition of *language.* But the photographic image is an absolutely explicit indicator; and this is both its strength and its weakness. It can show everything that is showable—and nothing else. The emotions it arouses are psychological "effects," in the strictest, most deterministic sense of the word. But an emotion that a word arouses cannot be considered the *effect* of that word. For the emotion immediately provoked by a word does not exhaust its meaning. The mind actively intervenes—clarifying, enriching, interpreting, and perhaps discarding the original reaction in order to comprehend the true significance of what has been uttered.

No trick of montage, no photographic inventiveness—nothing can change the essential and necessary fact that the cinematographic image is an imprint. Nothing can promote it from the status of a sign to that of a symbol. It cannot become a kind of word; it cannot *signify more than itself.* Nothing can turn a sequence of cinematic images into a sort of discourse. It can never be more than a group of pictures that have been juxtaposed for the purpose of imitating a *real event;* and the only effect it can have on the spectator is the evocation of emotions *similar* to those that could have been aroused by the real event. There is no device or technique by which a series of cinematic images can pass from the sphere of the imitative and the external to the intrinsically different sphere of coherent discourse, through which we endeavor to achieve logical order, acknowledging the mind's imperative to discover the rational in every experience.

If by reason we mean significant order, clear and coherent expression, then the universe of words (and certainly the universe of art) is governed by reason. Or, to put it differently, it is ruled by a necessity other than that of the physical or material world. But the realm of images is controlled by chance, by the way events and things happen in reality; and while series of images can cleverly imitate, reconstruct, and accentuate reality, they do not require us to ask why things happen the way they do. Reason has no role in a sequence of images; its place has been taken by actuality, which needs no reasons. The realm of discourse, however, is entirely occupied by thoughts and questions. Since one word cannot follow another without a reason, we cannot avoid asking ourselves why this is said or that is thought, and what motivates the mind to say this and think that. In the sphere of language we cannot limit ourselves to the machine-like registration of events, because the mind cannot function without ordering and evaluating. But images can only be registered; otherwise, we strip them of their essential virtue—indisputable evidence.

In one of Alberto Moravia's film reviews, which abound in acute observations, he argues along the same line:

The suggestiveness of a word is much less immediate and overwhelming than that of the cinematographic image; yet it is deeper and more persistent. Cinematographic images can be compared to mirages that are seen so frequently in the desert. When the thirsty explorer sees a well surrounded by palm trees in the distance, he rushes towards it without stopping to think. But as soon as he discovers that instead of a spring there is nothing but the same stretch of burning sand, he realizes that the image has left no mark on his spirit. For, after all, it was an illusion of the senses, not of the feelings. The word, on the contrary, works on the mind and consequently on the emotions; it "persuades."

In other words, the cinematographic image acts on the senses somewhat as alcohol, drugs, and other chemical compounds do. And perhaps that is why the laws dealing with the use of these intoxicants have always been so severe; just as those concerning the movies have been. But, after all, images leave things as they found them just as intoxicants do (if we except, of course, the damage they have done to the body). All that can happen to us after looking at images is that we rub our eyes and say, "I have been dreaming." How different is the effect of words. From them there can never be an awakening. Only another word can dissipate the effect of a word.

One could not express more succinctly and with greater acumen what there is to be said about image, word, and the cinema as an art. But when Moravia discusses a particular film in detail, there is nothing in his language to indicate that he is speaking about images and not words, movies and not books. Still, if the cinematographic image is an illusion and a fleeting mirage, while words "persuade," penetrate the mind, and have effects "from which there is never an awakening," it would seem that a critic should take this fundamental difference into account. How, then, can Moravia, a novelist, speak of a film as if it were some kind of novel, loading it with an intellectual content that he himself says only words can have?

For example, he tries to use the Marxist notion of alienation as the basis of his judgments of Resnais's and Robbe-Grillet's *Last Year at Marienbad* and Antonioni's *Eclipse*. According to Moravia, the two French directors look at reality as if they were men from Mars, and "refuse to give meaning to the lack of meaning peculiar to an alienated world. . . . They declare themselves satisfied with things as they stand." Hence, their movie "is a film consisting of nothing but images, that is, of insignificant images emptied of everything that lies under their surface, of everything but their beauty . . . on these images a love-story is superimposed." Whereas, in the Italian film:

the camera's eye . . . is the eye of a European intellectual of bourgeois origin . . . not a Martian. This intellectual is not a Marxist but a humanistic moralist, psychologist, and sociologist. He refused to accept the situation of alienation, which to him is profoundly abnormal and hence a source of suffering. He shows that the alienating element is money (symbolized by the Stock Exchange) which worms its way into all relationships, including the sexual one. . . . And in the sequence of the eclipse which closes the film, the religious-humanistic moralism of our intellectual is emphasized. Here we even see an allusion, perhaps an unconscious one, to the Biblical image of the sun that became "black as sackcloth of hair."

Moravia concludes by saying that in the French film "alienation is accepted, and, in a certain sense, ignored; therefore, all ends well. Whereas in *Eclipse* it is denounced; so all ends badly. Thus Resnais is an alienated being, or tries to be; while Antonioni is a moralist and treats alienation realistically."

Let me say at once that I regard *Last Year at Marienbad* and *Eclipse* as perfect representatives of a type of false and tedious film which presumes to use images as if they were words full of profound meaning. Now, of course, everybody is free to read as many meanings as he wishes into a series of photographs; or to enjoy as many meanings as they evoke in his mind. In a certain sense the function of the image has always been to spur the mind to reverie.

But the main question raised by Moravia's comments is a different one. The question is where, in what images or sequence of images, not only Moravia but we, too, can find the concept of alienation clearly present in Antonioni's film and clearly absent from Resnais's. As for me, all I saw in *Last Year at Marienbad* was a series of images that were sometimes precious and always unbearably "significant." But I am sure that if I had wanted to, I could have discovered the concept of alienation, too. In fact, all one needs is some familiarity with the premises of the *école du regard* and with the novels of Robbe-Grillet, for example, to understand that, by means of the systematic destruction of the synchronization of word and image, the director's aim is to give the illusion of an immediate experience in which *reality seems to be abstract* and intangible: a mixture of the present and the *past*; a kind of limbo with no exit. "Alienated," one might well say; but if one has not read Robbe-Grillet's novels and is not familiar with his theories (and there is absolutely no reason why a moviegoer should be), *Last Year at Marienbad* will simply be seen for what it is—an excessively slow, misty, mawkish love story. All the rest is just superimposed.

On the whole, *Eclipse* is the same kind of thing—a long-drawn-out, murky, preposterously sentimental love story. The fact that there is no happy ending does not alter this. If, as Moravia would have us believe, the concept of alienation is also lurking in *Eclipse*, then all we can say is that a "superimposed" would-be intellectuality has been added to the sentimentality. For a spectator who is not preoccupied with the notion of "alienation," it is difficult to find a clear meaning in the juxtaposition of images showing the meetings, pawings, and partings of a young man and a young woman, plus a few fine shots of the pandemonium of the Stock Exchange. Nor can we see why a picture of a woman staring fixedly out of a window should be considered an image of alienation; or what idea is supposed to be suggested by the recurrent photograph of a piece of wood floating in a barrel of water. The difference between the spectator who is willing to read profound meanings and symbols into the film and the uninitiated spectator who has no such predisposition reaches a point where in the final sequence the former discerns an image of the apocalypse, while the latter perceives only fatuously long, slow shots of nightfall or some kind of darkness covering a section of Rome. There is absolutely nothing in the images themselves to tell us *we are witnessing an eclipse*.

Our age has been called "the civilization of the image," and with reason. It has almost irreparably confused word with image, as it has confused a presence that is directly perceived with a photographic or phonographic replica. Caught off guard by the suggestive power of the new mechanical means of communication, most people come to believe that an image "says" much more than a word, and is infinitely more suggestive. Now, it is not surprising that untrained spectators fall into this trap, but when intellectuals, the guardians of rational language, confound confusion by giving it a theoretical basis, the situation becomes serious. For when, in their analysis of movies, they talk about words and images as if they were identical, they are adding the persuasive power of words to the suggestive force of images, justifying the belief of ordinary people in the reality of their mirages. So it is only natural that makers of films begin to think of a film as a kind of novel or poem, and by the same token begin to consider themselves writers, or even sociologists, moralists, and reformers. They have fallen victim to the cinematic fallacy: the assumption that complex emotions and subtle ideas, which can be expressed *adequately only in language,* can be rendered in *moving photographs.* And they turn out films in which they use images as if they were words pregnant with profound, if vague, meanings instead of employing them to create the *illusion of a real event.*

However, since cinematic images can never have the value of words, no matter how masterly the director's technique or how sophisticated his intentions, these movies are distinguished by the boredom they arouse in an audience, keeping it interminably waiting for a meaning that is never given. The film time passes emptily, without action or events; this is exactly the opposite of what should happen at the cinema.

If we disregard what we actually see, hear, and feel, we can, of course, affirm anything whatever, defend any thesis whatever, and claim to have seen, heard, and felt anything we care to. In the case of the films this is particularly easy, as the cinematic image can blend with, absorb, and adapt itself to practically any meaning we wish to impose on it. The reason is that, never being able to signify anything other than itself, impervious and indifferent to verbal meanings, the cinematic image can support interpretations that are absolutely contradictory. But in order to impose intellectual or symbolic meaning on a succession of images that have been combined in a particular fashion, we are obliged to "read" the film as if it were a series of separate, static, abstract pictures, and not the deliberately continuous, forward-moving composition of images it is supposed to be. That was the Surrealists' way of reading films and also of making them, with results that were at times striking.

But it is a fact that the meaning of a single image in a film depends entirely on its cinematic context (provided that a tree is not made to represent a mountain or a locomotive). Pudovkin, in developing his theory of montage, explains this very well. He also shows clearly how the art of the director consists in compelling the spectator to experience a particular feeling, arousing in him the desired emotional reflex by means of a certain juxtaposition of images and groups of images. Conversely, what the spectator accepts as the film's plot or meaning is simply the order the director has given to a definite selection of images.

However, the spectator of a movie sees what the director means him to only if certain gestures and certain combinations of images evoke the required emotions, and signify what they were intended to, immediately. In other words, the effectiveness of a movie depends on the same kind of complicity between director and spectator that binds orator and crowd, journalist and newspaper reader. The success of a film is rooted in a certain contemporaneity: the feeling of immediacy it arouses.

All we have to do is to see a film twenty years old to realize how ephemeral the cinematic idiom is. The movies, which at first glance seem to speak the most realistic and unequivocal language, quickly become stiff, mannered, and unreal. Not only will the action of an old movie seem absurdly slow or preposterously fast; the plot itself will be far from clear. The smile that so often comes to our lips when we view such a film is caused precisely by our awareness of the disparity between the meaning which the director originally led his public to find in it and the one it assumes for us as it breaks up into a series of stylized and arbitrary images. The interpretation of a succession of gestures and movements which once was so obvious that the resultant emotion became a simple reflex is no longer valid; or at any rate it no longer holds the center of our attention. The single images scatter like the beads of a broken necklace; and each one seems to disclose only its own meaning. For what are they but feeble shadows of a life that is over, relics of a "time" that is not just past but dead, existing only in the immediacy of fugitive gestures.

Yet cinematic images are fascinating in themselves, apart from the story they tell. For one thing, they imperiously occupy the field of consciousness, even when they do not really interest us. Under their domination, the eye wanders in search of curious or suggestive details, which it always manages to find. Everyone has had the experience of getting through a tedious movie by observing details at random. When all is said and done, one sequence of moving images is as entertaining as another. Since there is action and change going on continuously, we can always find something to look at on the screen. Fundamentally, the fascination the cinema exercises over us comes from the fact that it presents us with facsimiles of real objects and real people moving and changing exactly as they do in real life, without our having to bear the burden of anxiety and suffering that accompany action in real life. And, above all, without the inevitable travail of participation, judgment, and responsibility which real life continually demands.

What I am saying is that highbrow and arty films, tedious as they may be because of their slowness and their insistent suggestion of hidden ideas, are not essentially different from movies filled with excitement and action. They, too, in the final analysis, present us with a certain number of images to look at. If we are not interested in the meanings the director meant the comings and goings of the characters to have, we can always look at the landscape, try to guess the location of the street the hero is loitering on so long; or scrutinize the furniture in rooms, or the star's clothes. In fact, we do exactly what we do when, obliged to wait for someone or something, we become idle spectators of life.

But the crucial problem is elsewhere, as Dina Dreyfus clearly shows in an article in *Diogenes* (No. 35) on the relation between cinema and language in films of the Resnais-Antonioni school. She believes that the problem lies in the "deliberate intention to minimize the meaningfulness of words in order to increase the importance of images; to dethrone the former in order to enthrone the latter; and, by discrediting language as such, to accredit the idea that there is such a thing as a language of images."

According to Dina Dreyfus, this project oscillates between contradictory claims.

On one hand, the cinema is considered objective. Which means that it approaches the human through the mediation of things; it tries to reach the internal through the mediation of the external. The image manifests itself with the total *opaqueness* that only a *thing* can have; and nothing can be seen through it. A desert isle does not signify human solitude and incomprehension. It *is* that solitude. A pile of clothes in the middle of a darkened room does not signify the love act. It *is* the act itself. The image has no other-world. Solitude becomes a thing; and the desert isle is not empty because man has momentarily departed, but because he is eternally absent from it.

Now this claim to objectivity is immediately denied and contradicted by another aim. The cinema wants to signify; it wants to *say* something; and it wants to say it in images and not in words. Verbal discourse is then inessential. But the image wants to transcend itself as image in order to signify *interiority*, which belongs only to human motives, intentions, thoughts, feelings, impressions, desires, the cinema cannot *express* without denying its own nature. . . . But since it

now becomes a question of *expressing* by means of the image a subjectivity that . . . cannot be transmitted as such into the image, the
latter is forced to transcend itself and take on a verbal or discoursive
meaning, without changing its nature. . . . The cinema attempts the
impossible synthesis of the immanent and the transcendent; the interior and the exterior. . . . The empty landscape and the train that
disappears over the horizon become symbols; we are back with the
Romantics' notion of the landscape that expresses a mood. . . . No
matter what path the cinema chooses, it is irresistibly drawn to the
opposite one. If it takes one direction, it sins by omission: the image
suggests or evokes, because it *cannot say*. Hence its ambiguity and its
inferiority to language proper. If it takes the other direction, it sins
by excess: the image suggests and evokes because, we think, it can
say much more, much better, and more fully than words can. Hence,
its presumed superiority to language proper . . . it can say *everything*.

This insuperable contradiction, which clearly reveals the limitations of cinematographic language, helps us to understand the experiments of directors like Resnais, Antonioni, and Bergman, as
well as the reasons for their inevitable failure. Attempting to distort the nature of the cinematic image by forcing it to express ideological or lyrical meaning can only result in pretentiousness and
emptiness. The image is irremediably external; it is absolutely incapable of representing inner life, subjectivity, or personality. It
can only allude to them, and try to "illustrate" them by the external signs which are its material. To ask for more than this is asking
too much. The idea that by combining the resources of the cinema with those of literature one can nullify their respective limitations is absurd. It really means the destruction of all limits.

What the cinema has discovered is the universe of external
signs, which is indubitable, certain, and self-contained, since it
leaves no gap between intention and act, and no place for ambiguity. In this universe motives, feelings, and ideas are completely
transmuted into corporeal signs (and this is how the mirage
arises). Since it is impossible to represent inner life on the screen,
the suggestive intensity of gesture, of immediate presence, and of
rapid, functional dialogue is exploited to make up for it. The
priests of the highbrow cinema resort to these devices; and the result is a deliberate debasement of the inner life. At the same time
they want the image to express the soul and its ineffable torments

(the *vague à l'âme*) with a concreteness that words never could achieve. Now it is simply not possible to have it both ways. The cinematographic image is a sign, not a symbol. It is the trace of subjectivity, not its expression.

Following this path *à rebours* from literature to cinema, we are thrown back to those films of the 1910's, based on "expressive" posing, mannered photography, and that tiresome immobility which is supposed to be pregnant with meanings (although they exist only in the director's mind). These films bore us to death. For every time that the camera pauses, and fatuously dwells on details not connected with an action that is immediately clear; every time that it does not prick our curiosity about what is going to happen next, the picture is simply tedious. In the period of silent movies some immobility was inevitable (except in scenes of slapstick comedy and breakneck action), and a slow pace was technically necessary, since the director had to get as much suggestive power out of the image as possible. Those who are now returning to such methods are guilty of aestheticism, for this movement backwards is a deliberate one, and its techniques are arty and pretentious in themselves.

But the grossness peculiar to motion pictures as a medium of expression automatically destroys every attempt to impose literary significance on them. The picture of a woman who stares and stares and stares into space simply makes us laugh, and so does all action that is unnaturally slow. It is not that the images themselves are comical, but that the intention of the director is inane, flagrantly contradicting, as it does, the nature of his medium. There is no escape from the essential simple-mindedness of the movies. The attempts of cinema intellectuals to express complex feelings necessarily end in coarse sentimentality. Their efforts to suggest ideas result in wringing abstruse meanings out of images, which by nature are deaf and dumb unless they are elements in a sequence of rapid actions.

The one thing a film cannot do is express complex ideas or meanings; and forcing it to do so puts a brake on movement (which is the very essence of the movies), slowing it down to a complete stop in order to suggest a significance that goes beyond the image. But in the movies there is nothing but a void beyond the image. So, for example, an empty street which is supposed to

indicate (who knows how or why) the state of mind of a character
—to say nothing of the ideas of the director—is simply a static
image. It indicates nothing. The picture of an empty street can be
superb as photography, but it is only the picture of an empty
street. Nor can technical tricks or ideological comment make it say
more than it does. What actually happens when a single image is
imposed on us for too long a time is that we are reduced to a state
of stupefaction, not knowing what we are supposed to feel. A
static image breaks the spell of the movies by betraying the expectation of uninterrupted action that has been aroused, and jolts us
from a moving world to a motionless one. The effect is disastrous,
for our mind begins to work on its own; either we are completely
distracted, or we start associating automatically on the theme,
"empty street." But more often we are just bored. And I can think
of no worse boredom.

At such moments we become aware of the fact that the movie
has the effect, not of directing and ordering the flow of our
thoughts around the themes suggested by the pictures on the
screen, but of stopping the flow completely, submerging it in a cas-
cade of images. It is as difficult to get back from them to the
theme as it is to awake from the effects of a drug. Furthermore,
the intellectual cinema uses actors not as sources of actions and
gestures but as suggestive and almost inanimate objects. Reduced
to the condition of things, actors find it more difficult than ever to
express emotions and moods. All they can do is to assume poses.

And the purpose of all this is to escape from the elementary fact
that poetry and cinematographic images are at opposite poles. Not
only does an image "express without saying," as Dina Dreyfus
writes, but it hurdles, so to speak, ordinary discourse in order to
achieve an indicatory and emotional force that common words—
les mots de la tribu—cannot possibly emulate. Obviously, the pal-
pitating image of a thing is infinitely more effective than its verbal
label.

Nevertheless, it has nothing to do with discourse and its logical
order, where feelings and ideas are mirrored, or with poetry. In
fact, the emotion aroused by a cinematic image is similar to that
aroused by a spectacle or an event which we happen to witness in
real life. For no matter how skillful film directors and actors are,
they do not use evocative symbols but images, the indicative une-

quivocal signs made by the imprint of objects on the screen. Through the cinematic images we can apprehend the world only from the outside, for because of their nature, they are unable to render subjective experience, or to penetrate the world seen through an idea, a conviction, a form, or a passion—which is the world of art as we have always understood it. The cinema can allude to the inner life only to the degree that movements of the body correspond to movements of the soul. But it is obvious that the body can express complex states of mind only very vaguely. We can photograph a motionless person, or a face with a fixed stare, in order to show anguish or sadness. But the image will never render the quality of the anguish or sadness, which is, after all, what matters. The cinema derives its power from its ability to arouse an emotional reaction that is both immediate and certain. Whereas a poem or a novel cannot come alive without the reader's elaboration; its power of suggestion is a construction of his mind, calling into play his sensibility, and his intellectual and imaginative faculties.

It is indeed because they are striving to achieve the allusiveness of poetry, encouraging the spectator to participate in the creation of meaning, that the intellectualistic film directors attempt to use cinematic images as if they were words; thus they keep them in a zone of crepuscular ambiguity, as far removed as possible from their obvious and apparent meaning. But they strive in vain. After all, a cinematic idiom, with its innumerable possibilities, does exist, even though it is qualitatively limited. It is the language of signs that describes the external, in all its certainty and completeness. In this language every sign is clear, the meaning of every gesture is immediately comprehensible, and vagueness is excluded by definition.

The resources of the cinema are enormously rich. It has at its disposal a realm where all is explicit and accessible, where act immediately follows on intention, and where real life is magically transformed into a series of clear and definite events. But it is certainly not through the cinema that we can explore what Heraclitus called the "confines of the soul."

Speaking of the relation between thought and image from the point of view of a scientific psychology, Alfred Binet once said that from an idea worth a hundred thousand francs we get images worth a sou. With images worth a sou, certain movie makers would like to get ideas worth a hundred thousand francs. The operation, however, cannot be reversed.

Encounter, January 1963

IMAGE

The composition of the screen image endows subject matter with connotations of feeling and style in addition to explicit meaning

ORNATE PICTORIALISM
The Scarlet Empress (1934), Josef von Sternberg

DRAMATIC EXPRESSIVENESS
Metropolis (1926), Fritz Lang

MOOD
The Student of Prague (1926), Henrik Galeen

ATMOSPHERE
Hamlet (1948), Laurence Olivier

HEIGHTENED REALITY
Naked City (1948), Jules Dassin

DYNAMIC POINT OF VIEW
Bullitt (1968), Peter Yates

RHYTHMIC PATTERN AND DESIGN
Que Viva Mexico (1933), Sergei Eisenstein

PSYCHOLOGICAL STATE OF MIND
Notorious (1946), Alfred Hitchcock

SUBJECTIVE FANTASY
At Land (1944), Maya Deren

THE FLOW OF DREAMS
The Cage (1948), Sidney Peterson

VISUAL PARODY
Viridiana (1961), Luis Buñuel

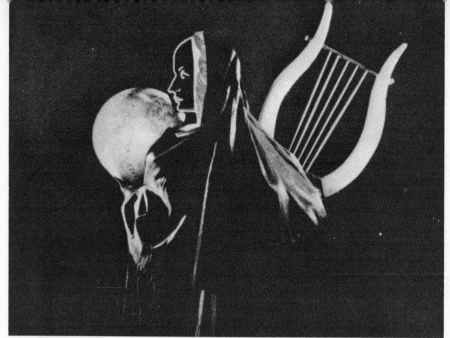

ALLEGORICAL IMPLICATIONS
Blood of a Poet (1931), Jean Cocteau

PSYCHIC IMPRESSIONS
House of Cards (1947), Josef Vogel

METAPHORIC STATEMENT
Eclipse (1962), Michelangelo Antonioni

SOCIAL COMMENT
La Chinoise (1967), Jean-Luc Godard

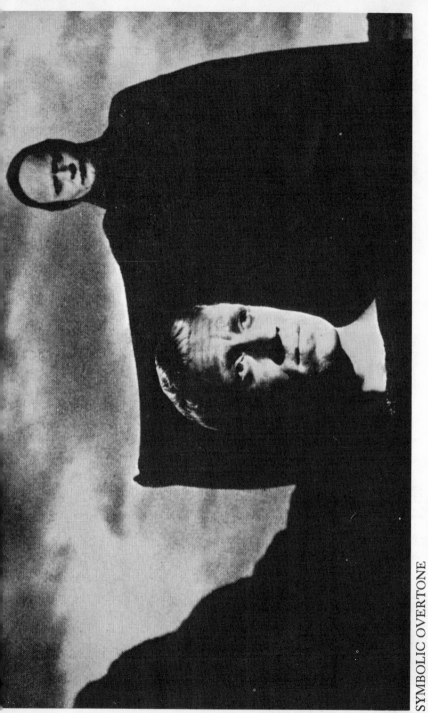

SYMBOLIC OVERTONE
The Seventh Seal (1956), Ingmar Bergman

The Subjective Camera

HERBERT A. LIGHTMAN

*T*he camera is the "eye" of the motion picture. It is not merely a mechanical thing of
cogs and wheels and optical glass that records an image on a strip
of film. Rather, it is an artistic tool—like a painter's brush, or a
sculptor's chisel. In the hands of a craftsman it becomes the instrument through which a dramatic story can be placed on film—
so that later on, in darkened theaters all over the world, vast audiences can see the film, react to it, and be entertained.

Psychologically, an audience responds as strongly to creative
camera work as it does to clever direction or powerful acting. For
the camera has "point of view" and the audience will see the story
only as the camera sees it. For this reason, the camera's approach
to a specific scene must be in key with the concept of that scene
as set down in the screenplay, and with the pattern of action
worked out by the director.

Usually the camera maintains the role of a detached observer of
the story. It is not, in itself, a part of the action—so it simply
stands by and records what goes on, assuming whatever angle will
best portray that action. When this is the case, and the camera remains apart from the action itself, we say that the camera is *objective*. A vast majority of the action in most photoplays is filmed
with this approach.

Occasionally, however, the camera steps out of its role as casual

observer and becomes a participant in the story. In so doing, it assumes the point of view of one of the characters, and what appears
on the screen is what that particular character sees in a certain
filmic situation. Thus, the camera actually becomes his "eye," and
when this is the case we say that the camera is *subjective*.

This technique, in itself, is not entirely new. Even back when
the movies were young, a character could scarcely be represented
on the screen as being drunk without the audience's being treated
to a revolving prism shot of his multiple d.t.'s. But, just as motion-picture technique in general has outgrown obvious forms of
trickery, the subjective treatment as used in Hollywood today has
become a smooth, subtle way of putting the audience into a character's "shoes." It is dynamic without being clumsy.

The psychological effect of this device on the audience is direct
and potent. The modern photoplay appeals principally to the emotions. For this reason, it is desirable that an audience participate
subconsciously in the action that is taking place on the screen.
When a person viewing a film can lose himself in the story and
react vicariously to the emotions of the actors—then he is quite
apt to leave the theater with the glow of satisfaction of having
seen an entertaining film.

The subjective approach, when well executed, tends to bring the
audience *into* the picture. The audience is allowed to see part of
the action as it appears to one of the characters, and it will subconsciously experience the same reactions he does.

In several recent Hollywood photoplays there have been some
excellent examples of this technique in use. In the film *The
Lodger*, directed by John Brahm and superbly photographed by
John Seitz, A.S.C., one sequence concerned the murder of a
dowdy London charwoman who had stopped by at the pub for an
"arf 'n' arf" before going home. Because of previously established
motivation, the audience knew that the killer was waiting in her
little shack. But when the camera followed her into her room the
murderer was not once shown. Instead, the woman started to re-
move her clothes, whirled about as she heard a sound off camera,
and registered fright when she realized that she was not alone. At
this point the camera subjectively assumed the point of view of
the killer. The frantic charwoman, directing her attention straight
at the lens, backed slowly away; while the camera, simulating the

lurching gait of the killer, began to close in on her. Terrified, the woman cowered against the wall as the camera lumbered ever closer, ending up in a stark close-up of her frenzied face. When the fade-out came, the killer had not once been shown, and yet the audience had had the unique jolting experience of having directly participated in a murder.

As with any original cinematic technique, the subjective treatment is sometimes misused. Attempts to go "arty" with the device only succeed in confusing the audience and clouding the dramatic significance of the subject matter.

For instance, some years ago a French film version of *Crime and Punishment* was released on the Continent and later shown in certain select theaters in America. Following the fade-in in one sequence, the audience found itself gazing up into the faces of three characters who were bending over the camera, gesticulating toward the lens, and discussing a fourth character. Over continuous dialogue, the scene then cut to a shot straight down at the face of a young man who was awakening. About this time the audience realized that it had been seeing the first three characters from the viewpoint of the young man who was just awakening and whom they were discussing.

This sequence utilized the subjective treatment—but its use in this particular instance was forced. When the scene faded in and the audience found itself gazing up at three strange characters, it is true that certain elements of surprise and suspense were established. But for several seconds the audience was lost, so that a good deal of the dialogue went by unnoticed while the audience struggled to orient itself. Obviously, whatever originality was achieved by the use of the device was outweighed by the confusion that followed and by the loss of dramatic meaning within the sequence.

A subjective scene cannot simply be tossed into a sequence at any point. It must be motivated by, and definitely linked to, the objective scenes that precede and follow it. For instance, if we had a sequence in which two men were engaged in an argument that was later to develop into a fistfight, we might have a straight objective shot showing the two men in their relationship to each other as the argument began. As the action mounted, over-the-shoulder close-ups would be intercut. Finally there would be a subjective shot of one of the men in close-up directing his dialogue straight at the camera, finally drawing back his fist and aiming it straight at the lens. There would be a quick cut to the other man's face as he received the impact of the blow, and our continuity would be complete.

In a case like this, the one subjective scene would not be merely a trick shot thrown in for haphazard effect, but a carefully planned dynamic device to make the audience experience the impact of the blow as it was struck.

Alfred Hitchcock, who not without good reason is known as the Master of Suspense, is one of the directors who has used the subjective camera to good advantage. In his precedent-breaking film *Lifeboat*, photographed by Glenn McWilliams, Tallulah Bankhead is shown sitting in the boat while John Hodiak, another victim of the shipwreck, swims toward her. She coolly takes up her hand movie camera and shoots some footage of him as he struggles to reach the boat. At this point, Mr. Hitchcock cut to a subjective angle showing the man as she saw him through the view finder of her camera.

In this instance, the device was used more for novelty than for any deep psychological effect, although it emphasized a certain facet of Miss Bankhead's character by showing the cool, detached manner in which she preferred to view the struggles of her fellow man. In a film such as *Lifeboat*, where the mobility of the camera was necessarily limited by the narrowness of the locale, a shot such as this added an element of variety and cinematic punch to an otherwise straightforward camera treatment.

Mr. Hitchcock, aided by the camera artistry of George Barnes, A.S.C., used the subjective approach even more effectively in one of his more recent films, *Spellbound*, a psychological love story. In one sequence the amnesia victim, played by Gregory Peck, is given a drugged glass of milk, and a good deal of the motivation at that point of the story depends upon whether or not he drinks the milk. After a series of straight objective shots narrowing down to a close-up of him raising the glass to his lips, a cut is made to a subjective shot showing what *he* sees as he drinks the glass of milk. As the glass is slowly tipped up, the action in the background becomes subordinated by the edge of the glass until the white liquid gurgles up around the lens, blanking out the scene for a fade-out.

Purists might complain that in this case the device was forced, but actually it added a good deal to the impression that this man was viewing his surroundings in a very narrow way, hemmed in, as he was, by amnesia. It helped the audience to assume his warped point of view.

Again, in the same film, the subjective device was used even more effectively. During the climactic sequence, when the exposed murderer is about to kill the young psychiatrist played by Ingrid Bergman, the camera becomes the murderer's eye. We see what he sees as he sits in his chair with his gun pointed at his victim. In a unique composition we see his hand and gun in the foreground of the frame, and Miss Bergman in the background as he slowly tracks her course of movement about the room. Then, as she convinces him that another murder can solve nothing, he slowly turns the gun on himself (i.e., at the camera) and fires.

The impact of this scene was amazing. Audiences viewing it become participants in expected murder (vicariously, of course) and then became victims of a suicide. They were drawn wholeheartedly into the action and allowed to participate. The suspense was masterfully built to a climax, and the denouement packed a wallop. *Spellbound* is a better film for so original a device.

Closely allied with this *visually* subjective type of scene is the kind of subjective sequence that pictures the *mental* conflicts suffered by a character. This type of sequence usually takes the form of a montage picturing either the distortions of a dream or the disconnected impressions of a deranged mind. An especially good example of this device was the almost-frightening subjective montage used to portray the nervous breakdown of a character in the film *Blues in the Night.*

This montage, technically one of the finest ever put on the screen, took a number of realistic objects from the life of the character, whirled them around, distorted them, and exaggerated certain details, just as a man's mind would do if he were suffering a mental crack-up.

Most dream sequences are not truly subjective—since the camera is still a detached observer, merely recording what the characters are supposedly dreaming. However, the surrealistic dream sequence designed by artist Salvador Dali for the film *Spellbound* held a certain subjective feeling because it showed impressions as they were received by the character, not realistic but distorted, and shown from his point of view.

Recently the author wrote the screenplay for a two-reel short subject which is entirely subjective. That is to say, everything that appears on the screen is shown as it is seen by the main character, so that obviously he himself is never seen until the climax of the film, when he appears before a mirror. The illusion of complete subjectivity is heightened by a stream-of-consciousness narration blended with direct dialogue.

It is, of course, self-evident that such a film could only be placed on the screen as a novelty short. A feature-length film done entirely with this approach would become monotonous. However, the use of single subjective scenes or sequences carefully motivated and executed in a feature-length screenplay (whose subject matter calls for such a device) can be of immense value in bringing the audience into the story. Properly used, it becomes an integral part of the overall approach of the film, and perfectly utilizes the camera as the "eye" of the motion picture.

American Cinematographer, February 1946

Composition of the Moving Image
Gregg Toland, A.S.C.

*A*ny discussion of composition in motion-picture camera work, as distinct from composition in still photography, must be predicated on the fact of *motion*. The accustomed compositional canons familiar to students of photography apply equally to cinematography. But interwoven with them must be an understanding of the uses and the dangers of movement as an aid or hindrance to composition.

Suppose, for example, a still and a motion photographer set their cameras up together to photograph a Western landscape. In the middle distance, against a background of flat plains and clouds, a herd of cattle browses. In the right foreground, a cowboy lazily stretches his length on the ground as, with his pony standing patiently beside him, he watches his herd.

In the still picture, clouds, prairie, and cattle alike form a background for the quiet figures of the cowboy and his horse, who are definitely the center of interest in the picture's composition. Everything combines to express quietude.

The movie cameraman's problem, even in filming this near still-life shot, is complicated by the necessity of foreseeing the effect of every possible bit of movement upon the compositional whole. For instance, will the natural movements of the grazing cattle in the middle distance distract attention from the more important but motionless figures of the cowboy and his horse? They can!

Will the natural movements of the horse—nodding its head, switching its tail, stamping its feet—divert attention from the figure of the man? They can! Further, suppose the action of the scene requires that the cowboy mount and ride away. In which direction is he to go? What will be the effect upon the composition of that movement? Should he come toward the camera, go away from it, or ride out to the right- or left-hand side of the frame? Should he walk his horse, trot, gallop, or run? Should he move in a straight line, a curve, or a diagonal? What will be left of the composition once the heavy, dark masses of that strategically placed man and horse are removed?

That, and a score of other questions, complicates the task of the pictorially minded cinematographer every time he makes a shot. Inevitably, they cannot all be solved at all times. But in the measure that they are considered and their effects planned for, will the resultant movie scene prove an effective example of cinematic composition? And also, let it be said right here that composition should have no rigidly fixed rules. Neither should any one individual's comments upon the subject be taken as an absolute criterion. Composition is in the truest analysis a matter of personal taste: what one person may consider well composed, another may criticize. Yet each could be right by his own standards.

From the time of Jay Hambridge's presentation of the principles of dynamic symmetry down to the latest analyses of the introspective Russian filmers, a great deal—almost too much—has been said and written about still and cinematic composition as a purely scientific proceeding, to the great danger of truly creative art. In every phase of pictorial endeavor today there are people who can discuss pictures learnedly in terms of geometric lines, forms, masses, and patterns but whose pictures seem lamentably stiff and stilted. There are others who, though they could never tell you what a supporting line is or whether chiaroscuro was something in a picture or in an Italian restaurant, have nevertheless the unfailing knack of producing pleasing pictures.

For this reason, the writer desires earnestly that his remarks will not be considered a formula to be followed slavishly, but rather informal notes which it is hoped will make screen composition easier for those who have had less experience than he, and which may perhaps point out some of the pitfalls that might entrap the unwary wielder of a motion-picture camera.

Composition in any medium—graphic or photographic, still or moving—is essentially a matter of arranging everything within the picture so it focuses the attention of the beholder wherever the picture maker wants that attention focused. Two means of getting the right attention are tonal contrast and position—common also to still photography. A third, peculiar to the movies, is motion.

POSITION OR ARRANGEMENT

Methods of focusing attention can be very broadly grouped under three main headings. The first of these is position or arrangement: the position within the frame of whatever may be desired as the chief object of interest, and correlatively, the relationship to it of everything else within the scene.

Speaking rather generally, the center of the picture is the most natural place for the object of greatest interest. This does not mean, however, that it should be at the exact mathematical center of the picture. Often a slight displacement will make for a more pleasing or interesting arrangement, without in any way detracting from the desired concentration of interest. This position of strongest interest should lie roughly along the diagonal from the lower left-hand corner of the frame to the upper right-hand corner, with the most favorable positions usually somewhere in the upper-right one-third of the frame area.

Inevitably, if one looks through any collection of pictorial stills or studies the composition of any well-photographed film scenes, exceptions to this rule will be found. They should be! But in almost every case it will be found that some secondarily prominent line, tone, or mass lies across this upward-slanting left-to-right diagonal to redirect the viewer's attention to any unconventional placement of the principal object of the composition.

The arrangement of the surrounding parts of the picture can play a very important part in guiding the viewer's eye to the chief object of interest. This is especially true in long shots. For example, in the scenic long shots which figure so importantly in most Western movies a much greater effect of depth and actuality is obtained if the composition is so planned that the picture has at least two strongly defined planes—foreground and distance. This is most easily done by arranging things so that the foreground—possibly in silhouette or semi-silhouette—provides a frame for the more distant view that is the object of chief interest. This frame may be a complete frame or only visible at one or two sides. A shot of the Grand Canyon or Yosemite Valley will be much more attractive, and give a much greater impression of depth and size, if taken through a foreground frame of rocks or branches, rather than if you simply step up to the edge of the cliff and shoot your scene *sans* foreground.

The same thing holds true of any long shots, including interior scenes made on a studio stage or movie interiors made in your own living room. If you can shoot through an arch from an adjoining room, or even through the frame of a reading lamp or similar piece of furniture, the effect will be far more attractive than a bare scene.

It may be mentioned, incidentally, that many of the professional cinematographers who specialize in exterior camera work, such as making Westerns and the like, go on location prepared to face the need of making such framed long shots in places where nature fails to provide such natural frames. They carry a tree branch or two, so they can put up their own compositional frame wherever it may be needed!

TONAL CONTRAST AND LIGHTING

A second important phase of focusing attention through composition is in accentuating it by means of tonal contrast and lighting. In most pictures, the lightest-toned area or object will almost automatically capture the beholder's attention first. This is true regardless of position. Therefore, if we see to it that the most important object, person, or area is also the lightest-toned, it is very likely to focus the audience's attention on itself at the outset. Add to this the advantages of commanding position, and it is almost sure to become the center of attraction.

In movies as in stills, there are two principal ways of achieving this effect. First and most obvious is to have the desired object inherently lightest in tone. For example, a girl in a light dress will stand out most prominently in the scene if her background, whether it is outdoor foliage or indoor walls, is darker-toned. Inevitably, she is the lightest-toned object in the scene, and the audience's eye is attracted to her.

That's why in so many Western pictures the cowboy hero wears a light shirt and rides a white horse, while the lesser players—and especially the villains—wear darker clothes and ride darker ponies. That is also why so many of our feminine stars and leading women are blondes, regardless of whether or not nature provided them with light hair. The blond locks capture audience attention!

To an increasing extent, we can achieve a roughly parallel result by means of lighting. If our central object of interest, whether a person, an object, or a landscape, is more strongly illuminated than the background or the surrounding objects *or other people*, it will photograph as the lightest-toned object, and hence be the most prominent part of the composition.

Watch the next movie you see, and notice how often this is done, not alone to make a person stand out more prominently against a darker-toned or less brilliantly illuminated background, but to make the star or principal player stand out more prominently in comparison to the other players.

This, by the way, brings up another unique complication of motion-picture composition: *continuity* of lighting. Things would be quite simple if each scene could be lighted solely for its own individual composition. Instead, however, each scene must be planned and executed with reference to those which precede and follow it. So although for one scene you might want to show a dark area on the screen to accentuate a given part of the composition, you have to weigh the value of the shade's effectiveness against the necessity of continuing that treatment for all the other scenes in that sequence.

ACCENTUATION THROUGH MOVEMENT

The third and in many ways the most potent and provoking phase of composition is accentuation through movement. This is solely a problem of motion-picture composition, of course.

Motion is the motion-picture photographer's prize asset, and—at the same time—his largest problem. For, like color in a still photograph, it can be amazingly beautiful or it can be most distracting. The main thing is to learn to understand and control the effects of motion.

Any moving object will attract attention in preference to a non-moving one. This is true regardless of the position of the non-moving object, its relative tonal value or illumination. So the cinematographer's problem is two-edged: on the one hand, he must plan things to give his principal subject the necessary eye-attracting movement. On the other, he must see to it that no irrelevant, incidental movement in any other part of the frame "steals the scene" from his real subject.

Distracting Motion. Hollywood actors quickly learn this fact, and some of them put it to thoroughly irritating use. A little, apparently natural movement has "stolen" many a film scene at a time when some other player *should* be carrying the chief dramatic (and compositional) interest in the scene. And these movements needn't be spectacular. One actor, for instance, when he wants to steal a scene from another player, often scratches himself; still another yawns; a third might "react" exaggeratedly to what the other actor is saying or doing. There are thousands of apparently natural acts like that which experienced troopers can and do use to distract attention from the other fellow.

The documentary movie maker seldom has to worry about tricks of this nature, but there are plenty of other ways in which undesired movement in the wrong place can weaken his carefully planned attempts at effective composition. Many a scene has been hurt by the inclusion of irrelevant movement in the background. For example, making a scene in a front yard, it is all too easy to overlook some disturbing movement taking place three or four doors down the street—until the resulting picture is screened. One of my friends made such a scene and forgot to watch the background. As a result, just as a pretty girl started to walk across the lawn in his shot, a car drove by along a cross street—and on the screen it looked precisely as though she were pushing the car!

Many other smaller, less obvious movements can intrude upon a composition. In a close shot of a person beside a horse, for instance, watch that the movements of the horse's head and tail don't distract attention from your horseman. In shots at the beach, the rhythmically moving white lines of the surf can often steal the scene from carefully composed shots of people. Even in interiors, distracting incidental movements have to be watched. Often the swinging of a clock pendulum or the flickering of a tiny candle flame, though unnoticed in the filming, can prove disturbing in the screened composition.

Planned Motion. But the use of motion in movie composition can be positive as well as negative. For example, movement along a definite line can tend to carry the audience's eye with it or even ahead of it, acting as a sort of compositional pointer. Imagine a New England landscape nicely framed in foreground foliage, with a white ribbon of road curving across the picture and leading toward a village. Ordinarily, the white line of the road itself would probably be the strongest factor in the composition. But suppose we have a car drive along the road in the direction of the village. The movement will tend strongly to send the audience's eyes racing along the road *ahead* of the car to focus on the village, logically setting the mental stage for following scenes made in the village itself. This, by the way, is true even if you only show the car moving along the road, without taking the time to have it completely traverse the frame and reach the village in that one shot. In the film *Stagecoach*, I remember Bert Glennon's surpassingly beautiful long shots of the stagecoach rumbling across the Arizona deserts. In those shots, despite the majesty of the scenery and the pictorial and excellently filtered cloud effects, the moving spot of the stagecoach—often dwarfed by the immensity of its surroundings—was always the commanding compositional element. We were always conscious of its progress, even though these long shots were seldom held on the screen long enough to show the coach completely traversing the road from one side of the frame to the other.

By showing in successive scenes different characters or objects moving across the screen in opposite directions, we can use composition and motion to build up the idea that they are approaching each other, possibly for conflict. When we see two trains thus rushing toward each other in successive scenes, our minds expect a head-on collision. Two men similarly approaching each other through successive scenes similarly build an impression of an eventful meeting and conflict, as the climaxes of innumerable Western films have proven.

Opposite motions within the same scene, whether along straight, curved, or diagonal paths, can aid composition in directing the eye to whatever point the two sets of motion may have in common. Concentric ripples in water, for instance, while in themselves moving outward, tend to focus one's attention on the central point where a pebble has been dropped. Lines of movement proceeding thus in circles concentrate attention on their center; two or more movements along well-marked paths, whether converging or diverging, tend to focus attention on the point where these paths of motion intersect.

Another important thing to remember about the use of motion is that, given several different movements in a single composition, it is the most *unusual* and unexpected motion that is likeliest to capture attention. For instance, in filming Niagara Falls, one might expect that the perpetual downward movement of the water roaring over the falls would inevitably be the paramount motion in the shot. Yet very often this is not true, for instead the unexpected *upward* motion of the misty spray which rises from the base of the falls captures attention.

It should also be remembered that a sudden cessation of motion, just like a sudden pause in a piece of symphonic music, can heighten the visual effect of screened action. Picture, for instance, a comedy scene in which a henpecked husband has gotten away from his wife and stolen down for a few free moments with the boys at the corner store, when his pursuing wife unexpectedly descends upon him. We would naturally compose our scene with the husband rather centrally located in the group, enjoying his visit with his cronies. Now, to make the wife's appearance more devastating, we would bring her into the picture in the foreground, for the position nearest the camera is almost always the commanding one. Then, as soon as she has rushed well into the frame, but before her spouse sees her, we could center attention on her. She could rush into the scene and then pause, all but motionless, as she "spotted" her wayward husband, and then—after drawing the audience's eyes to her by her sudden change of pace—descend unexpectedly on the errant man.

SCREEN PROPORTIONS

No comments on cinematic composition could be concluded without at least some mention of the peculiarities of the screen's fixed, yet constantly varying, proportion. In still photography we can, through use of the camera's revolving back, through cropping, trimming, and the like, suit our picture format to the needs of the composition. We can make it square, rectangular, oblong, horizontal, or vertical, as may seem best. But in motion pictures—35 mm. or wide-screen—our frame is an unalterable, horizontal.

We can and do vary the effect of this by composing our shots so that areas at the sides, top, or bottom may be effectively masked by shadows, but the rectangular proportion remains always the foundation of screen composition.[1]

Therefore, it is an important part of the motion-picture cameraman's task to plan his compositions for the full-frame area and proportion, but to arrange them so that they will not suffer too badly if part of the picture is framed off. Admittedly, this is not easy, but it can be done, and should be if a satisfactory standard of screen composition is to be maintained. With a fixed frame and motion to cope with, the motion-picture photographer has many compositional problems—but none so insurmountable that it cannot be solved by thought and good taste.

The Complete Photographer, No. 16

[1] The recent development of the device known as multi-image projection, which breaks up the screen area into a mosaic of multiple shots in multiple shapes, frees the filmmaker, to a certain extent, from the unalterable horizontal shape and proportions of the rectangular screen (Editor).

II. MOVEMENT

Movement: Real and Cinematic

LEWIS JACOBS

Next to imagery, movement is the most important element of motion-picture structure. The very name of the screen medium stresses this. In life, movement is connected with action interpreted through physical manipulation—speech, gesture, motion, the act of changing place or position in time and space. But on the screen there is no real movement, only an appearance of it. When a strip of film consisting of a series of static photographs depicting progressively altered positions or changes of places passes through the projector at a certain rate of speed, the optical effect is of continuous, uninterrupted motion. This is produced because of the faculty of the human eye to retain the visual impression it has received, until it is succeeded by another visual impression. The progressive advance and displacement of images propel the motion forward in the mind of the viewer. It is a phenomenon scientifically described as "persistence of vision," and accounts for the translation, by the brain, of what is seen, into thoughts, feelings, and emotions.

This constant fusion of images, representing successive phases and different aspects of movement, is central to the characteristic means of film expression. It is here that the significance of the term "movement," in all its manifold implications, exists, offering the filmmaker a powerful resource to control and heighten what is seen (and heard) with emotional expressiveness and stylistic distinction.

There are four major types of movement on the screen: (1) the movement of people and objects before the camera; (2) the motion of the camera itself, obtained by placing it on a moving vehicle or on a flexible tripod head which can "pan" or "tilt" the camera horizontally or vertically; (3) movement produced optically by shifting the lens from out of focus to sharp focus, by distortion prisms that multiply or divide the image and can be manipulated to give a sense of motion, or by a zoom lens which permits the camera to simulate a gradual or sudden approach or withdrawal from a subject; (4) movement obtained structurally by editing which modifies and organizes all types of motion into a rhythmic whole.

Each of the medium's ways of representing movement has its own application and values. In the movement of people and objects before the static camera, the filmmaker's preoccupation with speech, sound effects, gesture, physical motion of the performers, various groupings and regroupings, and panoramic and vast mass effects grants him the power through pictorial composition and *mise-en-scène* to exploit a wide range of moving forms that can instill an illusionary sense of motion in the film.

The foremost exponent of this technique is William Wyler. *The Little Foxes* (1941), *The Best Years of Our Lives* (1946), *The Heiress* (1949), and *Sister Carrie* (1952) reveal an exceptional dexterity in "deep-focus" *mise-en-scène*, obtained by a continuous and skillful staging of inherent and imposed movement of the performers in a prearranged relationship to the camera position and angle. Because of the skillful manner in which Wyler breaks down the performers' actions and reactions into different stages of movement through the background and foreground, by grouping and regrouping to obtain different degrees of emphasis (through differences of size, light and shade, contrasts of shape), the viewer is forced to look from one character to the other and from one part of the screen to another, thus generating a strong, subtle sense of flow and motion derived from a single viewpoint and stationary camera.

When a subject that is still or in motion is photographed by a camera in motion, the viewer readily identifies himself as the observer which the camera represents. By moving with the action photographed—following it, preceding it, drawing close or away from it—the viewer is conveyed through successive stages of motion into the very center of the screen happenings. The value of such fluid screen activity lies in its ability to impart a quality of immediacy, actuality, and increased physical participation.

The German filmmakers of the 1920's were the first to exploit this mobile-camera technique. In *The Last Laugh* (1925) the camera traveled down the descending elevator, through the lobby, in and out of the revolving door, through streets, up and down houses, around rooms, through hallways, doors, and windows, like a living organism. It was as though the viewer were actually transported into the very midst of the doorman's activities and so given a keener sense of participation, emotional identification, and involvement in the story.

This same technique is developed later with great ingenuity and invention into a tour de force by Hitchcock in *Rope* (1948). With what seems an endless mobility and flexibility of camera action, the director devises a continuous, fluid treatment. The entire film—eighty minutes in length—is executed in a single, apparently uninterrupted traveling camera shot, without a cut, dissolve, or other typical type of transistion.

Another type of camera motion is obtained without altering the position of the camera itself. This is made possible by a flexible tripod head that allows the camera to be turned in any direction, to move across "pan" or up and down "tilt" in a continuous flow, without interruption. "Pans" and "tilts" are often used at the opening of a sequence to "describe" the locale or atmosphere, to orient the viewer as to what is to follow, or simply to supply movement to a scenic view that otherwise would be static. A "pan" or "tilt" can be an effective means to heighten suspense and create dramatic surprise by withholding the meaning of a movement until the shot's end. For example, in *Shadow of a Doubt* (1942) two men are chasing a third, who runs into a yard and out again. After a moment his pursuers appear. They stop and look about in bewilderment, searching for their man. The camera, which has been tilting down on the scene from a height, now pans away and tilts up from the searchers to a roof and there comes to a stop on the fugitive, who is peering down apprehensively at his pursuers.

When the moving camera represents a neutral point of view and merely shows what is taking place, the viewer remains a detached observer. But when the fluid camera sheds its objectivity by assuming the point of view of a character on the screen, the viewer identifies more directly with him. What is photographed then is seen as the character's reaction to what is happening to him. The moving camera—swaying, rocking, turning, blurring, zooming— takes on a subjective point of view and presents the actor's physical and emotional state, reproducing what he sees and feels: dizziness, faintness, drunkenness, terror, or whatever.

An early example of camera movement suggesting a subjective experience is found in *Variety* (1925). Here the mobile camera is used as the inner eye of an emotionally distraught trapeze artist. Placed on a flying trapeze, the camera sways back and forth over the set, and the viewer experiences what the performer sees and feels.

A sudden shift in point of view can greatly intensify and more physically convey the impact of a moving camera. A dramatic application of this technique is found in Hitchcock's *The Birds* (1963). Mrs. Brenner, played by Jessica Tandy, upset by the extreme destructiveness of some flocks of birds, drives out to her farm to make sure everything is in order. She finds the house open and goes in, calling the farm hand. There is no answer and she is about to leave when she notices some broken tea cups still hanging from their hooks. Puzzled, she hurries to the bedroom. Inside, she stops short, seeing the condition of the room. At this point there is an abrupt change in camera viewpoint. The lens focuses on what Mrs. Brenner sees: broken bric-a-brac, wrecked furniture, a dead gull, a smashed window, an empty, disheveled bed. The scene climaxes with a rapid movement of the camera into a close shot of the body of the farmer pecked to death by birds. The camera then reverts back to its former viewpoint and catches the woman beginning to retch and stagger out of the room. The switch from objective to subjective viewpoint and back again, and from static camera to a moving one, makes the viewer by turn a witness, then a participant in the situation, forcing him to experience both the shock and the anguish of the woman.

The third type of movement—that obtained optically by shifting the camera lens to bring a subject in and out of focus—functions best as a conjunction of different points of interest in the same shot. A typical use of this device is in scenes where a person in the foreground is talking to someone in the background. By alternating the focus from one figure to the other during their dialogue, the film draws attention to the desired point of emphasis and at the same time introduces a sense of dramatized motion in what otherwise might be a static scene.

The indistinctness of the in-focus and out-of-focus technique can also be used to create psychological effects, to suggest blurred vision, dreams, and other experiences of a subjective nature. In Eisenstein's *The Old and the New* (1929), the technique is used to build suspense in a scene in which peasants crowd around a cream-separating machine, curious to see if it will do mechanically what they have been doing manually all their lives. To suggest their unfamiliarity with the machine, the director shows it out of focus at first—a confused glittering of lights reflected in the polished aluminum body. Then, as it does its job, the machine comes gradually into focus—as though slowly penetrating the peasants' consciousness; finally it grows clear and sharp in an optical projection of their new knowledge and satisfied, eager acceptance.

Variation of lens manipulation, obtained by special prisms placed before the camera lens, can multiply or divide the image, and when the lens is shifted, vibrated, shaken, revolved, or given other forms of mobility, can create an interplay of motion within the shot. Memorable examples are found in the experimental film *Lot in Sodom* (1933–34), which utilizes distortion prisms combined with moving lights and multiple exposures (predating today's strobe and kaleidescopic light shows) to endow realistic images with a multiform, gelatinous, melting quality that makes them flow in and out of each other with extraordinary iridescence.

A comparatively recent device that makes it possible to produce motion within the shot is the zoom lens. A sense of movement is obtained by changing the relative size of the subject from close-up to wide-angle view, or the reverse, from a stationary camera position. Properly used, the zoom provides a striking means to shift attention, to obtain emphasis, to give the impression the subject is being followed, or to suggest that the zoom's movement is building toward some climax by withholding the highest point of the shot's interest until the motion is completed.

In *Sweet Love, Bitter* (1967), there is a zoom shot that enlarges the field of vision to link dramatically two seemingly unrelated actions in a climactic confrontation: an Easter parade of pedestrians blithely showing off their finery, and two disheveled actors—one black, the other white—engaged in some private conflict, who expose their anguish to the paraders with unconcern for feelings and with grandiloquent gestures.

The shot begins with a close view of a cab coming to a stop. Out of it steps Dick Gregory, a strutting figure in ridiculous Bermuda shorts, knobby legs, and pot belly, swaggering forward, swinging a closed umbrella and intent on telling the white world to "go to hell." He is followed by his distraught friend, Don Murray, who is trying to placate him. During this, the lens zooms back to a larger view, revealing the scene to be Fifth Avenue, crowded with Easter strollers dressed in the height of fashion. Gregory is now clumsily pushing his way through startled groups of people who stare at him with supercilious smiles, or outraged shock, while Murray pursues him, with an attempt to preserve a vestige of decorum. The zoom pulls back further and finally comes to a stop—as though looking down from an upper floor of a building. We see a vast panoramic view of the avenue and several side streets, embracing a tide of sightseers and lines of buses, cabs, and moving traffic, in the center of which Gregory is now the focus of attention. He is aiming his umbrella like a rifle and frantically shooting and cursing everyone and everything in sight, while Murray stands by, embarrassed and dumbstruck.

Movement that is the result of editing is the most difficult to achieve, the most subtle, and the most to be admired since it derives entirely from relationships of the visual and aural components of the shot. For the directors of silent films this was perhaps the richest attribute the screen medium had to offer. Technically, this kind of movement can be produced merely by changing from one camera viewpoint to another, thus evoking a sense of motion. A dramatic or rhythmic flow is introduced by organizing the subject matter in such a way that, in addition to serving a thematic end, it also serves a formal purpose, as a link in a structure built from a succession of shots.

In this kind of movement, the shots must be planned in advance (where possible) and then arranged so as to give the viewer a visual and aural direction to follow, by presenting his eye, ear, and brain with a particular design, order, and rate of speed of shots in sequence. Here a sense of movement can derive from the composition of the *mise-en-scène* within the shot, or the motion of people and objects, or the motion of the camera, or the motion obtained optically, or any combination of these factors in a manner that will join shots visually and/or aurally in a mobile continuity. Shots may be bound together by including in each some motion, actual or implied, which refers the viewer's eye or ear to preceding and following shots. It may be a gesture, the abrupt break or continuation of a line of dialogue, or sound; the matching, overlapping, or juxtaposition of action of a figure or group; the repeated motion of the camera; a similarity or contrast in the association of objects or of such compositional elements as size, shape, light and shade, lines, masses, colors and changes of angle; or an association of ideas—anything visual, aural, or symbolical—that can motivate the progress and interchange of subject matter from one shot to another toward a mobile succession in which each shot has an optimum duration.

The movement resulting from a series of such changes generates various degrees of tension, introducing a dynamism which, when accented by variations of shot duration and sequences of expressive tempo, produces multiple rhythms. Because the motion picture is a plastic art, its rhythmic order and dimensions—created from a synthesis of movements—add physical and emotional overtones that endow films with vitality, form, and style.

Movement and rhythm achieved through editing are brilliantly demonstrated in Eisenstein's film *Potemkin* (1925). In *Notes of a Film Director* (published in Moscow, 1958), he analyzes the Odessa steps sequence from this plastic point of view. The scene begins with two opposing actions: crowds cheering the battleship *Potemkin* from a harbor stairway, and a platoon of Cossacks with fixed bayonets standing by. "Let's see how one of the structural and compositional means—movement—is used to express mounting emotional intensity," Eisenstein writes.

First, there are *close-ups* of human figures rushing chaotically. Then *long shots* of the same scene. The *chaotic movement* is next superseded by shots showing the feet of soldiers as they march *rhythmically* down the steps.

Tempo increases. Rhythm accelerates.

And then, as the *downward* movement reaches its culmination, the movement is suddenly reversed; instead of the headlong rush of the *crowd* down the steps we see the *solitary* figure of a mother carrying her dead son, *slowly* and *solemnly going up* the steps.

Mass. Headlong rush, *downward*. And all of a sudden—a *solitary* figure, slow and solemn, *going up*. But only for a moment. Then again a *change* in the *reverse direction, downward* movement.

Rhythm accelerates, tempo increases.

The shot of *the rushing crowd* is suddenly followed by one showing a baby carriage *hurtling* down the steps. This is more than just different tempos. This is a jump in the method of representation—from the abstract to the physical—and gives another aspect of *downward* movement.

Close-ups give way to *long shots*. The *chaotic* rush of the mass is succeeded by the *rhythmic* march of the soldiers. One aspect of movement—people *running, falling, tumbling* down the steps—gives way to another—the *rolling* carriage. *Descent* gives place to *ascent*. *Many* volleys of *many* rifles gives place to *one* shot from *one* of the battleship's guns.

At each step there is a change from one dimension to another, from one quality to another, until finally the changes affect not one individual action but the entire structure. . . .

Thus the steady, machine-like motion of the Cossacks, the wild movement of the scattering crowds, the broken, faltering motion of the descending baby carriage are organized into a complex whole of mobile patterns. The ballet-like precision of timing increases tension and raises the viewer's emotions from one level of excitement to another.

Today many of the younger filmmakers have submitted themselves to this aesthetic discipline with varying degrees of effectiveness. There is also much experimentation in the concept of structured movement in new genres of film—"loops," computerized movies, dynamic framing, multiple screens, and mixed media—in which often the subject matter is made completely subordinate to the kinesthetic sensations derived from techniques such as single-frame cutting, jump cuts, juxtaposition of black and white frames, multiple exposures, alternation of negative and positive imagery, repetition of moving and static images, and kaleidoscopic color separation. The expanding scale and diversity of these adventurous techniques, the convictions, audacity, and energy of the newer film-makers such as Jean-Luc Godard, Alain Resnais, Federico Fellini, Saul Bass, Stan Brakhage, Bruce Braille, Hilary Harris, Gregory Markopulous, and others give ample evidence that rhythmic movement has become in itself an active enterprise for aesthetic consideration.

Movement in Movies

EZRA GOODMAN

Slavko Vorkapich is a rather exotic name and the word "montage" seems to be on the esoteric side. But Vorkapich, the former M-G-M montage expert who directed some of the best of the *This Is America* series for R.K.O. is an outspoken man who talks good common sense about motion pictures.

"Montage," in Hollywood, has a special meaning. When Vorkapich was working for M-G-M, he devised montages for numerous pictures, mainly to get across a point economically or to bridge a time lapse. In a matter of moments, with images cascading across the screen, he was able to show Jeanette MacDonald's rise to fame as an opera star in *Maytime* (1938), the beginning of the revolution in *Viva Villa!* (1934), the famine and exodus of *The Good Earth* (1937), or the plague sequence of *Romeo and Juliet* (1936).

But the theory behind montage, according to Vorkapich, has wider applications and can be used to tell an entire screen story, not just an isolated moment in it. This theory is the rather familiar one that movies should move, that motion pictures are a visual medium, and that the camera is the means with which the screen creator expresses himself. Although this theory has been set forth frequently, it has too rarely been put into effect. Most movies today, Vorkapich contends, are merely extensions of stage tech-

85

nique. They are based on a theatrical use of dialogue, and the camera, through no fault of the cameraman, records the action passively instead of participating actively in the proceedings.

These are generalizations composed of fairly big words. To get down to concrete cases, Vorkapich avers that motion pictures were initially devised to record movement—whether of horses, trains, or custard-pie wielders—and that the word "movie" is indicative of the nature of the medium. Vorkapich's theory is that movement arouses an involuntary visceral reaction in the spectator, and that different movements can evoke different types of responses. An upward movement, for instance, usually represents aspiration or exaltation. A descending movement is symbolic of heaviness or danger. A circular, revolving movement is emblematic of a cheerful mood. A pendulum movement conveys monotony and relentlessness. And a diagonal, dynamic movement stands for the overcoming of obstacles.

These are physiological facts promulgated by the behaviorist school of philosophy. Since becoming a part of the picture industry in 1928, Vorkapich has experimented with these various ideas and has found them to be true. He wants to make it clear that he does not believe in motion for its own sake: too many directors today use dolly and boom shots simply to have so-called movement in a movie. Vorkapich says that there must be a reason for each movement, arising out of the subject matter. In the pioneer days of the screen, slapstick comedies and Westerns made use of a crude form of this technique. Vorkapich wants to see it applied to more complex ends in order to convey subtleties of mood, reaction, and motivation.

In 1934, Vorkapich did two montages at the Astoria studios in New York for Hecht and MacArthur's *Crime without Passion*. He cites one of these, dealing with the symbolic unleashing of the Furies, as a sort of master manual of visual screen technique. This sequence, in its original form, ran to only 300 feet of film, but it encompassed most of the things that can be done with a camera and film.

The sequence opened with Claude Rains shooting Margo. The initial shot was a full-screen close-up of one of Margo's eyes as she stared into the gun. Vorkapich shot this close-up as a still picture in order to have the reverse of movement, with the resultant feeling of holding one's breath. Vorkapich points out that the absence of movement can be as important to an artist as movement itself: all life is composed of contrasts. From this static close-up, he dissolved to a close-up of the muzzle of the gun in an exact overlap that found the gun in the same place on the screen as the eye had been. He cut back to the eye, this time showing a slight twitch. The next shot was again of the barrel of the gun. The firing of the gun was expressed visually by a number of quick flashes, an all-black frame alternating with a white one. Each of these shots was held on the screen for only two frames. In this way, the rapid, volatile effect required was attained visually.

Vorkapich adds that the sound of the gun shooting was on the sound track but that the result was all the more powerful for being a welding of the visual and the aural. He observes that the creative use of sound is important to a motion picture. Sound on the contemporary screen consists mostly of dialogue or obvious sound effects. I remember a picture Alfred Hitchcock made in England in 1937 called *The Woman Alone*. In one scene Sylvia Sidney is shown about to murder her husband, Oscar Homolka, with a kitchen knife. There is a deathly silence on the screen as Miss Sidney picks up the knife, almost without realizing it. Then, as she sees that she is holding the knife, she lets it fall back on the plate, where it makes a disproportionately loud noise. In this case, Hitchcock manipulated sound just as he did the camera, with excellent results.

To continue with the montage from *Crime without Passion:* the next shot was of Margo's eyes wincing in sudden pain, followed by an out-of-focus shot of smoke leaving the gun, and the man behind the gun. Vorkapich explains that in an out-of-focus shot the spectator's eye strains to bring the picture into focus and that this effort physically almost forces tears into the observer's eyes. Then, in order to prolong the feeling of agony, there is a slow-motion shot of the woman falling to the ground. One of the things the screen can do is stretch time or compress it for dramatic purposes. The march of the police down the Odessa steps in the Russian film *Potemkin* takes perhaps ten minutes to run on the screen. Actually, such a march would have taken only a few minutes in real life. Director Sergei Eisenstein prolonged the scene purposely to wring the last drop of suspense out of it.

Before Margo was shown hitting the ground in *Crime without Passion*, Vorkapich cut to a close-up of a drop of blood hitting the ground. Then out of the blood of the victim the symbolic Furies were shown rising and flying over the city. Vorkapich filmed this scene with the Furies stationary and the camera shooting from above and passing them as it headed down. Since on the screen all space is relative, the Furies seem to be in motion. When I was at the Astoria studios where *Crime without Passion* was shot, I remember looking at some of the sets stored away in one corner of the studio. The sets were flimsy and incomplete. Hecht and MacArthur, and Lee Garmes the cameraman, had no use for expensive, cumbersome sets. They knew just what effects they wanted to obtain and they were able to get those effects easily and inexpensively by using their ingenuity.

I cite this montage from *Crime without Passion* not necessarily because it is flawless but because it represents an approach to movie making that has been either forgotten or relegated to the background in recent years. Most of the shots I have mentioned are quite obvious ones, and the point I am making is almost a truism. It has been made many times before. I am making it once more because no one seems to pay any attention to what appears to be the obvious thing. The screen as an artistic medium has certain inherent characteristics. It can do things that other artistic mediums cannot. But these advantages of the screen are rarely put to use today. It is a wonderful vast field that has barely been touched. As Vorkapich says, the world of color is the domain of painting, the world of tone is the province of music, and the world of movement is the characteristic of film. The full range of movie movement—through cutting, dissolving, moving shots, pan shots, slow motion, reverse action, and the many other things the camera can do—can be used to probe the most complex and subtle moods and situations. Movement does not have to deal only with physical movement. It can deal also with action within people.

Vorkapich says that the trouble with most motion-picture scripts is they are written in terms of theatrical dialogue. He would like to see a scenario written in two sections. On one side of the page would be the dialogue, and on the other would be a detailed résumé of the action and camera manipulation. If the action does not speak for itself, he says, then something is lacking in the script. Such a scenario technique would require that the writer be thoroughly trained in the ABC's of motion-picture production before he sits down at the typewriter. It would mean that the writer would think visually instead of from a literary standpoint, and would consult experienced cameramen, would practically collaborate with cameramen in writing the action for his story.

Another thing Vorkapich requires of a movie is rhythm. Not the kind of rhythm that is musical or even, but an overall rhythm that arises out of the juxtaposition of the different shots, I will cite another instance, the picture *The Clock*. To my mind, the most moving scene in the picture is one that is told solely in terms of the camera and that could have been only briefly indicated by the writers. The boy and girl are in the park at night. Suddenly, looking at one another, they are drawn toward each other as if by some inner compulsion. The director and cameraman handled this scene almost as if it were a ballet. By some dexterous cutting and camera movement, and without a word being spoken, the couple move toward each other tremulously and gravely. It was not the usual love scene that is seen on the screen. Handled with talent and imagination, it had overtones that words could not approximate. The result was the overall combination of the different shots, the rhythm of the scene.

"Montage," Vorkapich says, "is French for any kind of mounting, assembling, putting together. Like many other words, it has a general and a special meaning. Thus, the making of a complete picture (assembling and putting together individual strips of film) is montage in its general meaning. So far, the possibilities of montage have been barely touched upon. Practically, it has proved to be a valuable economical device in regular productions. Artistically, it could become a true filmic form of expression. Montage is not just a jumble of camera tricks. They are tricks only when they are used for their own sake and not as the most graphic means of expressing something. Montage is in reality a film style of its own, and a very elastic one at that, which uses purely visual means, including all the possibilities of the camera, of movement, of rhythm, and of cutting to express feeling and thoughts to tell stories."

American Cinematographer, June 1945

Thoughts on Movement

HILARY HARRIS

The most exciting thing in film is movement. The rhythmic, pulsing, changing progression of images on the screen in a darkened room can be endowed with all the power and magic or delicacy that one can imagine. Out of our eyes all things move and express themselves in their movement. The action of shapes in reality or the abstract can have a wonderful range and depth of communication, from the flick of a cat's tail to the majesty of the earth's rotation. When you begin to think about it, every mood, character, animal, or place has its kind of movement, and, conversely, every movement expresses something.

As for my own work, the abstract film to me is the most purely emotional and engrossing, whereas the experimental film of concrete images is most revealing and provoking. It is extraordinary how film is capable of borrowing and using the images of all the other arts. It borrows the images but it cannot borrow the forms of the other arts. Film as an art has its own unique basis of expression, which has to do with movement and the manipulation of images in time. A good film, no matter what type, should have its own inner integrity, which is its own filmic form. Since the advent of the sound film thirty years back, film form has been dominated by the theater. This has held back the development of a more purely filmic form, which was begun in the silent era and then later advanced by the documentary movement. This does not mean fine films are not produced, but even the best dramatic films often seem to rattle in a vacuum of visual integrity or form. The task of developing a more excellent, powerful, and exciting kind of film falls largely to the experimental filmmaker, because usually the form of his work is more filmic and less dependent on other arts. The development of a true filmic form for each of his works is his biggest job.

There seems to be a considerable amount of confusion as to what is an experimental film. Many films have an experimental nature without being experimental films. A director may use many new, inventive, unusual elements in a film, but if he uses for his underlying form a story line or a literal development of ideas, then he has not made a true experimental film. A film whose underlying form comes out of a more purely visual experience is an experimental film. Some of the films made at the height of the documentary movement, such as *Song of Ceylon*, are of such a non-literal quality that they would now be more accurately called experimental films, in the light of the direction that the documentary eventually took. We should not confuse the adjective "experimental" with the noun "experimental." Perhaps this same kind of mistake was made when the term "art nouveau" was first used. It should be clear that experimental film is a distinct kind of film. Apart from dramatic films and documentaries, many excellent films may be difficult to categorize as to type because of the mixture of modes; but let that not negate the fact that most experimental films fall rather easily, if a bit loosely, into a distinct group whose form or "life" is a non-literal and non-dramatic visual experience. To avoid the confusion, perhaps we should try to change the name to "illiterate films" or "eye films" or "filmic films." It may be a good number of years before this, I think, good name attains the measure of dignity it deserves in the public eye.

At the moment, there are no great sweeping movements in the world of film. The work of the many isolated experimental filmmakers in various places is doing more than anything else to further the development of the filmic form. Certainly, out of America, the largest film-producing country, could come in the near future a real movement of important film works.

Modern Uses of the Moving Camera

STANLEY J. SOLOMON

*O*ne of the most important developments in film during the last few years has been the increasingly frequent use of a moving camera in scenes which traditionally have been photographed from fixed camera positions. Nothing is more characteristic of contemporary filming than the attempt to convey visual imagery with a mobile camera by panning, tilting, tracking, dollying, craning, and recently zooming.[1] Some of this would have to be considered experimental cinematography, as it certainly is with several New Wave directors, but in Hollywood as well as in Europe the practice is already common.

What is happening is not merely a change in technique but an essential transformation in the approach to visual expression. A film that employs a large number of moving shots requires from a director a different order of thinking than a film which relies mainly on stationary camera set-ups. Although the use of the moving camera is evidently haphazard, uncalled for, and pretentious in almost every ordinary film made in the last five or six years, there can be no doubt that some directors are discovering new and valid uses for this approach, especially since Kurosawa's brilliant track-

---

[1] In a zoom shot, the camera itself of course does not move, but the effect of simulating motion is aimed at, and thus zoom shots may be classified as a kind of moving shot.

ing shots through the forest in *Rashomon* made their impression on the film world.

I would like to examine some of the contemporary uses of the moving camera, paying particular attention to four films: Jacques Demy's *The Umbrellas of Cherbourg*, François Truffaut's *Jules and Jim*, John Frankenheimer's *The Train*, and Michelangelo Antonioni's *The Red Desert*. These films represent some of the more thoughtful conceptions (at times unsuccessful) of what this new tendency in filming might lead to.

In spite of the usual slowing down of the tempo, somehow the effect of liveliness is apparent in several contemporary films in which the camera moves continually, such as Jacques Demy's *The Umbrellas of Cherbourg*, where the effect is achieved in spite of some rather torpid editing. More remarkable, if we consider Demy's film an outstanding representative of this tendency, liveliness is accomplished in spite of some rather dull—or at least slow —physical movement on the part of the actors. Nothing much happens in Demy's film, visually, aside from the coloring (a static aspect of filming), and certainly the trivial plot and the thematic shallowness could not endear the film to American audiences. Still, there are few slow moments in this picture. The question, then, is how does Demy get away with his material and produce what most people thought was a lively film, including of course many people who wouldn't be caught dead at an opera.

It seems to me that, in *The Umbrellas of Cherbourg* and numerous films from Jean-Luc Godard's *Breathless* on, the effect is achieved by an unrestrained use of a technique of older master filmmakers (e.g., René Clair in his 1931 films, *Le Million* and *A Nous La Liberté*), who first discovered, but developed only in part, a principle of the moving camera. This principle is that in spite of the intrinsic slowness of panning a camera about, wheeling it in or around, craning it up or down, when the camera moves upon living subjects, the audience experiences a sense of participation somewhat greater than that experienced when viewing the classic works of film art in which the formal objectivity of the filmmaker prevents an emotional identification as easily and as thoroughly induced as in *The Umbrellas*. We are, in Demy's film, "thrust" into the lives of four characters no more interesting than the characters in the most banal Hollywood movie; but the sense of participation, the sense of increased emotional involvement, helps to enliven Demy's material and to disguise its essential weaknesses.

Has it ever been pointed out how Brechtian are most of the screen's *formal* masterpieces: e.g., Chaplin's *Monsieur Verdoux*, Eisenstein's *Potemkin*, Renoir's *Rules of the Game*, Lang's *M*, Kurosawa's *Seven Samurai*, Bergman's *The Seventh Seal*, or even, on a somewhat lower level, any Hitchcock film? By Brechtian, I refer to the objectivity of the presentation, the external viewpoint of action presented within (or filtered through) a carefully delineated framework. While the result is never the critical detachment that Brecht himself pretended to advocate—but of course was too much the artist to achieve—we do experience, if we are intellectually prepared, a less than total emotional involvement. This is because in a masterpiece there is more to look at than the emotional crises of particular characters or their dilemmas, loves, frustrations, and joys. There is form, a framework to which a spectator can attach himself and so gaze upon the scene without losing himself in it. One takes hold "intellectually" no matter how emotionally powerful a scene is, and thus a spectator is not swamped by the spectacle. I find this true even in the most overpoweringly emotional scenes in great films: for instance, in the gripping flagellation sequence from *The Seventh Seal*, a gasping spectator still keeps in mind that "Bergman has done this superbly." We continually come back to an appreciation of form, assuming an order of intelligence behind the choice of scenes which we do not bother to think about in films like Demy's. Instead, we suspend one part—the intellectual part—of our critical faculty so as to enjoy *The Umbrellas of Cherbourg*.

But Demy is certainly a film artist, though not on the very highest level. He does know what he is doing, and the use of a moving camera in *The Umbrellas* is a modern device peculiarly suited to his slight material. As the camera continually swings around, the audience itself is transported to a position in the center of the room in which the actors are performing. Traditionally, the film audience, like the stage audience, is given a "ringside" view, close to the action but outside of it. With the camera swinging about, we are brought not only up to the action but inside it; we turn from one wall to another constantly, as if we were in the room itself, glancing about it. As a result, our immediate presence has the effect of animating the world in which we have entered and participated.

In keeping with the musical nature of the film, the camera practically imitates the movement of a dancer, gracefully moving about in a confined space, the world of the umbrella shop and the gas station. However, even if we grant that Demy's use of the camera is appropriate, we ought to recognize that any values achieved with it are at least partially balanced by what is lost: the objective frame of reference which encloses the microcosmic world of most films and distances the audience from the life presented on screen. This objective frame, it seems to me, is the formal and orderly presentation of the visual imagery—and is characteristic of those films generally recognized as the greatest achievements in the art form.

Aside from liveliness, another value that might be claimed for relying heavily on the moving camera is that this technique is particularly appropriate in depicting the chaotic existence of contemporary life. If absurdity and chaos are now values to be aimed at in contemporary drama and literature and painting, we will probably have to admit that they will serve equally well in contemporary film.

Since the film has always existed in an age of chaos, it has long had its methods of depicting the troubles of its day. D. W. Griffith's way was the rapid cross-cutting of two actions (usually parallel in intention, though not in structure): Lillian Gish is caught on the ice flow and Richard Barthelmess is out looking for her. Eisenstein would build up pictorial elements in conflict within shots and from one shot to another. Similarly, Lang and Renoir, by paying attention to horizontal and vertical lines, could induce vivid effects of tension by pictorial conflicts. For example, in *The Rules of the Game* (1939) there are shots of steps leading to a terrace. When no person is in camera range, the image resembles a beautiful abstract photograph: perfect calmness established by preponderant horizontal lines. But when a character suddenly walks into camera range and up or down the stairs, an effect of tremendous

tension is produced simply by the introduction of a vertical line in
motion. This effect could not be achieved if a moving camera were
to follow the approaching character before he reached the steps.

The contemporary method for inducing in the spectator a feeling of a disoriented or unstable society is to employ a freely moving camera. One of the more popular films illustrating this tendency is *Jules and Jim*. Throughout it, Truffaut's camera seems
frenetic, hardly ever remaining at rest for longer than a shot or
two. The world of the three main characters, a world of war and
neuroses, is constantly unsettled, aimless, shifting—as is the camera. A spectator cannot watch this film intelligently without being continually reminded of the filmmaker's presence, which indeed seems to many admirers of the New Wave films the highest
virtue of film art, to be striven for even at the expense of seeming
obtrusive.

It is a peculiarity of *Jules and Jim* that at times even the transitions between sequences are achieved by the movement of the
camera. The physical phenomenon of a fast-moving camera (not
true of the human eye) is the reproduction of a blurred visual perception. This blur is sometimes used by Truffaut to effect changes
of scene, and as such it becomes a substitute for the traditional
methods: (1) cutting; (2) fading or dissolving; (3) using insert titles (e.g., Godard's *Vivre Sa Vie*) or a narrative voice (e.g., *Tom
Jones*); (4) using optical devices such as the "wipe." These traditional linking devices have long since exhausted whatever ingenuity may once have belonged to them. They have through continual
usage become entirely functional, not attractive or meaningful in
themselves, except for the sake of parody; in general, they are visually nonexistent, for most spectators never notice them. Not so
with Truffaut's rapidly swinging camera blurs. Because this technique is unusual, it calls attention to itself, and it is used so frequently in *Jules and Jim* that it constitutes a large part of what
many will remember of that film's visual design.

Blurring, however, is just an extreme instance of what Truffaut
does much more moderately throughout the film. Two or three
characters may be talking, while Truffaut, abjuring the usual
method of cutting back and forth among speakers and listeners,
pans around the set or whirls the camera from one character to another. The effect of this motion is often to present the visual form

(frenzied, perhaps chaotic) in direct conflict with the content of the dialogue and action in the same sequence (the dialogue being often calm and low-pitched). It is not unusual in any art for content and form to conflict; however, generally it is the content which stands out, while in a film such as *Jules and Jim* the form is almost always more striking than the materials being presented.

When watching films by many of the interesting younger directors, particularly the French directors, we cannot help wondering just how important the content is anyway. That is, technique, camera work, pace, and other formal aspects of film seem to count for almost everything. We always have the feeling—and this is often a refreshing feeling, not a criticism—that the directors are continually experimenting. The use of a moving camera therefore symbolizes the flux of their own artistic sensibilities as well as that of the filmic worlds they create.

The modern reliance on the moving camera is not limited only to experimentalists or French directors paying homage to Monogram Films. We find it now in recent works by long-established directors like John Ford and Vittorio De Sica. And among the newer contemporary directors like John Frankenheimer and Michelangelo Antonioni who are definitely committed to "intellectual art," directors of whom we could never assert that they were more concerned to experiment with techniques than to present what they had to say—even here we find a surprisingly large number of moving camera shots.

The cinematography of Frankenheimer's film *The Train* is at least as frenzied as Truffaut's in *Jules and Jim*. Presumably, Frankenheimer is as much a socially committed director as he is a film artist since he has consistently selected politico-sociological scripts like *Birdman of Alcatraz* (1962), *The Manchurian Candidate* (1962), *Seven Days in May* (1964), and *The Train* (1965). It is then to be expected that the form of his films will be pretty much in line with the significance of the material—that he will usually not proceed by establishing tension between the form and content of his films.[2]

---

[2] The possible exception, *The Manchurian Candidate*, is another kind of problem. Here the form *is* the meaning; the parody (of the basic comic idea of a Manchurian candidate) is probably less important than the subtler irony evoked by the deliberately melodramatic structure in every sequence.

In *The Train*, the rhythm of the first sequence after the titles sets the tone for the entire film: a room crowded with German soldiers crating paintings to be shipped out of Paris and behind their lines on the eve of the Allied forces' arrival in that city. The camera moves rather quickly through the midst of the activity, the audience receiving general impressions of commotion and haste instead of specific details of the hurried crating. Thus, from the outset, the filmic pace symbolizes the action of the narrative, which is made up of rushing soldiers, fleeing Resistance fighters, and the speeding train. Zooming, tracking, and panning shots are used continually to represent a moving world in which deliberation is impossible, decisions must be made quickly and carried out desperately by both sides.

The audience itself is psychologically drawn into the situation so that no spectator is enabled to reflect on the action while watching the film—we are swept along with the camera and forced unintentionally to suspend intellectual judgment on what we see. Frankenheimer's technical success in giving us a frantic ride on that train is achieved at great cost. For it is virtually impossible to watch the film as anything more than a good adventure movie—a sacrifice, probably, for a director whose work in the past has often been characterized by a somewhat heavy-handed social criticism.

The very ending of *The Train* is an ingenious attempt to restore some intellectual balance, and in its melodramatic surprise it succeeds. The agitated camera motion is entirely and abruptly stilled in the last few shots to show us pictures—they have the effect of photographs—of the final senseless carnage, dead bodies of Frenchmen killed purposelessly, as was the leading German officer in the scenes preceding this final sequence. Derived from the last minute of the film, the theme becomes an implied condemnation of unthinking actions taken by desperate men forced by the situation of war into brutal spur-of-the-moment decisions.

Although there is nothing I can recall in any film quite like the ending of *The Train*, I have considerable reservations about the value of the ending. From observation, I have seen the audience shocked by the sudden rhythmic change at the end (which is the equivalent of ending a sentence with five exclamation marks), and remain seated for several seconds after the lights have been turned on. Yet Frankenheimer was undoubtedly not aiming at just the shock effect of showing us a few final pictures of the stillness of death. I am convinced that he was commenting on the entire structure of the action, though it seems dubious that a few pictures at the end will cause many spectators to re-think an entire film which was entertaining and exciting throughout but which hardly seemed to be leading to any provocative ideas.

One of the values of the moving camera is its capacity to involve us emotionally in the environment, but at the same time it limits our ability to perceive significant ideas. When we are moving, we are probably not thinking, and when we are moving very quickly, when we are in fact "breathless," we may not even be feeling correctly.

The most successful recent use of the mobile camera occurs in *The Red Desert*, in which Antonioni approaches his material in a manner exactly opposite to Demy's in *The Umbrellas of Cherbourg*. Where Demy's camera attempted to depict the energetic liveliness of his characters' existences, Antonioni's camera moves in to examine a modern industrial wasteland, the physical stagnation of which symbolizes the stagnation of the characters' lives. Thus, the pace of *The Red Desert* is consistently deliberate, and the moving camera with its slow explorations of the decayed natural environment—such as a river turned into thick mud by chemical waste or the entire atmosphere polluted by yellow gases pouring out of the monstrous factories—hovers relentlessly over motionless images in pursuit of the symbols of society's death.

What Antonioni accomplishes by the numerous moving outdoor shots is to suggest to us that the man-made destructive forces contain a latent power of their own; that is, the ominous ships and machines have somehow eluded human control, and (like Frankenstein's monster) having received life of their own, are no longer slaves of their inventors. We observe very few human beings actually working the machinery of modern life, and even when we are shown a few, such as the men constructing the fantastically large experimental equipment for the University of Bologna, they are amazingly insignificant beside the structures they have built.

In developing the theme, the camera scans powerful machines, which, of course, lack the necessary intelligence to order their force against man. Perhaps the most emphatic images of this occur when Antonioni follows the metallic jumble of tubes and pipes—one time in particular when the camera explores some steel maze aboard a ship, tilting up and up on this abstracted complexity, which finally twists itself downwards; and the camera continuing to analyze it on its downward course surprises us by comically ending up exactly where it began.

In contrast, Antonioni presents a picture of men who have the intelligence, but not apparently the power or will, to order their lives so as to make a sensible stand against the industrial age. Thus, *The Red Desert* presents a nightmarish world engaged in a meaningless conflict of man and machine, meaningless in that no characters recognize the antagonism in their environment (though they all sense it). One of the most effective symbols of this is the brainless boy monster wheeling aimlessly back and forth while presiding over the bedroom of the young child. A threat—but one still latent, though it is emphasized that while the child sleeps, the monster's eyes remain alight, keeping watch.

Antonioni's formal problem was how to engage us emotionally in a world that is veering toward emotional death. (Most of the characters in the film, aside from the two main characters, are depicted as emotionless—even in the scene in the shack by the pier where six characters lie on a bed, a few pretending to be sexually involved but actually too bored to make more than some feeble gestures of involvement.) His solution was to use the moving camera with considerable restraint, but to use it often. Much of the movement does not attempt to take us into the characters' situation or the environment but instead moves us (sideways, craning or panning) *away* from the action. This is necessary, for the subject matter is complex, and the filmmaker could not possibly succeed with his numerous symbols if we were completely caught up in the lives of his characters, as we usually will be if we are not properly distanced from the story.

Exclusive use of either alternative—the objective or the subjective camera—could not encompass the aims of Antonioni in this film. If we are not at all concerned with the plight of Monica Vitti, then of course our objectivity will prevent us from emotionally grasping the significance of the various threats to psychological stability pervading this society. On the other hand, if we are ourselves lost in the highly subjective world in which the heroine because of her mental condition must exist, then we cannot take any intelligent notice of the symbols. A spectator may not lose too much if he fails to notice that outdoors the sky is always overcast in this film; but if he also fails to notice that indoors the external drabness is duplicated by bare walls and ugly railings and unaesthetic (though functional) living space, then the spectator has missed the film's point. In other words, the background which contains the characters must be observed in as much detail as the facial expressions or human movements in the center of the frame.

The Red Desert could not, therefore, maintain a moving camera for any number of consecutive shots. The camera continually arrives at points of rest where rigidly formal arrangements of photographic elements are beautifully used in a manner reminiscent of the best work of Carl Dreyer or Fritz Lang, but including experimental variations in lens focal length, which is not characteristic of any older director. In the style of Renoir, Antonioni permits characters to walk beyond camera range or out of focus. Sometimes characters appear to leave under the extremely unusual condition of walking in and out of medium or close shots. In fact, there is often much more movement on the part of characters photographed from a fixed camera set-up than from a moving camera arrangement. However, moving camera shots are frequently used to follow Monica Vitti from a short distance, framing her from head to waist or from head to shoulders. Such camera movement can hardly be effective in most films because a moving actor photographed by a close-following camera will occupy practically the entire frame (the background will be out of focus) and thus will appear in a somewhat confused relationship with his blurred environment. With these shots of Miss Vitti, Antonioni is consciously trying to show both her confinement in the unfocused world around her and her alienation from it. She moves without much awareness of other people, who are no more aware of her, and Antonioni emphasizes this by continually isolating her with his moving camera.

The four films that I have referred to by Antonioni, Frankenheimer, Truffaut, and Demy are of course entirely unlike one another, and unlike any other films in recent years. But they are all typical of the increasing modern preference for the moving camera. What this means for film aesthetics is that the normal mode of expression is changing, though it is too early to judge whether the change will result in an expansion or deterioration of contemporary film language. We have been conditioned by our critics to accept experimentation in films as a desirable end in itself—and this comes not only from the *Film Culture* critics but from critics on leading women's magazines and *Time* itself. Obviously, in a generation where millions of people are going to art theaters to see "something new," questions of quality in regard to the form of film art are less important than the immediate impact of topical subject matter or experimental style. When a film like *One Potato, Two Potato* can be generously praised because of its interesting subject matter, even though it is in form a piece of ineptitude, we realize that aesthetic criteria in this art medium are nowhere generally understood.

Part of the problem lies in the reluctance of critics to deal with the new methods of filmic expression, preferring to evaluate content and characterization as if these matters were only loosely affected by the form in which they are presented. It is an important function of our critical faculty not only to judge how well a particular scene has been done but to question whether the same material could have been filmed more powerfully, with more visual interest, if changes had been made in rhythm, editing, camera placement, and camera movement. Since there is much experimentation going on presently with the moving camera, it seems that critics are afforded excellent opportunities for evaluation and comparison. It should, however, always be kept in mind that camera movement is not merely, or even mainly, a technical matter of academic concern: it is, on the contrary, one of the essential considerations in the expression of visual meaning.

Film Heritage, Winter 1965–66

MOVEMENT

Movement generates various degrees of tension and sets up the dynamics of film structure

MOTION BEFORE THE CAMERA
The Boston Strangler (1968), Richard Fleischer

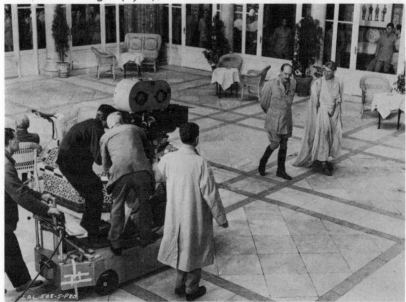

CAMERA MOTION
Lawrence of Arabia (1962), David Lean

MOTION PRODUCED
OPTICALLY: THE ZOOM
LENS
Romeo and Juliet (1968),
Franco Zeffirelli

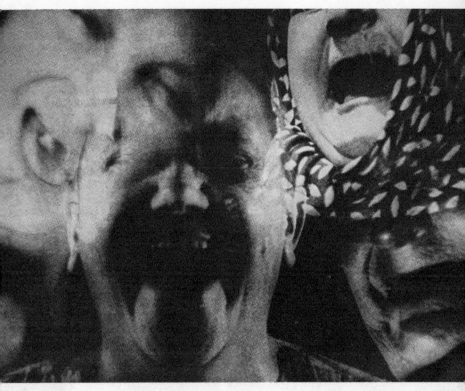

PRISMS
The Last Laugh (1925), Fred Murnau

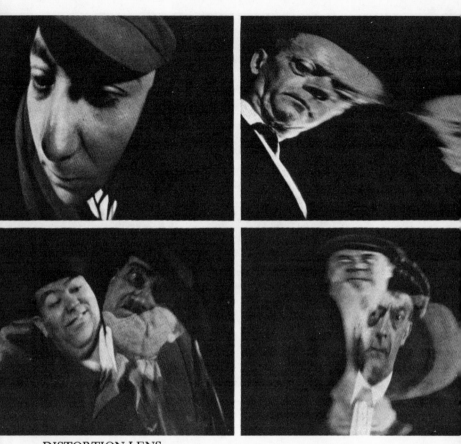

DISTORTION LENS
Uberfall (1929), Erno Metzner

MEASURED INCREASE OF
VISUAL QUANTITIES
Soil (1930), Alexander Dovzhenko

MULTIPLE EXPOSURE
Dreams That Money Can Buy (1947),
Hans Richter

CONTRAST OF
ANGLES
Strike (1925), Sergei
Eisenstein

SEQUENTIAL EVOLUTION OF AN IDEA THROUGH THEMATIC FORMS
Crime without Passion (1934),
Slavko Vorkapitch

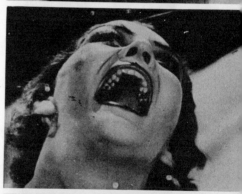

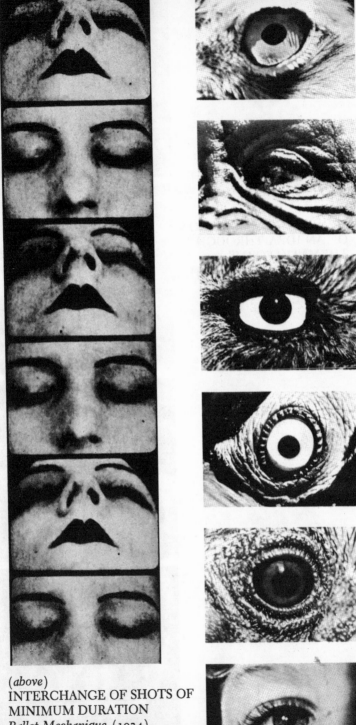

(*above*)
INTERCHANGE OF SHOTS OF
MINIMUM DURATION
Ballet Mechanique (1924),
Fernand Leger and Dudley Murphy

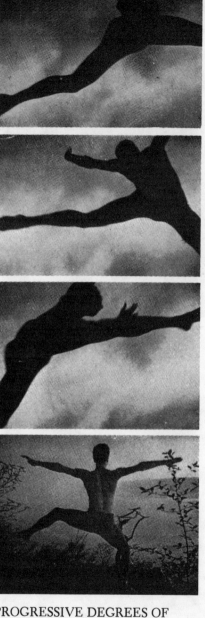

(opposite right)
THROUGH REPEATED SHAPES
The Searching Eye (1964), Saul Bass
Associates

PROGRESSIVE DEGREES OF
CHANGING, MATCHING, OR
OVERLAPPING ACTION
*A Study in Choreography for the
Camera* (1945), Maya Deren

COMPARISON OR CONTRAST OF QUALITIES
Mother (1926), V. Pudovkin

Change of Camera Viewpoint

Irving Pichel

*I*t is typical of all forms of spectacle before the motion picture—the theater, the circus, the sports field—that the spectator remains in a fixed position at a determined distance from the action he sees. The spectator at a football game watches the movement of the two teams in relation to their respective goalposts. The goals remain at fixed distances from him. Only the players move. The spectator participates in their movement insofar as he turns his head to follow that movement. His mind participates in that movement as it estimates the distance of the moving players from the goal toward which they move. Since he knows the rules of the game, this distance has significance for him. If he is concerned with the fortunes of one of the opposing teams, the lessening distance between the players and a goal induces excitement which may produce sympathetic movement on his part. He may jump to his feet, wave his arms, shout, cheer, or groan.

A newsreel photographer high above the field might photograph a game with so comprehensive a shot that both goals would be simultaneously visible. For parts of the game, as when the teams run the length of the field, only such a viewpoint can adequately convey the significance of the play. However, from this distance the players appear so small that details of the action cannot be seen, players cannot be identified, and the ball is invisible. The cameraman, therefore, after a time moves closer or changes the lens on his camera. More detail can now be seen, but his shot includes only half the field. Since the players are all at that end of the field, approaching one of the goals, this is a much more satisfactory viewpoint. In moving his camera he has, in effect, moved the spectator. When the newsreel is shown in the theater, the first comprehensive shot will be followed by the closer shot. Though the action will be continuous, the viewpoint of the spectator will change instantaneously. Then, as a player runs with the ball toward the far end of the field, the camera viewpoint will shift again to the more distant position so that the larger sweep of play can be seen and the significant relationship of players to distant goal be realized and measurable.

Changing the position of the camera during action to a closer position, without any apparent interruption in the continuous flow of the spectacle, was the first technical advance that was to make of motion pictures a new and unique form of visual experience. The fixed relationship between spectator and spectacle was broken down. The action could be brought closer or moved away, or, stated conversely, the spectator could have every sensation of moving closer except that of motility.

It will be noted that this instant change of viewpoint to one more advantageous occurs, in a projected film, not in the action pictured, or in the actual position of a person watching the film, but in the film itself. This is *movement*, though not action. As the screenplay developed, this filmic movement was to take many forms: the abridged movement implied in the cuts from shot to shot—from long shot forward to medium shot, and still nearer to a close shot; the movement of point of view from one character in a group scene to another; and the much greater movements implied in cuts from one locale to another.

The convention which asked an audience to take for granted these instantaneous changes of viewpoint was easy to establish, since, first, it exploited in a larger sense fundamental film characteristics of movement; and, second, it represented not too inaccurately the operation of the spectator's imagination. This structural motion in film objectifies fairly closely the manner in which the eye seeks out of any occurrence or spectacle the most interesting person or action and follows it, to the exclusion of other elements presented at the same time. It operates as the mind does when one reads a story, visualizing with the author's account the actions now of one character and now of another, the events now in one place and now in another, the observing of large panoramas and then of minute details. It also objectifies magically, as no other medium can, the wish to be able to come closer, to see more clearly and intimately than life or the earlier forms of theater art have allowed.

Let us return for a moment to our football game. We shall assume that the cameraman is in the closer position, his lens covering only half the field. Through the finder he sees a player start with the ball on a run down the field to the farther goal. He swings his camera, following the runner, exactly as a spectator turns his head to watch the play. Instead of an *instantaneous* move to a viewpoint from which the action can be seen, there is a movement *simultaneous* with the action. The movement, timed with the action, occurs not in the film but in the seeing organ, the eye, the camera.

With the development of screen technique, camera movement has been elaborated. Mounted on wheels, the camera can precede or follow a character. Set on a crane, it can be lifted high above the action. It can recede from a detail to a full shot or, conversely, move from a full shot into a close-up of a single character selected out of the scene. Camera movement, it will be noted, takes place at a much slower tempo than filmic movement and has a different aim. Its rate is related either to that of the spectator's eye or to that of a moving person or object as the spectator's eye follows that movement in the scene being filmed. Its aim likewise is twofold. It seeks either to imitate the eye movement the spectator would perform if he were present at the scene being photographed, as in most "pan" shots, or it undertakes to convey to the spectator the illusion that he himself shares the movement of the camera.

A person walking has the sense that he is approaching a distant landmark which remains rooted at a definite place. The tree grows in one spot, although its size and relationship to other objects in that landscape modify as the pedestrian draws nearer. Some part of his own motility transfers itself to the tree. As he draws nearer, the focus of his eye changes, the tilt of his head is greater as he looks toward the tree's top. His approach causes him to bring into play a different set of muscles, to alter his relation to what he sees. He has the sense that, as he shortens the distance between himself and the tree, it is the tree that alters its aspect. He will say, "The tree grew taller" (as he approached), or "The tree loomed larger."

If he approaches a fixed object in a vehicle, an automobile let us say, in which his own physical effort is eliminated, he is likely to attribute the movement not to the vehicle or to himself but to his surroundings. He will say, "The country flowed by," or "The house drew nearer."

Something equivalent occurs when the camera is moved while photographing action. The moving character or object is centered in the finder and remains virtually stationary on the screen, and the background becomes fluid. Landscape or buildings flow past and, on the assumption that the spectator identifies himself with the moving character, his relationship to the background is in flux while he himself is actually motionless.

In photographing a character in motion, it must be decided which is more important, the movement or the closeness of the point of view. Obviously, if the camera moves with a moving character, as in dolly shots, movement is negated, since, as has been noted above, the character remains centered on the screen and the background passes by. Comment on this fact will be amplified later in this discussion.

Before attempting to make generalizations concerning the use of camera movement, it is important to clarify the function of the camera. It is not enough to say that it is the machine by which a screenplay is photographed. The chain of instrumentalities which begins with the camera and its negative film and passes through the developing machine and the printing machine, the development of the positive and the projection of the positive print on a screen, is too closely identified with an important human sense to be regarded simply as a mechanism. The camera, by which for brevity we mean the entire mechanism, is an eye. Like the microscope or the telescope or field glasses, it extends the capacity of the human eye. It is an eye that functions in a special way for a special purpose. Whose eye do we conceive the camera to be? And how is it to be used? The answer to the second question will be provided by our answer to the first. Most commonly, since the images photographed by the camera are to be viewed by a spectator, the camera is treated as an extension of the spectator's eye. It sees what the spectator could see if he were himself present at the events photographed. It reports as a newsreel does. It satisfies at each moment the spectator's wish or unconscious need to see now in general and now in particular the places, the people, their faces, their hands, their weapons, their action toward each other, which compose into an organic dramatic or narrative whole. Through filmic movement, it is endowed with selectivity. As a theatergoer with opera glasses will focus them now on one character and now on another, the camera, instantly eliding intervening motion, goes from person to person, from image to image. Exhausting for the moment the interest of one locale and its characters, it can go instantaneously to another group in another place to see how they are faring. It may accompany a character in an automobile or an airplane or go under the sea in a submarine. It may walk with sweethearts and overhear their most intimate conversation. It may accompany a criminal to the gallows. If the camera is used as a substitute for or an extension of the spectator's vision, it is limited only by the obligation to maintain at all times feasible human viewpoints.

If the camera is thought of, however, not as a projection of the spectator's viewpoint, but of the narrator's, it may move with greater freedom and latitude. Like the eye of a novelist, the camera then partakes of the character, personality, and approach of the narrator. It has, like a storyteller, omniscience and omnipresence, or, more exactly, the ability to see only what it wants to see and to be only where it needs to be in order to tell its particular fable. It has selectivity, seeing only those instants in the life of various images which add up to a continuity of time, spatial relationships and causative relationships which the natural eye is incapable of seeing. Conversely, it has the ability to avoid seeing everything in the lives of the fable's characters which is not germane to the telling of the fable. In this use of the camera a complete personality is created who, though not appearing before the audience's eyes, is yet real and definite and as highly personalized as the real storyteller, be he writer or director, who employs it. With this concept of the use of the camera, the director can achieve personal style as definite as that of a writer. (The term "director" is here used generically, as the word "camera" is used generically. By director we mean the individual who creates or the group of individuals who collaborate in the conception, writing, directing, and editing of a film.) The camera will "see" the story as he sees it and will relate it to an audience through his eyes. It will select shots which for that director have acute expressiveness. Shot will be related to shot in a sequence which has special significance to him. If the camera moves, it will move where he wishes to direct the interest and attention of the spectator.

Attempts have been made also to personify the camera more subjectively by conceiving of it as a character in the story, a narrator using the first person; in other words, as the eyes of a participant in the events it describes. Rouben Mamoulian opened his film *Dr. Jekyll and Mr. Hyde* with a long introductory sequence in which the camera represented the eyes of Dr. Jekyll. However, since the film play was not a story told by Dr. Jekyll, but a story about him, the device had to be abandoned after a few hundred feet.

In a film I directed a few years ago, called *The Great Commandment*, the camera was used in two sequences in the first person to represent the eyes of Jesus. Since the Nazarene appeared in only two short episodes, of which He was the focus, and since the story dealt not with Him but with a number of characters who encountered Him, the device accomplished two important results unobtainable in any other way. The first and less important was to avoid attempting to represent a Presence which could not be visualized satisfactorily for a large proportion of the spectators; and the second, to enable the camera to see intimately and feel the effect of that Presence on the story's principal characters.

Certain limitations become immediately apparent when the camera is used in this manner as an actual participant. The fact that characters speaking to the character represented by the camera must look directly into the lens means that they look directly from the screen into the eyes of the spectator. Thus the spectator is identified with the character assumed by the camera. In the denouement of Hitchcock's *Spellbound* the camera becomes momentarily the eyes of Dr. Murchison. It follows Ingrid Bergman as she crosses the room to the door and hesitates under the camera in the exact center of the screen. Following her as she crosses, we see Murchison's hand holding the revolver. When the door closes behind her, the hand slowly turns the revolver away from the door, pauses, then turns it directly into the lens and shoots—the spectator. Such a twist may defeat the very aim of the device. Further, scenes must be played without cut in continuous action, and the point of view is unalterably that of an individual, and can be moved or changed only at the pace and within the range of the physical mobility of the individual represented by the camera. It is aware only of what he can see and know. Orson Welles had planned as his first picture in Hollywood the production of Joseph Conrad's *The Heart of Darkness*, to be told in the first person with the camera as the eyewitness and narrator, but the plan was defeated by some such considerations as these.

The camera may be used in another way. It is not conceived of as having a personality of its own but as being simply an instrument in the hands of the director, capable of highly flexible expressiveness, as a violin is when played upon by a virtuoso. In this sense the camera is not so much an extension of the narrator's eye or mind as it is a wholly new kind of sight instrument, as fabulous as radar and free from most of the limitations that hedge about human sight. The director uses the camera, if this is his concept of its function, quite arbitrarily. It goes where no human eye could possibly go. It moves according to laws, if any, which apply not to the human eye or the human consciousness but to itself. A number of directors use the camera with this virtuosity, achieving extraordinary effects. One recalls von Sternberg's use of the camera in *The Scarlet Empress*, or that of Orson Welles in *Citizen Kane*. In the most skillful hands, virtuosity of the camera may enhance dramatic effect and produce a work as uniquely conditioned by the fact that it is transmitted through a camera as a violin concerto is conditioned by the fact that it is transmitted by a violin. The dangers attending this use of the camera are easy to define: it offers a constant temptation to place the camera arbitrarily, on the premise that a striking viewpoint or a striking composition is justification in itself, or that camera movement predicated wholly on the capacities of the machine requires no further motivation. To be sure, the end composition will have meaning which in the eyes of the director seems justification enough for the means employed to arrive at that end.

Surely a purely cinematic use of the camera is warranted in semi-abstract treatments of non-dramatic subjects or moments in dramatic films, as, for example, in the photography of musical or dance numbers. The camera movement may have a real or fancied relationship to the music or choreographic pattern, but often enough it simply employs an arbitrarily selected variety of angles and moves with no other object than constantly to refresh the spectator's interest in what he is seeing.

In actual directorial practice no compact is made with the spectator concerning the camera's function. He is not asked to recognize the camera either as his eye or as the narrator's eye or as that of a participant in the action, or to identify himself with a participant in that action. Commonly, no principle in the use of the camera is constantly adhered to by the director. He uses the camera at one moment as though it were the spectator, at another to score a point of his own as the storyteller, or again, impersonally, as a tool for the achievement of an "effect." He justifies movement of the camera as the pursuit of "fluidity," or adheres to the idea that frequent change of angle gives "life" to the film or that sustained master scenes have a special value. These may all be warrantable generalizations under certain circumstances, but they ignore the fundamental that the camera acts as a living organ rather than as a tool.

For all that, the camera is governed by laws of optics, as the eye is also. In function it partakes far more of the biological and psychological aspects of sight than of the purely mechanical, physical aspect. Only a few directors exhibit a clear concept of a continuous understanding between themselves and the spectator concerning the function of the camera. Thus it would seem to the writer that John Ford uses the camera as the spectator's eye. He rarely causes the camera to move, thus permitting the spectator to orient himself in a stable world in which the people and not the landscape or the architecture are animate. There is a minimum use of close-ups, and close shots are achieved more often by causing the characters to approach the camera than by moving the camera closer to the characters. Ford holds that camera movement destroys reality, which is his recognition of the fact that the illusion of movement on the spectator's part cannot be supported by his physical experience as he watches the film. This gives to the rare shots in which he does cause the camera to move an uncommon effectiveness and meaning. In *The Grapes of Wrath* one recalls the wobbling progress of the camera through the Okie settlement when momentarily the camera took the point of view of the Joad family as its truck drove into the camp. Or the shot in *How Green Was My Valley* when, for a moment, Ford became the storyteller and moved the camera away from the faces of Mr. and Mrs. Morgan to the street to the left of them, to show the two sons leaving home. It is as though he were content to let the spectator see the story as an eyewitness, with occasional comment from the director —comment so infrequent that it gives pith and validity from the very detachment and objectivity with which the rest of the story is told. In Leo McCarey's *The Bells of St. Mary's* the camera is moved not more than half a dozen times—only when it is panned, as the spectator might follow with his eyes a character moving purposively from one part of the scene to another.

There are other directors whose camera technique is more fluid because they employ the camera as a storyteller employs words. The point of view is primarily their own. Although it is shared with the spectator, they seem to say, "Let me show you what I saw." They act as gentle guides leading the spectator from place to place, wittily or poignantly pointing to this or that character. Not infrequently their point of view is revealed with an element of surprise. The camera maintains a credible viewpoint, but one somewhat superior to and in advance of the spectator's. It knows, although the spectator does not, where it is going and what it is going to reveal. It has a self-evident sense of plan and foresight. It tells a tale in which not even the accidents are accidental. To illustrate, a picture directed by Lubitsch is told consciously as a tale to amuse or to move the spectator, and the question of the reality of the occurrences shown is secondary. The aesthetic goal is not the illusion of immediacy but the pleasure of an engaging tale.

A skillful craftsman, regardless of his general philosophy concerning the use of the camera, will be governed by one fundamental consideration—that in every shot the content shall be more important than the manner in which it is transmitted. The story comes first, and every shot deals with characters and what they do. If what they do at a given moment is stated in terms of physical action, the camera will set up space for the action and fixed points of reference. If the physical action is casual and secondary to what the character is saying or thinking, the camera will hold the character in the center of the screen whether he is moving or standing still. If his words or the intention that can be read in his face are important and interesting enough, the movement of the camera as it follows him will go unperceived. If, however, the character is stationary and the camera moves toward or away from him, the movement of the camera is bound to be perceived and must then have meaning in itself, saying, in effect, "Watch this man!" or, "We may now leave this person's thoughts and draw back to a place where we can observe his actions." If this preparation through movement or an act of attention on the spectator's part heightens dramatic effect, it is warranted. If it accomplishes merely mechanical readjustment of viewpoint, it draws attention to itself as movement and diminishes the importance of the content of the scene.

With the exception of pan shots which simulate the turn of the spectator's head, camera movement is of two sorts: either (1) the movement of the camera is motivated by and synchronized with the movement of a character or characters; or (2) the movement of the camera is not synchronized with movement on the screen.

It has already been pointed out that camera movement synchronized with physical movement is justified when it is more important to fix audience attention upon the moving character than upon his movement with relation to other characters or the background. Generally speaking, such movement does not change the initial distance relationship between the spectator and the image on the screen.

In camera movement which is not physically motivated, a proper justification can be found only in the imitation or symbolic reproduction of movements taking place in the imagination either of the storyteller or of the spectator. Such movements may be classified roughly as follows: (1) movement from a longer to a closer angle, (2) movement from a closer angle to a longer one, (3) movement from a scene to a detail, (4) movement from a detail to a scene. If such movements have some correspondence with the emotional participation by the spectator in the action, drawing him closer to characters or retracting him to a fuller scene, directing his attention to an inserted detail or drawing his attention from a detail to the characters to whom the detail relates in some significant way, the movement may be justified. It may be observed, however, that these same alterations of viewpoint can be achieved filmically, that is, through direct cuts, more quickly and usually with less awareness of the move itself. Camera movement used in this fashion decreases the pace at which the film moves. The reduction in tempo may have emotional value in itself, though it should be noted that the primary emotional responses of an audience are to the content of the shot, and the enhancement of these responses through the addition of camera movement is achieved, if at all, at the cost of an arbitrary transferral of motion from the scene to the spectator's eye. Whatever value such movement may have in terms of rhythm or imagination, it must be observed that the effect attained depends not upon an imaginative adjustment of the spectator's point of view, as in the direct cut, but upon an adjustment which inevitably relates itself more closely to the spectator's capacity for physical movement. That is to say, the imaginary journey on which the spectator is taken proceeds at a pace of the body, not of the mind. When this is true, such arbitrary movement defeats the end for which it was planned. The tempi of screen action are set up in the scene itself. Filmic movement can accelerate these tempi; synchronous camera movement can retard or negate them. It is an open question whether camera movement not synchronized to physical movement on the screen or to a normal act of spectator attention adds effect to the screen play. Certainly, if the director doubts whether an effect can be better achieved by moving a camera or by letting it stand, he will let it stand.

The Hollywood Quarterly of Film, Radio and Television
(now *Film Quarterly*),
Winter 1946

III. TIME AND SPACE

The Expression of Time and Space

Lewis Jacobs

TIME

*B*ecause the motion picture is a time art and is concerned with the problems of how to present real or actual time—events happening in the present, past, or future, or happening simultaneously or at different intervals—the element of time is of major importance in achieving clarity and effectiveness of expression on the screen.

Actually, the totality of a film can never be apprehended in any one instant, for while the eye is observing the progress of an image, an associative memory is relating and apprehending its meaning in sequence with other images through time. At any moment in time, as one views a film, only a fragment of sense impression is immediate. Other fragments are stored, held in the offing, dependent upon the succession that is not fully fixed until the unfolding of the whole is completed.

This progress from one point to another depends upon units of real time, the actual length of time it takes for each foot of film to unreel. Here time is constant, unchanging, regulated by the motion-picture camera and projector at the rate of a foot and a half a second, or ninety feet a minute—no more, no less.

In the real world, time cannot be changed, cannot be made longer or shorter: a minute is always sixty seconds; an hour, sixty minutes; time is fixed and unalterable. But in a film whose events may extend over several weeks but whose screen time is seldom more than two hours, real time of course cannot prevail. Real time can only be suggested. How this is done was first described by the Soviet director V. Pudovkin in his pioneering book *Film Technique* (1928), in which he pointed out that the laws of real time do not apply to motion pictures: "After the cutting and joining of the separate pieces of film, there arises not that real time embraced by the action as it takes place before the camera, but a newer, filmic time, conditioned only by the speed of perception and controlled by the number and duration of the separate elements [shots] selected for the filmic representation of the action."

Implicit in Pudovkin's observation is the fact that screen time is not fixed as in nature, but is alterable. This makes it possible for the filmmaker to deal with time as freely as the novelist does. He can manipulate it in ways not possible in real life, transcending or modifying arbitrary and conventional time concepts. The measures and dimensions of the real world can be compressed, extended, prolonged, even arrested.

As Pudovkin indicated, the breaking up of action into units of shots photographed from different positions and angles makes of each shot a different moment of real time, fixed in an unchanging physical linear time as in nature. Then, in editing, the filmmaker eliminates certain shots and shortens and assembles others in different ways to reconstruct the original action, so that a new temporal order arises from the altered duration of the selected shots which make up the new whole.

This is the characteristic method of controlling the flow of time and the speed of events on the screen. As an example of the condensation of continuous time to propel the subject forward, consider the typical scene of a man driving to the airport, parking his car, rushing to catch a plane, flying to a foreign country, and upon arriving there, disembarking and being driven by cab to a hotel. Involved in this action in real life are a series of intervals uniting the various points of passage from one place to another in a fixed order to time. On the screen, however, the time of this progress is not rigid, since the shots which constitute the action can be manipulated at will, their number and length dependent upon the importance of the action to other parts of the story. The filmmaker need not show all the separate intervals, but only those necessary for clarity. Thus the dimensions of continuous, real time can be compressed (by editing) to a matter of moments—a condensation impossible in the real world.

Another example—in this case the bringing together of discontinuous and different periods of time—is found in pictures whose story depicts events spread over a period of months or years which must be presented within a reasonable projection time. *Citizen Kane* (1941), which portrays the life span of its chief character, stands out as a model of such compression. An incredible number of events in the present and the past can be readily communicated by breaking into the chronological sequence of the present to reveal through "flashback," events that take place in the past. What is omitted—months, a year, or more—is simply suggested by the skillful change from one shot to another in a straight cut, a dissolve, or some other visual or aural device which acts as a transition to link any time span desired.

A more complex use of the time dimension is that in which events taking place in widely separated periods of time are brought together and made to appear simultaneous in a dramatic proximity impossible in actuality. The classic example is Griffith's *Intolerance* (1916). Here four stories from different historical periods are presented as if they were happening all at the same time. The duration of each story within a controlled time, and the periodic interplay of the stories through parallel and contrasting editing, utilizes the temporal factor not only to direct attention more vividly to what is significant and characteristic of each period but to galvanize the structure as well. This is most dynamically evident in the climax, where the screen duration of each segment is prolonged by repetition but is constantly contracted in ever shortening intervals in such a manner as to make time itself the dominant dynamic that unifies the four stories and the internal movement of the film itself.

The filmmaker's freedom to treat clock time as he may see fit and give its chronology any pattern that will produce the effect he wants can be reinforced with another device that extends time. Extension of time is generally obtained through the extension of screen space. If different shots of an action are photographed from different angles so that, after editing, it is not apparent that the identical area has been photographed each time, the action can be sustained beyond its normal duration in real life.

The famous steps sequence in *Potemkin* (1925) is an apt illustration of such extended space-time manipulation to create a nerve-racking climax. Here the steady descent of the Cossacks, which in real life would have taken two or three minutes, has been extended to ten minutes or more, through repetition and intercutting of other components, in order to intensify the mounting tension and terror of the scene to panic-stricken proportions.

Editing, which affects the duration and order of the subject matter, is one of several means to modify the dimensions of time. Changing the camera's normal shooting speed of twenty-four frames a second to one, ten, or a thousand frames a second or more, taken at intervals of minutes, hours, or days, or photographed continuously, also allows the director to alter time—in this case, of the subject itself.

Changing the camera's normal shooting speed is put to a humorous use in Lester's *The Knack* (1965). The hero, fleeing from scantily dressed girls who have taken over his bathroom, dashes frantically down three flights of stairs. In actuality, it is only a single flight, but the director has the actor repeat the action three times, photographing each descent at subnormal speed to achieve the effect of an accelerated, mile-a-minute motion, thus giving the scene a Sennett-like flavor.

This kind of camera manipulation is part of the organic structure of the shot. Technically known as speeded-up or slowed-down photography, stop-motion, and time-lapse photography, these camera devices can accelerate or decelerate the unchanging nature of physical time by slowing down, speeding up, telescoping or stretching out to remarkable lengths, or even "freezing," the movement of the subject for dramatic, humorous, or scientific purposes.

Time-lapse photography, for example, can show the evolution of a skyscraper from foundation to forty stories in as many seconds. Conversely, high-speed photography will slow down the flight of a bullet so that it seems to crawl into a sheet of splintering glass. Slow-motion photography, occasionally used for dream and fantasy effects, makes time seem interminable and imparts a somnambulistic quality to movement. Accelerated motion, used since the silent days for comic chases, enables performers to weave in, out, and around moving vehicles—careening at impossible, breakneck speeds—with a split-second timing that adds a ballet-like brilliance to action.

Time can also be extended or arrested by the device known as "freeze frame." This is achieved by reprinting a single frame of a motion-picture shot, the effect of which is to stop an image in mid-motion so that it resembles a still photograph. The frozen picture thus represents a moment of arrested action extracted from physical time which, depending on its contextual relationship, can either prolong or stop the flow of time until the frame "unfreezes" and the picture proceeds.

A dramatic example of the "freeze frame" appears in the last moments of Truffaut's *The 400 Blows* (1959). Here the delinquent boy, running from home, from school, and from society in general, has come to the sea. At that instant the director suddenly moves into an extreme close-up of the boy's frustrated and anguished face and "freezes" the image, ending the film. The effect is startling; it delays the resolution of the boy's plight and forces the viewer to look within himself for the answer to the boy's dilemma and for the person who is responsible for his condition.

In recent years, directors such as Alain Resnais, Ingmar Bergman, Federico Fellini, and some of the younger, avant-garde filmmakers—Chris Marker, Stan Brakhage, Peter Kubelka, Michael Snow, among others—have become interested in a more radical approach to time. The objective temporal sequence of past, present, and future, common in dramatic and chronological clock time, is abandoned for heterogeneous time. Time is regarded as multi-dimensional; the temporal dimensions that are ordinarily divided according to some objective metric system are here fused and continuous. In films such as *Hiroshima, Mon Amour* (1959), *Last Year at Marienbad* (1961), *8½* (1963), *Juliet of the Spirits* (1965), *Persona* (1967), *Hour of the Wolf* (1968), *La Jetée* (1964), *Art of Vision* (1965), *Unsere Afrikaneise* (1966), and *Wave-length* (1968), feelings, memories, dreams, fantasies, desires, and events in real time function as a succession of qualitative changes merging in and out of each other without regard for chronological time, thus carrying characters and events forward and backward in a precise temporal sequence. Time has been reshaped into a dynamic, free-flowing force as it is actually experienced in subjective human awareness, with a complete interweaving of the "before" and "after." The past is imminent in the present, and time has the "timeless" logic of free association, part of a continuous stream of consciousness.

A further expressive use of time is the measurement of time as it serves to produce rhythm. Rhythm is not an ornament but a vigorous resource that can unleash added power to heighten cinematic expression.

Rhythm is generally recognized as repeated motion experienced through patterns of duration, separated by intervals of time. The word is often used to suggest tempo. In film, however, tempo applies to the rate of duration of the shots—fast, slow, or moderate. Rhythm has to do with the regular or irregular distribution of such patterns of shots. For example, a succession of shots each of five seconds' duration creates a slower tempo than a series of shots lasting only one second each. The repetition of two or more such series would trace the development of a pattern or division of rhythm. Varying the shot durations or tempo and their measured intervals extends the complexity of the rhythmic design. It is of course impossible to suggest all the potential combinations of shot patterns or all the rhythmic designs that can be woven out of controlled durations and measured intervals of time. But it should be emphasized that a rhythmic development based on a repeated regularity can become fairly obvious. Tempo and pattern then seem purely mechanical: mere repetition is unlikely to sustain interest for any length of time. By means of arrangements that vary tempo and the rate of intervals—gradually increasing or decreasing measured divisions in different combinations and with recurring periodicity deepened by slight variations that avoid chronometric measurement—rhythmic compositions can be given an unlimited diversity.

Thus rhythm can act as a catalyst to heighten anticipation and build emotion. It propels the film forward and endows familiar subject matter with unexpected overtones and new relationships.

SPACE

Space is generally conceived of as an unlimited continuity extending in three dimensions. This notion of space in the real world—length, width, and height—is based on a binocular vision that is limited and changes as one moves from place to place or as different areas of space are isolated by concentrated attention (even though adjoining areas remain visible peripherally). Experience has shown that, in nature, physical space is tangible and intractable. There are no sudden breaks in real space; every action takes place in an uninterrupted spatial sequence. A person moving from a garden to a kitchen must pass through a certain amount of intervening space from outside to inside to reach the desired destination. In life, this given area—whatever its actual spatial dimensions from exterior to interior—is fixed. It cannot be made smaller or larger. Its physical spatial continuity cannot be broken, fragmented, or changed.

In movies, space loses its multidimensionality, no longer serves merely to surround objects, but rather appears as a two-dimensional modification of real space on a flat surface. The physical space is given visual proportions and limits by different camera positions, by lenses of different focal lengths, and by the filmmaker's selective vision. Space thus is concerned with the arrangement of subject matter enclosed within the boundaries of the motion-picture screen. Space becomes a pictorial component directly related to the composition and efficacy of the shot.

Sensitively handled, pictorial space can be one of the dynamics of a shot's expressiveness, endowing a subject with additional emotional and stylistic value. There are many examples of films among whose distinguishing traits is a pictorialism that lifts them above the average. Outstanding is Dreyer's *The Passion of Joan of Arc* (1928). In this film, pictorial space is flattened out for the sake of a stylization that places extraordinary emphasis on the close-up as a mass, in strong contrast to background areas treated in graphic patterns of white, gray, and black. The compact pictorial arrangement pulls the viewer bodily into the emotional framework of the tense drama and engulfs him in a powerful sense of oppressive tension and strain.

Conversely, in Orson Welles's *Citizen Kane* (1941) there is an unfettered, imaginative use of pictorial space which frames his compositions in dramatic new ways. The imaginative staging, steeped in deep-focus pools of light and shade, molds and shapes the film images with a spatial plasticity and atmospheric mystique that strikingly underscores the dramatic situation and arouses the viewer's psychological responses.

In Robert Flaherty's *The Land* (1941), it is the special capacity of the wide-angle lens to expand spatial perspective which enables the director to exaggerate the vastness of the panoramic stretches of eroded countryside and so more forcefully involves the viewer in the urgent need for soil conservation.

Spatial distortion as a valuable asset of a shot's force and intent is found in Mike Nichols's *The Graduate* (1967). To prolong Dustin Hoffman's frantic effort to get to the church in time to stop his girl's wedding, the director photographs the scene from a distance, but with a very large telephoto lens that makes the running youth appear to be quite close. At the same time, the telephoto lens greatly diminishes spatial perspective and produces the impression that, despite Hoffman's desperation, his running is getting him nowhere. Instead, he seems imprisoned in a spatial vacuum.

Just as pictorial space operates within the context of individual shots in terms of the visual representation of the subject matter, so does filmic space operate in the relationship between shots and their order and arrangement in time. Filmic space violates the laws of real space in the same way that screen time violates real time, and enables the filmmaker to break up spatial reality and reconstruct it to suit his own purpose. The motion-picture camera constantly interferes with physical space, selecting portions and areas from the whole and reproducing these segments from different spatial distances and viewpoints. The terms "long shot," "medium shot," and "close shot" designate the spatial distance between subject matter and camera. Each of these camera positions represents a different segment of spatial reality, lifted from the whole, which gives physical limits to the subject without regard to its actual spatial dimensions. What emerges is a visual spatial awareness, showing the subject multidimensionally from the various viewpoints of the different shots taken separately, none of which may have an exclusive viewpoint.

The original idea of breaking up real space and reconstructing it by joining separate camera shots can be traced back to the primitive efforts of Edwin S. Porter's two seminal films: *The Life of an American Fireman* (1902) and *The Great Train Robbery* (1903). The method was further expanded and brought to artistic fulfillment by Griffith in the years 1908 to 1916. But it was Pudovkin who first articulated the basic difference between real and film space. "By the junction of the separate shots, the director builds a filmic space entirely his own. He unites and compresses the separate elements that have recorded different points of real, actual space, into one filmic space."

As an example, Pudovkin records a brief experiment filmed by the director Lev Kuleshov (Pudovkin's teacher). It was a scene consisting of five shots, each taken separately in a different location, but which, when assembled in a particular sequence, created a unity of space that had no existence in reality. The film showed a boy approaching a girl, their meeting, the boy pointing to a building in the distance, the two starting off toward the building, and finally both climbing up a broad expanse of steps together. The first three shots were photographed in different sections of Moscow. The fourth was a picture of the White House taken from an old American movie. The fifth shot was photographed at the steps of a church in Leningrad. When the shots were joined, places which in actuality are thousands of miles apart were brought together and made to look as though they were concentrated in a small area that could be covered in a few paces by the actors.

It was this cinematic convention—using selected shots, photographed at the same site or at different sites, to unite different, separate aspects of real space—that led to the art of editing and made possible the illusion of a spatial continuity not found in nature. By shortening, lengthening, or eliminating intervals and uniting what in reality may be separated by physical distance (feet, miles, or even light years), editing allows actual space to be manipulated and reassembled with a plasticity capable of limitless changes and a rationale indigenous only to itself. The process enables the filmmaker to transport the viewer from one spatial area to another, one country to another, even one historical period to another in a spatial discontinuity that defies all logic and reality.

Classic examples of the modification of space to create affinities —connotations, juxtapositions, or associations that do not in fact exist—are found in the climax of Griffith's two major films. In *The Birth of a Nation* (1915), three spatially isolated actions are intercut and made to appear to be happening at the same time: the ride of the Klansmen, the flight of Negro terrorists, and the flight of the refugees to the marshes. In *Intolerance* (1916), four stories that take place in different parts of the world (and in different times) are linked through parallel action. The commanding feature of both films is the extraordinary facility with which widely separated and different spatial areas are altered, juxtaposed, and rearranged in new spatial sequences so that the spatial alteration becomes a dominant force in strengthening the dramatic impact.

Recently, a seemingly new and fresh approach to spatial control has been introduced. At the 1964 World's Fair and at Expo '67 in Montreal, the viewer was exposed to two processes that extend the medium's characteristic method of linking one shot at a time by cutting back and forth, to a more arresting and complex technique: linking combined multiple shots by presenting them simultaneously in a continuity that binds the various combinations of shots in a thematic unity. The first process, called the "multiple-screen device," employed shots from three, six, ten, or more screens placed side by side. At times each screen contained a different picture; at other times the different images merged into a single picture. The second process, the "multi-image system," employed a single screen, greatly enlarged, whose area was broken up into a mosaic of five, ten, twenty, or more diverse shots brought together simultaneously in different combinations, sizes, and shapes, but united by a single idea.

Although both techniques have been used before with varying degrees of effectiveness—Abel Gance, the French director, employed a three-paneled, multi-screen device in *Napoleon* (1926), for the battle scenes; René Clair, in *Two Timid Souls* (1928), divided the conventional screen into three segments to show concurrent actions in three different bedrooms—the techniques were ignored for the most part until after the enthusiastic, world-wide response at the two world fairs.

Since then, many contemporary directors have become intrigued with multi-image technique as a highly effective means of controlling the space (and time) element of continuity in exciting new ways. Norman Jewison, in *The Thomas Crown Affair* (1968), divides the screen into an enormous assemblage of forty segments or more to show the various aspects of a polo game simultaneously and then suddenly climaxes the effect with a single full-screen close-up of the polo ball for a startling dramatic impact.

Ralph Nelson, in *Charly* (1968), uses a split-screen device, instead of cutting back and forth, to include both the actions and reactions of a boy and girl in conversation, and so gains an added freshness and stimulates a deeper involvement by the viewer.

Richard Fleischer, in *The Boston Strangler* (1968), employs the multi-image screen to dramatize the growing panic in a community by portraying simultaneously a number of incidents that are occurring at the same time, thus achieving an emotional effect in the briefest time. In another sequence he pictures collectively on a fragmented screen two or three angles of the strangler, to emphasize his broken and disconnected personality.

The spatial flexibility of the multi-screen and multi-image techniques has enhanced the technical legacy handed down by Griffith. Through the simultaneous juxtaposition and relationship of different images on different areas of the screen or screens (brought together in a diversity of compositions, sizes, shapes, colors, and thematic ideas), a more inclusive and more powerful sense of reality can be evoked than was heretofore believed possible. As a result, screen space has acquired the verisimilitude of real space evoked in memory, dreams, and imagination.

The Faces of Time

ROBERT GESSNER

Students of drama, a many-colored phrase that covers the human race from Atkinson to Zooey, have become increasingly aware of cinema as a sisterly art, although there may be confusion as to how brotherly the relationship is. A devotee of theatrical drama, while acknowledging the occasional arrival of an exceptional film, may be puzzled by his enthusiasm, which he might fear is disloyal. He might prefer to claim the theater a superior art form in all respects, and yet quietly suspect he's being unfair.

How much of cinema is derivative of drama? In what way is cinema unique? These are the questions which are more frequently asked than answered.

The recent debate of Tyrone Guthrie and Carl Foreman in *The New York Times Magazine* of April 29 [1962] missed the point on two scores: first, it is not pertinent to compare the poorer plays or films to the best examples of the other medium. Rank commercialism can ruin plays and films as it has on occasion cheapened the novel, coarsened the dance, and even emasculated architecture. No one art has a monopoly on the evils of box-office or monetary domination.

It's quite pointless, second, to assert that "the screen is far more capable" of holding "a mirror up to life" than the stage (Foreman), as it is to believe (Guthrie) that the movies "are only photographs; and, as Puck says, 'the best in this kind are but shadows.'" A "live" performance on the stage may be more "dead" than that of a great actress creating illusion on a screen. After all, talent is recognizable in any medium, whether it be writing or acting talent. Shakespeare's *Measure for Measure* focuses more sharply on the motivations of immoralists than Fellini's *La Dolce Vita*. Conversely, Buñuel's *Viridiana* offers a more vibrant mirror of human frailties than Rattigan's *Ross*. Obviously, such comparisons are meaningless; a work of art stands on its own authority.

It is a popular, but limited, view that the greatest difference between stage and screen is to be found in the visual ratio between audience and scene. The purchase of an admission ticket, it has been truly observed, determines in the traditional theater whether, if you sit in the balcony, for example, your entire evening is to be spent in viewing long shots or, if you sit in the front rows, in viewing close-ups. Your purse decides your perspective. Whereas, in cinema, the camera is your constant usher, regardless of where you sit. Whether you lie outstretched on a home sofa or sit upright before a public screen, you may be transported from a long shot of open scenery into the intimate proximity of a close-up without paying more money or moving leg muscles. This flexible ratio between the action and the audience, which alters the size and shape of the proscenium, is called frame movement. Specifically, frame movement subdivides into pans (panoramic sweep from a fixed pivot), trucks (traveling forward, backward, sideways), tilts, and zooms.

Unique as these movements are to cinema, they do not comprise the whole of what is *sui generis* in this art form. Actually, frame motion is only one of the seven possible movements that are basic in cinema and which I will discuss in the course of this essay. Of these seven fundamental types of rhythm there is but one—it must be emphasized—which coincides with the stage; namely, subject movement within the frame. This means the action that is observed and the dialogue that is heard during a single shot (one camera operation) and without frame movement. This rhythm parallels the action and dialogue which are observed when the curtain is up. From the point of view of cinema, this normal motion of time is recorded movement, the least manipulative of the seven faces of time which comprise the multicountenance of the art. In subject movement within the frame, time is not manipulated; similarly, the time spent on the stage between the rising and falling of a curtain—or blackouts (a cinematic acquisition)—approximates the watches of the audience.

This unique capability for juggling time forward, backward, parallel, and at slower or faster rates enables cinema to be independent of theatrical inheritances from the traditional stage. Moreover, it enables cinema to treat emotions and ideas in revolutionary ways, evoking responses not experienced heretofore. This evocation and control of motion, which in turn affects objects in space, needs to be more fully appreciated by students of both drama and cinema.

Motion is the touchstone that turns craft into art. As much as it's the magic wand, vitalizing and coordinating objects and their meaning, motion in cinema needs to be considered in association with light. Illumination by itself produces still photography, but light when touched by motion becomes fluid. The shape and compositional control of actors and setting are the results of measured motions of director and editor, who are the masters (or preferably the master) in charge of rhythm and light. Thus a fresh definition of this art might read: cinema is the creation of rhythms amid illuminated objects and accompanying sounds to express meaning and emotion.

The drama- or literary-minded differs from the cinematic-oriented student in the frame of reference he employs to express his responses; the former, for instance, is prone to recall scenes while the latter refers pragmatically to shots (camera operations) and cuts (juxtaposition of adjoining shots). Cinema, more than drama, is a fluid mosaic, composed of 300 to 500 fragments, coordinated and connected. The cinema-minded is shot-conscious.

Alain Resnais, for example, is the master fragmentalist in contemporary cinema. A study of his translation of Marguerite Duras's script of *Hiroshima, Mon Amour* (1959) into images reveals how, through direction and editing, he composed rhythms and light as the means of controlling objects and actors. Duras's words —"ashes, rain, dew, or sweat"—were not lumped into one shot, but were the idea behind a transitional scene of four shots, all medium close-ups. In the first, the skin texture of a man's back and a

girl's arms is extremely rough; in the second shot, this texture of
the lovers' bodies has a bubbly and sparkling quality as though the
forms were molded from volcanic ash; in the third, the skin texture has a heavy layer of perspiration; in the fourth, the skin is
normal, with a slight trace of perspiration. Thus, in these opening
shots, movement in the mind of the viewer is created by interrela-
tionships in terms of linear perspective coordinated with shade,
the interrelationship blending and evolving through the juxtaposition of four images. The viewer may see symbolism in sweat turning to atomic sparkles and back to sweat. Resnais, in composing
and editing his shots, relied solely on rhythms in mass and
rhythms with light to convey his theme.

In *Last Year at Marienbad* (1961) Resnais conducted his particular orchestration from a text by novelist Alain Robbe-Grillet, and
again attempted to transcend time, largely by movements (via editing) back to previous scenes, all fragmented in surface textures of
rare depth, precision, and beauty. The camera traveled in trucks
and pans to depict a static existence within a massive mausoleum;
organ music summoned memories of departed encounters. A sense
of failure accumulates with the excess of the experiment, the varied movement after the first half hour becoming less compelling as
the emotional motivations become less precise. The first half hour
had the stylized grace of a chess game; motion was then adventurous, the cuts were like provocative tests and probes, the traveling
shots were exploratory; life was baroque. However, when motion
came to depend on the style or vintage of a woman's gown to distinguish past from present, the emotional texture of film had departed. The illogic of a dream had taken over completely and we
were confused observers; Resnais no longer cared whether anyone
understood wholly or felt with comprehension. His viewer-be-
damned philosophy has precedents, of course, and possibly we
might reach a state—as we have with Joyce and Picasso—when
we'll be thankful for comprehending three out of four of Resnais's
shots. We should be grateful for dreamers.

Within a more limited area of experimentation, the non-charac-
ter film, Ian Hugo creates multiple motion unlike any ever seen.
Motion within the frame is captured and controlled by superimpo-
sitions, sometimes more than the eye can consciously record; the
whole blends and flows in unique patterns. A painter and an

etcher, Hugo as a cinema artist makes color move in association with rhythm of line and rhythm in mass. His *Bells of Atlantis* (1954) is cinematic poetry, a perfection of mood; V*enice, Etude Number One* (1961) is a masterpiece of motion, visual and aural, utilizing at times as many as seven impositions.

In less complicated fashion but more self-conscious of being experimental, Maya Deren, in her film *A Study in Choreography for Camera* (1945), created "dances choreographed for and performed by the camera and by human beings together." Also, Miss Deren employed normal and slow camera speeds in recording her images. Camera speeds are variations of subject movement, the motion that occurs within the frame. In cinema, subject motion may be fast and reverse as well as normal and slow. In Méliès's *The Doctor's Secret* (*c*. 1900) the use of stop motion (trick photography) in coordination with fast motion created a new comic fantasy which Mack Sennett later applied to the chase, automotive and ambulatory.

Artificial motion can be comic or fantastic, whereas reality is normal motion. Actually, normal frame movements of creditable characters, emotionally authentic, can evoke a more intense degree of identification than the same shot done without trucking. For example, in Malle's *The Lovers* (1959) the frame movements under the moonlight through the trees, over the fields, along the river of the lovers, strolling and boating, were so exquisitely fluid and sensual that for the first time (halfway through the reels) we believed momentarily in the romance.

Since we see in cinema before we hear—the opposite of traditional theatrical drama—visual motion inevitably affects dialogue, sound effects, songs, background music, and their combinations; often it controls them. In *Citizen Kane* (1941), an open gold mine of excellent examples, there is a singing-lesson scene between an exasperated maestro and the inept Susan. The shot has an extreme depth of field, similar to a stage setting, in which Susan and the maestro are in the foreground by the piano, with Kane in the far background at the door. It is Kane's slow movement forward which intensifies the drama; we await his reaction to the maestro's inability to teach the talentless Susan, Kane's second wife. By the time Kane arrives in the foreground, we know that the lessons will continue. His forward motion (subject movement) dominates. Although this example is more dramatic than cinematic, in that the action is recorded by camera, the steady, self-assured approach of Kane, by dominating the scene, heightens the suspense. How much more effective when the motion is cinematic. When Kane dies in the opening sequence, the camera cuts from an extreme close-up of the dark lips of Kane, uttering "Rosebud," to a close-up of a glass ball containing "snow" and a miniature house. The movement from one composition to another makes a thematic link, its symbolism being the key to the mysterious word—"Rosebud." Kane's hand relaxes in death, the glass ball drops to the floor and breaks. In this close-up the house is on its side, and, reflected in the distorted glass, the figure of a nurse in white enters where the room is dark. In this combined close-up of the ball she comes forward in the background like a long shot. The cut is to a medium shot from her point of view, in which she pulls a white sheet over the dark face. In these continuity cuts—all in silence since the word was uttered—how death-like become the black and white compositional rhythms, unique to this art. Light and rhythm dominate sound in the subsequent satire in the March of Time projection-room scene. The anonymous reporters are in shadow while the editor, front-lighted (we are shooting at his back), omnipotently orders his men in garbled sounds "to bring back Rosebud, dead or alive."

By panning his camera right and left and reverse, Orson Welles created frame movements which, coordinating with the breakfast dialogue of Kane and his first wife, depicted the decline of that marriage. By trucking in, altering size and perspective, he underscored the credo of Kane instead of relying solely on words and acting; this example refers to a scene in the newspaper office when an outraged Thatcher, lawyer-guardian, is upbraiding his ward. The shot is medium in size, shooting over Thatcher's shoulder at Kane, leaning back in a chair and grinning with pleasure. The guardian's lecture is not unusual, nor is it unexpected. Thatcher sits down; there is no cut. The camera trucks slowly into a profile shot of Thatcher, very angry. Now Kane begins to describe his editorial intentions, his face firm, the words aflame; whereupon the camera quickly moves closer, giving a visual force to what Kane says. All this is in one shot. There are in *Citizen Kane* approximately 500 shots in two hours, or an average of one shot every 14.5

seconds, all of which attests to an exceptional fluidity, reminiscent in pace of the climactic passages in *The Birth of a Nation* (1915) and *Intolerance* (1916). Undoubtedly the engrossing quality of an action thriller, *The Guns of Navarone* (1961), can be traced to the extraordinary tempo of its editing, executed on an average of one shot every 12 seconds, a total of 763 shots in 155 minutes. Another clue to the power of subject, frame, and edited movements in *The Guns of Navarone* may be found in another startling statistic—though no artistic success is based on a mathematical analysis —namely, that in a script of 157 pages there are only 89 which contain dialogue.

By the above examples I am not suggesting that pure cinema is silent cinema; the utterance of words is normal, though not always wise. Characters in dramatic art forms do talk— "But any attempt to convey thought and feeling exclusively, or even primarily, by speech," Professor Erwin Panofsky observed in the early days of "sound pictures" (1934), "leaves us with a feeling of embarrassment, boredom, or both."

Of motion achieved through editing, the most common cinematic rhythm is *the cut for continuous action* (continuity). Actually, subject movement sets the pace for this ordinary edit, which in turn generally alters the size of the subject movement in accordance with a shift of locale or perspective. Also, the insertion of a close-up may intensify the flow of continuing time.

Next in frequency of use is *the cut for accelerated action* (rapid or jump editing). This is the motion which contrives to compress less than sixty seconds to the minute, so that action leaps forward beyond normal expectation. These cuts intend to create a feeling of contemporary tempo, especially if the subject movement within the frames lacks dynamic power; such seemed to be the intention of Antonioni in *La Notte* (1961). When subject motion is highly motivated in emotional and visual terms, an accelerated pace that omits the pedestrian and the obvious can have enormous excitement. Witness in *A View from the Bridge* (1962) the scene in which the niece and her fiancé dance before her incestuous uncle.

Parallel motion permits the viewer to be in two or more places concurrently; this type of editing may be called *the cut for simultaneous action* (cross-cut). In the classic ride-to-the-rescue or a classic chase that involves hound and hare, an omnipotence is conferred on the viewer; he may be in two locales at identical times. In Griffith's *Intolerance*, the master of the cross-cut had us in four different countries and in four different centuries simultaneously. Time is thematically related by the depiction of historical dramas in which man was intolerant to man; chronological time was ignored. It might be argued that *Intolerance*, thematically, is still ahead of our time.

The cut to previous action (flashback) seems to be employed currently for stylistic effect, whereas Griffith used it regularly for simple narrative values. Remembrance of previous actions could be established by having a fade-out on a character, say Elsie Stoneman in *The Birth of a Nation*, and a fade-in on Elsie and the Little Colonel in a tender embrace, a vignette by itself; then back to Elsie recovering from her reverie. The contemporary flashback as utilized by Alain Resnais in *Hiroshima, Mon Amour* and in *Last Year at Marienbad* more often echoes in intent, if not in execution, the cross-cutting in *Intolerance*; that is, motion cuts across time and place barriers. Fragments of the Frenchwoman's romance with her German soldier lover are inserted now during her embraces with her Japanese lover; the effect, thematically, is an intellectual awareness of a Christian doctrine without preachment; namely, the love one should feel for one's enemy who is similarly one's victim. In *Last Year at Marienbad* the sequences involving time previous in juxtaposition to sequences of time present are so intricately blended cinematically that time becomes meaningless; all that appears to matter is a dream-like *motion* that has a mysterious, psychological *flow*. In this aesthetic sense, the film is successful. The girl X is the sum of her past; Riva, the Frenchwoman, is similarly the maiden with her young German and the mature woman with her Japanese architect. Past and present are one, Nevers and Hiroshima are one. This is superb artistry, thanks to an imaginative employment of the flashback.

Finally, the least common cinematic rhythm is *the cut for decelerated action*. Unlike slow motion of subject elements within the frame, time is slowed through editing, usually by repeating parts of previous shots so that a minute seems longer than sixty seconds. Holding back the clock is a technique opposite to jumping the clock forward, which is the method in *the cut for accelerated ac-*

tion. A classic example of prolonging time through repetitious cuts is the series of shots depicting the descent of a tall fir in *The River* (1937). Nature lovers would wish to hold back time and the tree, and for a few precious seconds Pare Lorentz grants our romantic urge. The crash of the giant tree hence is doubly painful. Fragmenting subject movement for the purpose of extracting every drop of emotional or intellectual meaning—a Griffith-Eisenstein technique—may extend time by actual count, but the aesthetic effect can be the opposite. That is, the time it takes for an irate sailor in *Potemkin* (1925) to smash the plate with its lettering, "Give us this day our daily bread," is a matter of two seconds in normal subject movement. By editing this action into nine shots, Eisenstein prolonged the actual motion, but the total impact so stimulated the eye that the doubled lapsed time of four seconds seemed less than two. By deceleration the moment is enlarged, not an unusual psychic phenomenon. Also, laboratory printing may create an illusion of retarded time by slowly dissolving cuts between shots.

These five basic cinematic rhythms, achieved through editing, coordinate with the equally basic subject motion and frame motion. The effectiveness of any given shot may depend not only on motion within and motion of the frame but on the motion evoked by juxtaposition. These seven fundamental rhythms make cinema the art of creating movement. Motion, in every shot, is based on two or more possible rhythms—subject motion, and at least one of the editing types of motion. The maximum combination would be three: subject, frame, and one of the editing types of motion. These rhythmic concepts may be called the Seven Faces of Time. They are not ends, obviously, but means employed with subjective qualities. They are not magical numbers that can be imposed arbitrarily, but an empirically valid convenience, useful for critic and creator.

Although Cinema, more than any art, manipulates physical objects and utilizes machinery, the problems confronting its artists are not unlike the challenges inherent in the classic arts. Once its luminous uniqueness is more fully understood, we shall have the means of evoking emotions and ideas in another language.

Theatre Arts, July 1962

Tempo and Tension

MAYA DEREN

*M*uch has been written on the techniques of shooting—exposure, lenses, lighting, angles, framing, etc.—with the result that the serious filmmaker can readily become a competent cameraman.

But relatively little attention has been given to the circumstance that he is also required to be his own cutter; and the fact that he must fill both functions *can* result in far finer filmmaking than where there is a strict division of labor between the two functions.

It means that he is in a position to shoot to cut. For, if he has the final, cut version of his film in mind, he can save footage by filming a room, for instance, from the one angle which would follow most logically from the previous shot, instead of shooting the same action from three different angles and then discarding two of them. More important, every detail of a shot—the direction of the light source, the rhythm and speed of the action, whether the person should enter the shot or should already be in the frame—can be meticulously designed to flow unbrokenly from the end of the previous shot, whether or not it has already been recorded. This complete control of one's film, if consciously exercised, makes possible a compelling continuity in the final product.

Certainly, it must be obvious that a motion picture does not consist of individual shots, however active, exciting, or interesting they may be, but that, in the end, the attention is held by the way shots are put together, by the relationship established between them. If the function of the camera can be spoken of as that of the seeing, registering eye, then the function of cutting can be said to be that of the thinking, understanding mind. By this I am saying that the meaning, the emotional value of individual impressions, the connection between individually observed facts, is, in the making of the film, the creative responsibility of cutting.

For example, the length of time which one permits a certain shot to continue is actually a statement of its importance. Let us imagine that one wishes to show a specific person entering a large building (an institution which must be identified in some way), in order to accomplish something there. This would probably call for two shots in succession: a wide-angle shot from across the street would be required to identify the building; and a close (possibly pan) shot would be required to show and identify the person who is going in. It is quite possible that the wide-angle shot of the building, its height exaggerated by a low perspective, might be much more interesting, pictorially speaking, than the close-shot pan. But one would never hold both shots for the same length of time on the screen.

If it was the action of entering the building which was important (as part of the plot, let us say), then any lengthy architectural treatment would delay the action and would give an importance to the actual appearance of the building which, relative to the action, was unwarranted. One would hold the building shot only long enough for it to be identified, and then cut back, as rapidly as possible, to the continuation of the action.

On the other hand, suppose that, in the action of the plot, the person has dreamed of coming to this spot—that the building (a university, perhaps) represented for him a place where hopes could be fulfilled, where he would make his home for a long time, or something of that sort. In such a case, the cutting time of the two shots would be exactly reversed, for the camera, as an eye, would stare and fix upon the building and perhaps even lovingly travel over its architecture. Pictorially, this long time spent upon the building would convey the idea that the structure itself, as a "place," was important to the person in question.

In the cutting process, then, duration not only serves to show or identify something; it is also a statement of value, of importance.

To determine the length of duration, the relative importance of each shot must be carefully weighed. And if this is done by the same person who is shooting, there will be a minimum of footage which ends up (or should end up) in the trash basket.

Timing, in the sense of duration, can actually become an even more active element when it creates tension. Here, it is a matter of the relationship between the duration of the object or action within the shot and the duration of the shot itself. I should be inclined to say that, in general (there may be, in specific cases, exceptions), whenever the duration of the shot exceeds the duration of the action, there is a decrease in tension, and vice versa. For this reason a static shot of a building will become boring if it is held longer than the identification or appreciation of the building requires; the active curiosity of the eye is very soon satisfied.

Moreover, in the static shot, we see something which, we know, lasts longer than the duration of the shot. We know that nothing critical will happen to the building after we no longer see it, and consequently there is no tension. But a static shot of a person balancing on one leg, for example, can be held much longer, for we know that that action must have some conclusion; and so, the longer we look, the more the tension increases, until, finally, the person actually falls, the action is completed, our anticipation has been satisfied, and we relax.

It is the phenomenon of duration as tension which explains why slow motion—which may have in it very little activity—often makes for greater tension than normal or rapid motion, for the tension consists in our desire to have our anticipations satisfied. An example of the use of duration as tension is the very last sequence of my short dance film, A Study in Choreography for Camera (1945). The dancer takes off from the ground for a leap, and the shot is cut off while his body is still ascending in the frame. This is followed by a shot against the sky of his legs traveling horizontally—the plateau of his leap. This is followed by a shot in which he moves descendingly through the frame, and this, in turn, is followed by one in which he lands on the ground. All this was filmed in slow motion; there is no sense of rapid or emphatic movement. Rather, the sequence has the quality of a slow floating. Yet I should say that it creates more tension than any other sequence in my four films, for the simple reason that, cinematically, the leap endures much longer than it could in actuality. During this stretch of time the audience is waiting for the dancer to come down to earth, as it knows he must, eventually.

The fact that this sequence consists of four shots does not contradict the idea of duration, for these are so identical, cinematographically, that, to all intents and purposes, they comprise a single shot. Essentially, the point remains the same; namely, that the image of leaping was given a duration which far exceeded the normal anticipation that was waiting to be satisfied.

It is also significant that this total duration of the sequence was achieved by not permitting any of the single shots to satisfy the normal necessity. That is, the first shot was cut off just at the point where the dancer began to descend, the second shot similarly, and the third was cut off just before the landing. In the second and third shots the ascent is also cut off, since, once he had leveled off, to show him rising again would have implied a fall in between shots. In other words, no single action was completed, and therefore the subsequent action was understood not as a new and independent action but as a continuation of the one which has not yet been completed.

In this sense, movement or action is carried "across the splice." This principle of cutting into an action is basic to the whole problem of the continuity of a film, even when the action is not so extreme as a leap. The failure to realize the importance of this technique accounts for the stuttering tempo of many films. Over and over, an action is shown through to its completion. Our anticipation is satisfied, not to say glutted. We relax, and the subsequent action is a new one which must begin at the bottom again, in commanding our interest and attention.

This is so important a contribution to intensity and continuity that a film should actually be so planned as to have a maximum of its cuts occur in action. Let us say that an incident consists of two periods of action separated by a pause, as when a person comes up to a table, pulls out a chair, and sits down. It is an action which must be filmed in two parts: a long shot showing the approach; and a closer shot showing, let us say, the details of the dinner which the person is about to eat.

Normally (and let us assume that we wish to render the action normally), there is a pause at the moment when the person arrives at the table, as he prepares to undertake the action of pulling out the chair. The temptation is to shoot his walk and arrival in long shot and to begin the close-up with his pulling out the chair, the cut taking place during the pause between these actions. But a much stronger continuity, tension, and interest would be created either by cutting off the long shot, just before he comes to a stop, and picking up the close shot with his arrival (entering the frame), then the pause and then his pulling out the chair—or by holding the long shot until he has started to pull out the chair, and letting the close-up cut in after the chair movement has already begun.

Obviously, such techniques demand that the cutting be decided upon before any shooting is done, unless, of course, one can afford to waste film by shooting the entire episode both in long shot and in close-up and later throwing away half of each. It is difficult to put the scissors to one's own film, but the sacrifice of a few frames of action—those frames which bring it to a stop—is justified by the smooth, compelling flow of the film which it will achieve.

It is impossible to overestimate the compelling continuity of duration which movement carried across the splice can create. Obviously a prerequisite of this technique is a consistency in the tempo or rhythm of the movement; but once this is achieved and carefully pointed up cinematographically (angle, light, etc.), it can be used to hold together even places which are completely separate in actuality.

In the dance film, the dancer appears in a long shot sharply defined against the sky, as he begins to lower his leg from a high position in the air. The pace of this action is well established by the time the leg reaches waist level. At this point there is a cut. Against an interior apartment background, we see a close-up (so that the movement dominates the locale) of a leg being lowered from the top of the frame at exactly the same rate of speed that governed the previous long shot. The effect is that the dancer has stepped from exterior to interior in a single movement, so completely does the action across the splice dominate both sides of the splice.

This technique can even be carried a step further (or, more precisely, in a different direction), to give a repetitive action the illusion of being a continued action. For, whenever a movement is not completed, we understand that the one which follows is a continuation of the incomplete movement. The leap of the dance film, which I described a moment ago, is an example of this; for, in actuality, the same leap was repeated four times and was made continuous by not being completed in the film until the end of the fourth shot.

The same technique creates a long fall at the end of my most recent film, *Ritual in Transfigured Time* (1946). In this case the person dropped from a considerable height four times against a blank background. Both the area covered and the action were repeated; but since the body fell vertically through the frame each time, so that the disappearance at the bottom of the frame was immediately followed by an appearance at the top of the frame in the next shot, the four shots joined together gave the effect of a continuous movement.

Both the leap and the fall occur against rather neutral backgrounds which cannot be identified as repeated areas. But so compelling is continuity of movement across a splice that even identifiable backgrounds become subordinate to it when assisted by a manipulation of angles. In an earlier film, *At Land* (1944), it was necessary to extend the time of a girl climbing up a large driftwood tree root, far beyond the time the action would actually take. The girl climbed the tree three times, entering at the bottom of the frame each time. The first shot was a downward angle, as if she were low; the second was a level angle, as if at eye height; and the third was an upward angle, as if she were overhead. The tree root was a very distinctive formation, and the shift in angle did not, actually, change its shapes beyond recognition, provided one expected to recognize it as a repeated area. But the movements through the frame and across the splice were so compelling that the three shots of the root seemed to be a continuation of an area which is only consistently similar in its construction. It is not recognized as being a repetition.

The furthest extension of this principle which I have thus far attempted occurs in the party sequence of *Ritual in Transfigured Time*. My idea was that the reason people go to parties is to establish personal, social relationships; that, if all the long static conversational pauses were omitted, there would emerge a sort of dance, consisting of people moving toward one another, passing one person in order to reach another, greeting each other, etc. Above all, I wished to convey the idea that all these different people were there for the same reason and were doing essentially the same thing and even, as it were, making the same movement—that the consistency of the total movement pattern transcended the variety of the individuals involved.

First I made a series of shots in which different persons approached each other, gestured to each other, clasped hands, etc., in approximately the same way. Then I cut together, for instance, one couple as they first recognized each other and started to approach each other, and followed this by a shot of another couple in a further development of the same movement; then came two other persons who meet, clasp hands, and start to turn; another couple finish a sort of turn about each other and start to separate; and then two persons, back to back, move in opposite directions.

Since the people are all different, and since it is not a cumulative action—in the sense of adding up to any narrative story—the only thing that crosses the splice and makes one shot seem to come from the previous one is the movement, which is never brought to a stop but is always continued by the following shot. If cutting into movement can be the principle of tension and continuity for one hundred and fifty feet of film which does not have a story direction, then surely it can do wonders for the solution of simpler sequences in which interest is also maintained by character action, story plot, and known characters.

Movie Makers, May 1947

TIME

The control of time is important for clarity, effectiveness, and emotional expression

SIMULTANEITY OF PAST AND PRESENT
Wild Strawberries (1957), Ingmar Bergman

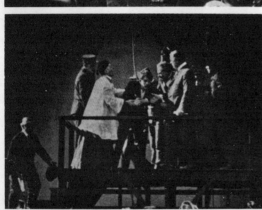

FOUR CONCURRENT TIME
PERIODS
Intolerance (1916), D. W. Griffith

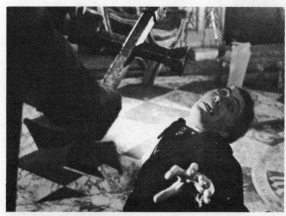

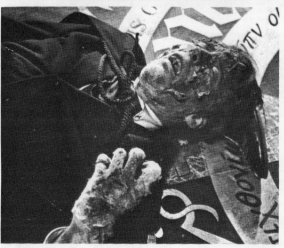

COMPRESSED TIME
Dracula (1952), Terrence Fisher

EXTENDED TIME
Potemkin (1925), partial sequence,
Sergei Eisenstein

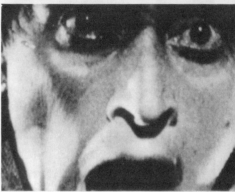

CHRONOLOGICAL TIME
At the Races (1914),
Charles Chaplin

SPEEDED-UP TIME
The Searching Eye (1964), Saul Bass Associates

SPACE

The controlled use of space provides emotional and stylistic values

FULL SHOT
Sweet Love, Bitter . . . (1967),
Herbert Danska

MEDIUM SHOT
Sweet Love, Bitter . . .

CLOSE SHOT
Sweet Love, Bitter . . .

SCALE AND DISTANCE
The Ghost That Never Returns (1929), Alexander Room

THREE-DIMENSIONAL PLASTICITY
Citizen Kane (1941), Orson Welles

PATTERN AND DESIGN
Last Year at Marienbad (1961), Alain Resnais

EXTENDED REALITY: SPLIT SCREEN
Two Timid Souls (1927), René Clair

ACTION AND REACTION: SPLIT SCREEN
Charly (1969), Ralph Nelson

Multi-image and multi-screen techniques extend the motion picture's spatial qualities and offer many ways of bringing together different aspects of a subject simultaneously

IMPRESSIONISTIC "MONTAGE": MULTIPLE SCREENS
City of Contrasts (1932), Irving Browning

THEMATIC ASSOCIATIONS: MULTI-SCREENS
To Be Alive (1964), Francis Thompson and Alexander Hammid

Time and Space

JOHN HOWARD LAWSON

*I*n *The Time Machine,* H. G. Wells wrote of a scientist who invents a vehicle that can carry him through time, back to the dinosaurs or forward into the mysteries of the future. There have been many similar fantasies, and Wells's Time Traveler makes the usual explanation:

Any real body must have extension in *four* directions: it must have Length, Breadth, Thickness, and—Duration . . . There are really four dimensions: three which we call the three planes of Space; and a fourth, Time. There is, however, a tendency to draw an unreal distinction between the former three dimensions and the latter, because it happens that our consciousness moves intermittently in one direction along the latter from the beginning to the end of our lives.

Wells wrote at the start of the twentieth century; he was intrigued by the naïve notions of the fourth dimension that were current at the time, but was perspicacious enough to note the distinction between time and space in their effect upon human existence. Our consciousness is constantly and intensely concerned with time because it is the inescapable condition of our being. The moments of our lives are the measure and test of all our actions; each moment as it passes is irreplaceable; the rhythm of our hearts is the rhythm of our days and years. The Time Traveler in Wells's

163

story shows his friends a set of pictures: "Here is a portrait of a
man at eight years old, another at fifteen, another at seventeen, another at twenty-three, and so on. All these are evidently sections,
as it were, Three-Dimensional representations of his Four-Dimen-
sional being, which is a fixed and unalterable thing."

The time and space factors are interwoven: if we see the child
in a happy home at the age of eight, if the man stands with his
bride in a church at the age of twenty-three, the place affects our
consciousness of the man and his consciousness of himself. But
the time pattern is primary in two ways. First, it provides the continuity or form which expresses—and as it were, encloses—everything that happened in the man's life. Second, it is fixed and unalterable. There are many actions or relationships that can be
changed or modified; we can reverse decisions *before it is too late*,
but time submits to no revision: it is always *too late* to go back to
the previous minute.

These two aspects of time have a unique effect on film. The
form of any narrative is to a large extent determined by the way in
which it presents time relationships. At an earlier point, I wrote:
"Film can place events in any time order, but it emphasizes their
immediate impact; it treats the past, and even the future, as if
they were in the present tense." Let us go back for a moment to
reexamine this statement.

What is the sense of the phrase I have just used?—"Let us go
back for a moment . . ." We can go back in space through the
pages of a book. The actual turning of the pages takes a few seconds. But the time in which I write the lines is separated from the
time in which the reader reads. I riffle the pages of the manuscript;
a year or many years later, the reader holds the volume, and may
or may not turn back the printed pages. If the reader looks back,
his consciousness covers only the time during which he has been
reading the book, while the author's consciousness covers the period occupied in writing. But there is a third area of time to which
we refer when we discuss the history of film. In a theoretical work,
this third area may be indeterminate, but it is self-evident that it is
prior to the act of writing. It would strain the reader's credulity if
I wrote: "I am looking at a film and the hero is just taking the
heroine in his arms."

In fiction, the distinction between the time of telling the story and the time when it happened is all-important. The novel is always concerned with the memory or contemplation of past events.

George Bluestone writes (in *Novels into Film*):

"Chronological time in the novel exists on three primary levels: the chronological duration of the reading; the chronological duration of the narrator's time; and the chronological span of the narrative events. . . . If the novelist chooses to chronicle a series of events up to the present moment, he discovers that by the time he commits a single event to paper, the present moment has slipped away."

The narrator can pause to refresh his memory or to deal with some other facet of remembered events. A diary or report can be written a few moments after something has occurred; it may be composed under the shadow of terror or the fear of what is to come. But there is a gap that cannot be closed between what took place and the act of describing it.

In the mid-nineteenth century, an American journalist wrote a series of stories purporting to tell the adventures of Davy Crockett, a Western hero whose exploits were legendary. This legendary character was supposed to have died in the defense of the Alamo, a Texas fortress captured by Mexican troops when Mexico was trying to prevent the American conquest of Texas. The last of the tales ends with Crockett's last moments in the beleaguered fortress. He writes that men are dying all around him. Then he tells us that he himself is mortally wounded, and dots indicate his agony as he reports, "I am losing blood . . . I am dying . . . These . . . are . . . my . . . last words . . ."

This is an amusing illustration of the problem noted by Bluestone: "Whenever a novelist chooses for his province a sequence of events which cannot be completed until the present moment, the three levels come into open conflict." The storyteller (the author or a character delegated by him to describe the events) plays an essential role, because he establishes the relationship of the three levels. He creates a bond between himself and the reader, so that the time-gap between them is bridged and they can share a common sense of the past.

The relevance and urgency of the past, as history or as emotional experience, determine the form of a work of fiction. There is nothing of a similar sort in stage or screen presentation. The theater has a more limited time range: our attendance in the playhouse presupposes our agreement that the action is really taking place before our eyes. We are in a dynamic present that is driving forward toward a denouement. The past may be described, but it is valid only in connection with the stage event. Film can develop an extended time pattern, but it is not mainly an art of remembrance like the novel, nor is it mainly an art of suspense like the theater. The novel is concerned with *what has happened*. The theater asks *what is about to happen*. The screen tells us that *what is happening* is all-important because it is not isolated—it is part of the past and future.

Film alone can weave a time pattern in which all the parts are equally vivid, all having the same audiovisual impact on our consciousness. This is suggested, in an elementary way, by Wells's description of the pictures of a man at different periods of his life. The camera does not distinguish between the various ages, and something happens between each of the portraits: a relationship is created.

In its appearance, the average film consists largely of shifts from one place to another, and this spatial movement is set in a more or less chronological time structure, covering a given period and jumping over the hours or years that are not important to the story. The impression that the picture simply moves ahead through time like a ship in the sea results from the filmmaker's dependence on narrative and theatrical techniques. But even in these cases the consciousness of time pervades the action. It affects the length and tempo of each shot. The exact length of a scene creates its emotional value, and the tensions between the scenes depend on whether the actions are simultaneous or consecutive or separated by a long period. The time span of the action determines the way it is organized and the relationship of all its parts.

This process, which occurs in every film, can be reduced to deceptively simple terms. Gilbert Seldes in *The Public Arts* describes it as "control of the time-sense by breaking any action into many parts, showing the audience some of it, skipping other portions." Seldes points out that "the art closest to the movies is music, because in each the element of time is so significant." He illustrates the detailed resemblance:

"In its simplest form, the note we hear is part of a sequence of notes which create the melody, and the woman's face we see at the window connects with the detective we have just seen looking for this woman and with the other man who will presently draw down the blind; and the length of time we see each of these shots and their grouping together create the rhythm of the picture, corresponding to the duration of and accent on the notes in music which create their time signature."

Seldes realizes that this procedure, which we take for granted in the films we see, has far-reaching implications: "The annihilation of ordinary time is one of the most extraordinary effects the movies can produce. Parallel to the invention of perspective in painting, the invention of cutting in the movies is a landmark in the history of art."

If film annihilates "ordinary time," what does it put in its place? Seldes gives a technical answer: "It may take half an hour to show the events of ten minutes, or a lifetime may be condensed into three hours."

If ten minutes is stretched to a cinematic half hour, or if the span of a life is compressed into three hours, we are clearly aware of the process; it does not challenge or annihilate our sense of ordinary time. However, there is such a challenge, amounting to an imperative and compulsive rejection of time, in the concept of alienation. Since our life is so bound up in time, and since our consciousness inevitably moves along it, people who hold that all experience is subjective cry out against the supremacy of time.

In the introduction to *Last Year at Marienbad*, Robbe-Grillet says that he was eager to work with Resnais because of their similar approach to art:

"I saw Resnais's work as an attempt to construct a purely mental space and time—those of dreams, perhaps, or of memory, those of any effective life—without excessive insistence on the traditional relations of cause and effect, or on the absolute time-sequence in narrative.

"Everyone knows the linear plots of the old-fashioned cinema, which never spare us a link in the chain of all-too-expected events . . . In reality, our mind goes faster—or slower, on occasion. Its style is more varied, richer and less reassuring: it skips certain passages, it preserves an exact record of certain 'unimportant' details, it repeats and doubles back on itself. And this *mental time*, with its peculiarities, its gaps, its obsessions, its obscure areas, is the one that interests us since it is the tempo of our emotions, of our *life*."

Robbe-Grillet's statement exposes the contradictions in his viewpoint. He is justified in rejecting "absolute time-sequence" and "linear plots"; his impatience with conventional cinema can be understood and applauded. Our memories of events do not correspond to the reality, and there is a complicated interplay between our cognition of time and its actual course. But mental time, divorced from cause and effect and from real time, has no existence outside itself, and this means that it has no existence outside the film. The screen has no extension, because the characters have no lives outside the momentary mental states that are expressed in the film. Robbe-Grillet is forced to the conclusion that there is only one kind of time, bounded and enclosed by what we see on the screen:

"In a film, there's no reality except that of the film, no time except that of the film. If people ask me, 'How long did *Marienbad* take to happen? Two years? One? Two months? Three days?' —I say, 'No. An hour and thirty-two minutes. The duration of the film.' The story of *Marienbad* doesn't exist apart from the way it's told."

This is an extremely literal statement, but it cannot be accepted literally. The theme of the film, as well as its title, relates to a previous and probably imaginary meeting of the lovers; although they may not have met "last year at Marienbad," the man's attempt to persuade the woman that they did creates the clash between consciousness and the real world that drives the action forward.

The obvious fact that man can move more freely in space than in time creates a whole spectrum of feeling regarding time. It is volatile and precious; it can be uncertain when it is filtered through the prism of memory, but it is inexorable in its passage and it has no mercy upon our whims or desires. In an English morality play of the Middle Ages, there is a bronze bell that clangs and an iron voice speaks: "Time is . . . time is . . . *Time was!*" Film can no more change the reality of time than it can raise the dead or bring back "the snows of yesteryear."

Film can move backward and forward in time, but it is not a magical machine that explores the highways and byways of history. Extension in time—one of the most potent, and most difficult, forms of cinematic expression—cannot transcend the requirements of the theme. Dziga Vertov rejoiced in the peripatetic adventures of the camera, citing examples from the film newspaper, *Kino-Pravda*, which he edited in the early twenties:

They are lowering the coffins of national heroes (shot in Astra-khan in 1918); they fill in the graves (Kronstadt, 1912); cannon salute (Petrograd, 1920); memorial service—hats come off (Moscow, 1922). . . . (See *Kino-Pravda*, No. 13.) Crowds greeting Lenin in different places at different times are also in this category. (See *Kino-Pravda*, No. 14.)

We can appreciate Vertov's enthusiasm, and hail the astonishing results he sometimes achieves. The effect, in the examples cited, arises from the simple thematic line that unifies the material. But Vertov underestimated the historical and aesthetic problems involved in any rearrangement of chronological time.

According to Lewis Jacobs, Griffith's invention of " 'the switch-back' freed the movie from its dependence on a rigid chronology of time and space." The switch-back as it was first employed by Griffith was a cross-cut from one scene to another to present two or more actions taking place simultaneously: in *The Birth of a Nation*, the Klan gathers while the Cameron family is besieged in a cabin and Lynch is forcing Elsie Stoneman to marry him; these three events happen at once, but the reality of time holds them together. The pressure is pushed to the ultimate limits of the time available for a rescue. It is an entirely different matter when the action moves back through time to envision past events in the familiar flashback. Griffith's feeling that there is almost no limit to the range of film experience led him to combine the two methods. In *Intolerance*, he goes back thousands of years, bringing stories that are far apart in time together in a simultaneous climax. *Intolerance* moves us by its power and rhythm, by the daring with which it attempts to encompass the story of mankind. But the climax violates the principle of simultaneity: the four actions are not interlocked by any immediate time relationship. Griffith asks us to believe that different periods of time can run parallel, but this is what they can never do, and our sense of real time rebels against the illusion. It is conceivable that a film could achieve the massive extension attempted in *Intolerance*, but if it did, it would have to master the time relationships of the different periods. In *Intolerance*, history does not move; it simply repeats parallel actions, from which we learn only that they are similar. There is no explosive contrast, no cinematic revelation, between the stories: it is hard to ignite a spark of passion across vast spaces of history.

Griffith's experience had proved to him that a film is a story. But he had also learned that it has a scope and movement that are unlike any other mode of telling or acting a story. In *Intolerance* he tries to achieve greater intensity by adding more stories. He endeavors to give emotional unity to the separate actions with the image of the woman rocking the cradle, but the image is "timeless" and has no emotional relationship to the time scheme. There are many technical lessons to be learned from *Intolerance*, and perhaps the most important relates to time: the links between each event in a film story are links in time, and the emotional linkage depends on real time relationships. The principle is expressed in terms of physical action in Griffith's use of the last-minute rescue: it cannot take place at a leisurely pace; it cannot involve an indeterminate period of time, and it cannot be spread out over centuries.

Real time becomes an insistent pressure as *Last Year at Marienbad* approaches its denouement. The woman pleads for time:

A: No, no. All I'm asking is that you wait a little. Next year, here, the same day, at the same hour . . . And I'll come with you, wherever you want.
X: Why wait, at this point?
A: Please. I have to. A year isn't too long.
X: (*Gently*) No . . . For me, it's nothing.

But X immediately shows that time means everything to him. He says: "Then you need more time. Until when? Until when?" And a moment later:

X: I can't put it off again.
A: No, of course not . . . A few hours is all I'm asking you for.
X: A few months, a few hours, a few minutes . . . (*A pause.*) A few seconds more . . .

The emotional pressure is bound up in the time pressure. We can imagine how the tension would evaporate if they agreed to wait for another year. If the film dissolved to the same situation a year later, it would be necessary to repeat the problem of time in exactly the same way: "A few hours, a few minutes . . . a few seconds more . . ."

Filmmakers generally avoid any break in time in the climactic development of a picture. They fear that a break will dissipate the tension. While this is often true, a jump in time may also intensify and magnify the action, provided the emotional connection is sufficiently strong to bridge the gap. The real duration of the intervening period determines its effect, for our consciousness of time is too sensitive to be trifled with.

Potemkin is conceived as a unified action taking place in a limited period. Let us suppose that the guns of the *Potemkin* suddenly became the guns of the *Aurora* firing on the Winter Palace. There is certainly a connection, which could be rendered creatively, between these events. But it would be an ill-considered intrusion on the action of the rebellious sailors: the intensity of their experience is determined by its exact time; the limits imposed on their situation, and on their consciousness and capabilities, cannot be transcended without diminishing their human stature and the meaning of their action. Eisenstein presents the revolt as a microcosm of the 1905 Revolution; this is accomplished by making it so potent and compelling within itself—within its own time span—that it suggests the whole character of the epoch. Extension beyond the immediate situation would dilute the emotion; it would force us to consider questions which cannot be answered in the context of the *Potemkin* revolt.

Both Eisenstein and Pudovkin faced the difficulties of a larger historical structure when they undertook to make films celebrating the tenth anniversary of the October Revolution. The theme demanded an epic form, which at the same time would evoke the passion and humanity of the event. When he began work on the project, Pudovkin followed a suggestion from his cameraman, Anatoli Golovnya, that the film cover two centuries of St. Petersburg history, through the years in which it became Petrograd and Leningrad. Zarkhi tried to develop a script which would go from the birth of the city to its revolutionary transformation. But, as Leyda points out in *Kino*, he "was defeated by the breadth of two centuries." Zarkhi reduced the time span and wrote a script entitled *Petersburg, Petrograd, Leningrad*, which was further revised as *The End of St. Petersburg*. Eisenstein also had to reduce the scale of his original plan. It was announced in November 1926 that his anniversary film would include "preparations for October, October at the centre (Petrograd) and other places, and episodes of the civil war." In its final form, *October* achieves its emotional effect by a more concentrated treatment of the historical situation.

Film tends to concentrate on periods of maximum intensity and meaning when our emotional experience affects our sense of time: although we know that time is fixed and unalterable, we *feel* that it moves more rapidly or slowly in accordance with our tensions and desires. The ten days of the October Revolution were so crowded with events that the pace must have seemed breathless to the participants. Yet there must have been moments when great decisions were awaited, when time seemed to "stand still." We have all experienced the sensation that "time seems to fly," or that "time is heavy on our hands." These variations in our attitude toward time do not mean that we escape from it or ignore its real duration, but rather that our sense of its reality is heightened. Film's ability to visualize our consciousness of time is obviously validated by changing the speed of the camera to speed up or slow down the action. But there are more subtle ways of achieving similar effects through cutting and the relationship of images.

In *Potemkin*, the moments of maximum intensity are heightened by making time stand still and then rush forward. Arthur Knight writes:

"Perhaps Eisenstein's greatest editorial discovery was the discrepancy between screen time and real time . . . Griffith had shown how to eliminate the inessentials, to concentrate the significant into a single dramatic close-up. Now Eisenstein proceeded to *expand* time, to accentuate the moment of peak significance."

Knight mentions the scene in which the young sailor picks up the platter with "Give us this day our daily bread" inscribed on it and hurls it to the floor:

"Eisenstein took the same action from a number of angles, then cut the shots together in a slightly overlapping progression. The result was to emphasize the action by the abrupt hail of shots, and to prolong it through overlaps . . . This cinematic expansion of time reaches its fullest, most complex expression in the scenes of the massacre on the Odessa steps."

The method is used to advantage in the scene showing the passage of the train in *The Clear Sky*. Louis Marcorelles objects to the sequence on the ground that it "lasts too long" and thus distorts time. If we adopt this literal conception of time, we must omit all temporal transitions, and also, for that matter, all transitions from one place to another, because every cut disarranges the time schedule.

If there is to be no discrepancy between screen time and real time, the action must take place in the same number of minutes that it takes to view it, and the critic can judge the result with a stop watch in his hand. The presentation of an action from a number of angles in order to accentuate its significance follows the principle of simultaneity discovered by Griffith. In showing two or more actions happening at the same time, Griffith prepared the way for the examination of the same action from different points of view. The method is as essential to the aesthetics of film as the close-up, with which it is intimately associated. Close-ups show the intensity of human feeling that must be related to the event which arouses the feeling. The close-up can be given greater sensitivity when it registers the individual's consciousness of time—the sense of fleeting seconds or of time delayed and immobilized.

In *The Clear Sky*, the flashes of faces watching the train rush by give the event an emotional extension which demands a corresponding amount of time for its expression.

While film expands time in terms of precious seconds at moments of tension, it also compresses time in order to sustain emotion over periods of comparative calm. There are situations in which tension grows gradually over years. Rudolph Arnheim observes: "A simple phrase like 'She lived absolutely alone in her cottage' is extraordinarily hard to express on the screen, because it does not indicate a passing event but a permanent condition which cannot be made clear in any momentary scene."

Film cannot portray the woman's loneliness if it attempts to build a series of crises in the manner of the theater, because each scene must involve other people or activities which contradict the main condition of the woman's life. The main condition is the passage of time, which cannot be expressed in "dramatic" terms. The cinematic imagination can make the repetitious details of the woman's experience painfully real. This can be done by intensifying the time, compressing the monotony of years into harsh moments of awareness. In *Citizen Kane*, there is a breakfast scene in which Kane and his first wife sit at a table; lapses of time, with changes of costume, show the estrangement of the couple over the years, but the dialogue continues from the first shot of an affectionate couple to the last, in which the wife hides her face behind a copy of the newspaper that is the rival of Kane's journal. The scene is not extraordinary in its characterization or detail; it is unusual only in its economical portrayal of a marriage and its use of time as an active force in the audiovisual scheme.

Citizen Kane has exerted a broad influence on film thought; its psychological tone, its emphasis on emotional frustration, its technical devices have been admired, studied, and imitated. The contribution made by Orson Welles and Herman Mankiewicz in freeing the film from subservience to a routine chronological progression has received less attention than it deserves. The film views a man's life, not as a movement from the cradle to the grave, but as a pattern of conflicting purposes and forces, orchestrating various themes that merge in a final thematic statement. Time seems to be the framework, the loom on which the themes are woven. The method is defined in the opening scenes, which are rich in promise—the main title appears in silence, followed by the events surrounding the death of the millionaire, and the sudden shift to the rapid welter of newsreel shots showing the highlights of his public life.

When the newspaper man declares that he intends to discover the truth about Kane, the excitement engendered by the opening is considerably abated: the reporter is not an interesting figure, nor does his plan to find out about Kane carry any note of passion. He is an observer who can have only a casual intellectual interest in the problem he sets out to solve. Yet the problem is the heart of the film, and the newspaperman's approach to it necessarily weakens the structure. He interviews people who were close to Kane, and their memories provide the rationale for the exploration of the millionaire's life. The interviews seem a harmless and not very inventive device to hold the story together. But they have a disastrous effect on the emotional force of the transitions from one period to another: they cushion the transitions so that what happens between the events, the lapse and pressure of time, the hidden links or explosive contrasts between one time and another, are dissipated.

The newspaperman is a symptom of a deeper trouble, one that relates to Kane himself. Kane is not shown as a person who changes and grows or deteriorates; this man who exerted a dynamic and sinister influence on history, who controlled great newspapers, who instigated wars and planned imperial adventures is pictured as a lonely and thwarted individual whose character is predetermined by an unhappy incident in his childhood. This concept of the protagonist makes it impossible to place him in a real system of time relationships. The promise of the newsreels at the opening is not fulfilled. We do not see Kane's life as a race against time, nor do we see him as an integral part, a significant manifestation, of the historic period in which he lived. The sense of history —personal or public—is missing.

There are moments in the film when Welles seems about to achieve moral passion, which is inseparable from moral judgment. There is such a moment—perhaps the most creative passage in the work—toward the conclusion, when the camera moves across the vast storeroom filled with miscellaneous commodities Kane has collected. The scene may be regarded as an intellectual comment on a life devoted to conspicuous accumulation, but it is a tragic and powerful summary of such a life. Its force would be magnified if it were linked more closely to the dead man's experience. However, the link to the past, concluding the scene, is the revelation of the sled with "Rosebud" written on it. This is the secret for which we have been searching throughout the film. We are asked to believe that Kane has driven relentlessly toward wealth and power because he was deprived of a sled when he was a boy.

The meaning of Kane's life is reduced to a Freudian epigram. By the same token, it ceases to be a system of meaningful and interlocking time relationships. In the last analysis, time has stood still for Kane. He has never gone beyond the childhood moment of bitterness when a prized possession was torn from his grasp.

In *Citizen Kane*, alienation is "the thief of time." It plays a similar role in recent films which relate past and present events. In *Hiroshima, Mon Amour*, there are two incompatible sets of time relationships. The connection between the lovers and the bombing of Hiroshima is real, because they are in the city where the destruction took place and the emotion that bridges the gap in time is a response to their environment. The connection with Nevers is subjective; it has nothing to do with chronological time or with intervening events: the woman explains that she ceased to live when the German soldier died, and alienation has destroyed time.

In *Wild Strawberries*, there are moments when the gap between past and present is visualized on the screen. The professor sits eating wild strawberries near the house where he lived as a young man, and it is suddenly transformed; the sun glitters on the windows and curtains sway in a gentle breeze. Isak sees his cousin as a girl; he calls, "Sara . . . It's me, your cousin Isak . . ." But she cannot hear him across the years. A boy strolls down the hill. It is Isak's brother, Siegfried, whom Isak sees kissing Sara. She is frightened, angry, and moved. Isak remembers the emotion he felt at the time, but his emotion as an old man looking back is made more poignant by the passage of years.

However, in the film as a whole, the insistence on Isak's inability to feel or communicate with others makes the time pattern repetitious and static. The imminence of death is the theme of the film, expressed at the beginning in Isak's dream of his own funeral. Isak searches the past to justify his life before it ends, but there can be no justification because there has been no energizing passion in his life. The denial of time is indicated in the opening dream, when a clock without a face appears. Later Isak looks at a childhood toy, a watch without hands, and recalls the dream: "The blank clock face and my own watch which lacked hands, the hearse and my dead self." The idea that his spirit (his real self) is dead negates the past movement of time and reduces the tension concerning his approaching death.

It is unfortunate that the importance of time in the cinematic structure has been so little recognized and that there has been so little experimentation with an imaginative use of time relationships. Variations in chronological time are introduced as a defiance of reality, as in *Hiroshima, Mon Amour*, or time is treated as the enemy of man, driving him toward his death, as in *Wild Strawber-*

ries. The flashback appears frequently as a plot device, but it is accomplished according to fixed conventions. A character speaks of other times, or muses or dreams; there is a moment when the images are blurred or whirl before us, and we know that we have been safely transported to an earlier period—without any of the shock or excitement that should accompany the voyage. Ordinary progression in time is also covered by familiar formulae—the close-up of a clock ticking, the calendar with changing dates, the leafless tree that becomes a tree in bloom.

These attempts to avoid the impact of time transitions indicate the filmmaker's recognition that time is a troublesome and difficult thing to handle. It does present difficulties, because it is the most sensitive and the most dynamic factor in the film story. Even if the story follows a simple and comparatively brief chronological pattern, time is the pressure that drives the story forward; the form is determined by the whole time span and the selection of periods of concentrated experience within the whole design. Transitions in space are so interwoven with time that they need not be considered separately. Each shift in the camera's position must be linked emotionally with the preceding shot, but the linkage cannot be purely in space. The scene must be later or earlier or simultaneous to the one that preceded it, and its place in the time scheme determines its effect.

Cinematic time is a conscious organization of real time. It must be constructed on the bedrock of actual chronology. Film is uniquely able to explore time relationships; the compression and extension of time are aspects of our experience. Time in its imminence and duration is the condition of our lives and history, moving with the ticking of seconds and the majestic passage of centuries. Film draws its tension and power from this reality. It cannot escape into a timeless dream. Cinematic time is not "a clock without hands."

Film: The Creative Process, 1964

Rhythm

IVOR MONTAGU

> "I'll tell you who Time ambles withal, who
> Time trots withal, who Time gallops withal,
> and who he stands still withal."—*Shakespeare*

*I*n motion pictures it is possible to construct, annihilate, rearrange time.

Shots can be taken out of order and arranged in a fresh succession that appears to be that of the development of the event depicted.

Also, just as we can omit unnecessary transitions in space by cutting from one image of interest to another image of interest, so we can omit transitions in time.

A man enters and crosses a room. We see him enter the door at one side of the room. If he passes completely out of the shot before the shot itself is taken from the screen or, to give a simpler effect still, if he is passing out of it as it leaves the screen, he can then be shown entering another part of the room without our seeing him cross the intervening space. This "speeds up" the action (and not necessarily with a change of rhythm). It eliminates a transition in time and space.[1] Similarly: suppose a man is going to bed. He walks to the bed. We end the long shot or middle shot and cut to a close-up of a bedside chair. Various articles of cloth-

[1] Distinguish the needs of this example, of course, from those of a case where the progress of a man is not just a transference from significant place to significant place, but itself the subject of the portrayal. Here it would be right to show the full passage and choose an angle (i.e., behind or head-on along a corridor) that would emphasize time.

ing are deposited on it by a person out of shot. A hand pulls back the bedclothes. The bedside lamp; a hand enters picture and switches it off. We understand perfectly what has happened; the totality of the action is fully apprehended, although its duration has been reduced by elimination of inessential parts of the action.

Note a point. I say: we understand perfectly what has happened. The man has gone to bed. But who is "we" here? "We" is anyone familiar with films. But we have had to see many films to "see" in terms of their expressive methods. Their language is no more naturally to be understood than a baby is born able to read and write. Just as everyone now "sees" incidents and phenomena and understands them as wholes when represented in a succession of parts of shots, though the spectators who first saw the result of Griffith's economizing innovation did not, so to "beginner" film audiences these transitions are sometimes hard to follow. The first great innovator to use parts of action and time to represent wholes, not merely for speeding the action—a method developed pragmatically and very soon a part and parcel of all skilled cinema technique—but as a witty expression, a sort of visual epigram, was the German, later American, director Ernst Lubitsch. But the ingenious pictorial condensations he achieved in his day are now so much a part of normal cinema expression, of general film culture, of the way anybody makes films, that his comedies perhaps survive worst of all classic pictures.

Consider the description we have given of a going to bed communicated visually by a hand depositing clothing on a chair. That was Lubitsch.[2] The idea of presenting the pomp and power of a ruler by having a caller pass through an endless succession of huge antechamber doors flung open in pairs at his approach—that was Lubitsch, in his *Forbidden Paradise*. The dignified unyielding lady whom we leave in fade-out courted by an irresistible Prince Charming and who next morning secretly smiles at the reflection, in the mirror of her dressing table, of a bruise on her white shoulder—that was Pauline Frederick, directed by Lubitsch. All these

---

[2] Incidentally, the late Edwin Greenwood, who knew a good thing when he saw it, copied this scene exactly in a film of his own a few months later. The British Board of Film Censors turned it down. "But you passed it in a Lubitsch film," protested Greenwood. "I know, Mr. Greenwood, but we wish to maintain a higher standard of morality in British pictures."

things and countless others sound banal in description—because we have seen them so often. But he did them first. Every ingenuity has become a cliché—he enriched film language so that we now take it for granted.

Conversely, Chinese films, especially those first made in China after the new dispensation, to us seem slow. The man who enters the room will open the door, come through the doorway, cross the length of the room—and we will watch him till he reaches the other side. Why? Not because Chinese filmmakers do not know how to make films. They make excellent films. But before 1950 no Chinese spectators outside those in the larger towns had ever seen films. When you are making films for a public of 650 million of whom only some 50 million have ever seen films before, you are right to assume that the conventions now second nature to those who have acquired them will in others take a modicum of getting used to.

We can halt on time, dwell upon it, repeat it for emphasis. The perfect type example, shown to film-study groups to this day, is Eisenstein's "raising of the bridges" sequence from *October*. In this sequence, at a moment of tension, the Provisional Government gives orders to raise the bridges over the Neva and so separate the administrative center of the city from the working-class factory districts. Machine-gun fire halts a crowd trying to cross, and one half of the bridge rises with a carriage on its end balanced by the dead horse hanging from its shafts, the other with a slain woman whose long streaming hair hangs, like the horse opposite, immediately over the division of the bridge. The two sections with their poignant images rise, rise unbearably, endlessly, the motion repeated again and again until at last horse and corpse fall from the now vertically raised bridge halves, abruptly completing the irrevocable separation. Here the repetition is used in a carefully composed form employing both graphic composition and content to raise the emotionality of the scene to a height of poetry. A more prosaic example of non-natural time development is to be seen in Hitchcock's *The Lodger,* where the assassin, striking indiscriminately at golden-haired women, turns out the lights of a ballroom before stabbing one of the dancers. A hand, in close-up, pulls down the switch and *then* the light goes out in long shot. There is here of course no poetry, no creation of a new time scale perceived and accepted. But this repetition of time is a like liberty taken with nature and, at least at a first viewing, works effectively to heighten the melodrama instead of being perceived as nonsense.

What we have instanced so far are film rearrangements of real time, but film time generally—the time created for the purpose of the film—is itself plastic and at our disposition for free modeling. The stage can compress a lapse of years into an interval of ten minutes or the raising and lowering of a curtain (or, in a certain type of experimental expressionist production, simply the switching off of a light in one box or compartment of the stage and the switching on of that in another—merely granting time enough in darkness for a character or two to pant up or down a pair of ladders). But the cinema has simpler, more direct means of punctuation: the fade-out (F.O.), fade-in (F.I.); gradual submergence of the scene into or emergence from darkness, at any speed desired beyond about half a second minimum; the mix (or lap dissolve); the slow blending of one whole scene into a fresh one; the wipe, where one scene is effaced, as quickly as you like, or breaks up, to disclose another, the new one appearing from one side or above or below or disclosed in an aperture of any regular or irregularly shaped margin. (Note, of course, that the more novel or unfamiliar the manner of punctuation, the more the engrossment of the spectator will be interrupted; the more familiar and conventional, the less the regular filmgoer will be aware of the interruption.)[3]

Priestley, in *Time and the Conways* and others of his "time plays," reverses time and jumps about from one period to another. On the stage he can do this, act by act or scene by scene. In film we can do this ad-lib, even shot by shot, in the device called flashback.

All these are examples of the arbitrary control of time. They are conveniences, chiefly, of expository construction. But more important for degree and intensification of effect, for *form* in the art communication, is the determination of tempo, the control of rhythm.

[3] Incidentally, film audiences are nowadays so familiar with time lapses that a sequence change often requires no punctuation other than a careful change of composition. (This is very well demonstrated throughout Richardson's *Tom Jones*, where the frequent use of jump cuts accelerates the tempo of narrative.) TV always prefers the jump cut to an F.O., F.I.

Perhaps the most simple and drastic example of the creation of content by arrangement of *shots* is another given by Pudovkin. Consider three pieces: (*a*) a face frightened; (*b*) a revolver pointing at it; (*c*) the same face smiling. The order *c b a* is apprehended as a coward; the order *a b c* as a hero.

But the right order is still no good unless the pieces are the right length. The scene analyzed below is from a film depicting a street accident.[4]

1. The street with cars in movement: a pedestrian crosses the street with his back to the camera; a passing motorcar hides him from view.

2. Very short flash: the face of the startled chauffeur as he steps on the brake.

3. Equally short flash: the face of the victim, his mouth open to scream.

4. Taken from above, from the chauffeur's seat: legs, glimpsed near the revolving wheels.

5. The sliding, braked wheels of the car.

6. The corpse by the stationary car.

Certainly this breakdown and synthesis of the event into shots should be more effective for the spectator than the whole thing filmed obscurely in one long shot. But note that its effect will be achieved only if the right *rhythm* is attained, including the right length of the pieces.

Suppose we show:

1. Man crossing street.

2. A startled chauffeur's face—very long, held a long time on screen.

3. The screaming face of the victim—also held long.

4. Etc. The braked wheels and everything else long.

The whole scene will disintegrate. It will not appear as a unity. We shall hardly perceive it as an accident at all.

The shots must be, as we have already provided in definition, the right length. But what is the right length? Is it a question of the absolute length of the pieces? Certainly not. The absolute length of the piece comes into it, but only as a factor. The absolute length governs the duration of the image. But the right length

---

[4] *Film Technique and Film Acting* (London: George Newnes, 1933).

depends on a relation between the form of the image, its content, *and* its duration.

There is only one special case I can think of where the absolute length is mandatory and that is in an experimental effect first introduced in *October* and since repeated to such exhaustion that it has become an unusable cliché—the rattling impression of machine-gun fire produced by repeated alternation of two shots, each two frames in length, of the machine gunner and his gun.

The point is that we are dealing with length of visual effects, and not just length of pieces: duration of the time it takes for apprehension of the content of a shot, as well as duration of the time the shot is upon the screen.

Consider the filming of an object in motion. Suppose we film an object passing across the lens of a stationary camera; say, a fast motorcar. If it is near and nearly fills or even momentarily obscures the screen, its passage will appear rapid but we may not even recognize the car. If it is far from the camera and tiny on the screen, we shall have plenty of time to see it, we may even be bored watching the vista, but the car will appear to pass slowly.

Suppose now the car is traveling toward us. For a period we show it doing so, but far away. During this period it changes in apparent size. The scene is not very exciting and again we may be bored by the background. If the period selected to show the car is between the two nearer positions, the apparent size change will be much greater; the image will be full of menace.

Suppose, again, that the vehicle is moving from left to right in relation to our lens but that the camera, instead of being stationary, is now itself mounted on a car moving parallel to the vehicle being filmed and at a similar speed. Now the first shot will be a slow-seeming, dull shot in which only a relatively small area of the image will be changing so as to indicate motion. With the second shot, we shall see distinctly the tiny car we are filming, and the major part of the image will be a blur.

In all these cases the object is traveling at the same speed. But its apparent speed will be different. The liveliness of the shot will be different. Equal absolute lengths of these pieces would have entirely different "tempo" effects on the rhythm of the succession of pieces in which they are included.

Why is ballet so difficult to film? In the theater the spectator of ballet has before him a whole spectacle proceeding at a tempo whose key is given to him by the music. Even if the whole corps is not engaged, but only the principals are proceeding at this tempo, it does not matter: the movements of the principals will insure that our attention will be only upon them. The tempo of the movements will still be identical with that which the sound dictates to us.

In cinema, things are more difficult. First, depth is harder to perceive and the movements insofar as they take place in depth will be within a space less apparent. For us to be conscious of the depth of *corps de ballet* movements, our viewpoint must rise above the level on which they take place. Only then will the tempo of movement in space be in some degree restored and the composition cease to be a jumble. But too high a viewpoint will distort the figures, so that though they will still comprise patterns at an approximately correct tempo, they will tend to become dehumanized.

A greater problem here is the change to the viewing of detail, a *pas de deux* or *seul* for example. The music still remains the guide. The actual movements of the dancers remain in time. *But each cut presents us with a graphic composition so novel compared to the last one that it takes a fractional moment to adjust ourselves to the new composition before we can begin to apprehend its contained movement.* The cutting intrinsic to cinema, and necessary to effective portrayal of any filmed process, here interrupts the rhythm if it is not taken into account. To set up a few cameras and join the resulting shots together, hoping that, because the actual process filmed proceeded rhythmically, the rhythm will automatically be immanent in the joined assemblage of shots, is to float a dead fish. The rhythm of the dance *can* be re-created, but only if, in combining shots, the filmmaker takes into account not only the actual speed of the dancers but the composition of the shots *and* the change of fresh shots.

Paul Czinner has done well with ballet, but real successes with dance rhythms are very rare. In Shengelaya's *Elisso* there is a much better Caucasian *lezginka* than Eisenstein achieved. Von Stroheim in *The Merry Widow* had a feeling for the waltz. The cancan has been often attempted, perhaps best realized in Pabst's

L'Atlantide. Basil Wright did well with a ritual rhythm in *Song of Ceylon*. The gang dancers in *West Side Story* were good, and even better is the brides' dance in *Seven Brides for Seven Brothers*. A most remarkable tour de force is the Cuban dance of African origin in the film *The Birth of a Ballet*, which took the Grand Prize at the Leipzig Festival of 1962. Here the most difficult feat is triumphantly attained—one I had not believed possible—the intermingling, in perfect continuous rhythm, of shots taken at normal speed and in slow motion. Composition, speed of shot, place of cut, absolute length, all these combine to make the rhythm immanent in the synthesized image, regardless alike of the action speeds in themselves and of the absolute lengths in themselves.

Eisenstein used to say that the determining factor in length is always movement. If there be no movement in the image, if the image be a static one, the determining factor is nonetheless a movement—that of the eye, passing over the parts of the picture to take it all in. A pretty conceit, but perhaps more than that, a good way of emphasizing that a change of shot always *is* movement, always requires a modicum of time to take in. The seen image cannot be taken in, and its content cannot be apprehended at all, under a minimum time, which will vary with the clarity of composition. (The two-frame alternations in the *October* machine-gun fire were perceptible only because they were repeated a multiplicity of times, and then they were apprehended as a combination, a sort of "rattling" double exposure; a single frame is hardly noticed at all.) A mix is always a slow element of tempo precisely because there is no sharp change (cut) to a new composition; the old composition lingers after its significance has ended, and the new one appears before it is significant.

A pan or track is likewise invariably slow. We discussed earlier, when introducing cutting as corresponding to the natural transfer of the gaze, the unnaturalness of most pans. This especially applies of course when the camera is identified with our wandering eye or the eye of a character and it roves around a static scene. So many graphic elements of the image remain unchanged or only slightly changed during its course. Even if, as is rare in such cases, the image is significant not only at the beginning and the end but in all its course, the change is so slow that a part of the composition area has always finished its usefulness, having been absorbed and then discarded from interest, long before it disappears in the course of the camera movement. We spoke of certain types of pans as being justified and picked out as such the type in which we follow not a particular viewpoint but a particular character or, for that matter, a thing, itself moving, and something we are particularly interested in. Even here, however, the thing watched, or its background, has to change enough to maintain our interest and conquer what would otherwise be monotony. A fine example of this is the remarkable pan in which Wajda introduces his central character to the underground group in A *Generation*. A lighted cigarette is passed round from hand to hand, the camera pans following it, pausing on each new figure as each refuses it or takes a puff. The pause on each person is clear and introduces us to his character. The pan is not a waste because the *cigarette-passing itself is the actual subject of the scene*, showing the poverty of resources of the group, their comradeship in sharing, and the ease of their respect for one another in that the "round" is taken as quite normal. If anyone refuses the cigarette, it is instantly passed on; there are no polite pressures or hesitations. But the difficulty is that, for all its holding interest here, the rhythm of the pan is still intractable. The pan per se has its own built-in rhythm. Wajda uses the scene as an episode on its own. You cannot readily use the pan as an element in a rhythm constructed by synthesis.

A proof of the element of movement in apprehending the static composition involved in the first sight of a shot is the fascination that can be exercised by films composed of still pictures, each held only for the time necessary for the impact of its content in the given graphic composition. Granted the right length of the pieces, such films are not in the least apprehended as "slow." Here the Eisenstein dictum comes true indeed: the eye undoubtedly wanders over the whole image, seeking to extract everything from within it. This is particularly true when these compilations of stills show historical rarities. We feel we are privileged for a moment to live in the real past, so long as the film grips, unconscious of the present that surrounds us. Excellent examples are Charles Eame's *Before the Fair* (Chicago), and, shown on television, Colin Low's *The City of Gold* (the Yukon gold rush), and the Granada suffragette and Boer War histories. An example of drawings used for such a historical reconstruction is Jean Gremillon's *Les Champs de l'existence.* For these are certainly films and something different in kind from magic-lantern shows, quite apart from the fact that their material is still pictures.[5] In a show on magic-lantern principles the *separation* of the still images is emphasized by the method of presentation—the wait for the apprehension to sink into the audience, the almost ceremonial click of the lecturer's instruction as he orders substitution of one image by the next after he considers his teaching to have sunk in. There is here a relation between pedagogue and taught analogous with that of live actor and audience. On the other hand, the automated—predetermined and fixed—mechanics of the relation of filmmaker to his spectators in the case of the films we describe, his nice calculation of the length of presentation of the image based not only on its content but on the time its comprehension and the emotional reaction to it are likely to require under the influence of its composition—the whole arrangement of the picture succession as *cuts*—determine that the aesthetic principles of this construction, and the relation of creative artist to captive spectator, shall be exactly the same as in "true" films; that is, records of movement.

As a sidelight on the point we were just discussing, the effect of pans, it is highly significant that the film studies of masterpieces of painting or draftsmanship, shot by a director sensitive to composition,[6] provide an exception to the boring effect of transitional movement. Many works of graphic art are so meticulously balanced and composed that almost any frame extraction presents a new scene perceived with a new eye, and the camera can, as it were, enter into a picture—even one we have seen often and know inside out, so to speak, in its own frame as a whole—extracting area after area, ever exploring and exposing, as it moves, new and hitherto unsuspected felicities.

A muddled composition with nothing clear in it, succeeded by another muddle—this will seem in any case slow because we are apprehending nothing clearly. A well-designed composition, clearly using contrasts of light and shade, black and white, foreground

---

[5] Nowadays the glass slides of the classic magic lantern are often replaced by a "film strip," but this is of course irrelevant. The single frames are each of a separate image, and presented separately, like slides.

[6] There are many recent examples: *Bosch*, Wright's *Leonardo*. Also, certain studies of three-dimensional graphic art; for example, Wright's lovely *Greek Sculpture*.

and background,[7] not only within itself but also—perhaps in the vertical, horizontal, or diagonal elements—in relation to the compositions that precede and succeed it, allied of course to the logical overtone relationships to which these compositional elements are directing attention, will be apprehended swiftly and its right length produce no feeling of slowness.

Can any recipe be given, any prescription made out, for determining all those features contributing to "rightness"? Alas, no. But they are all bound up in the effect nonetheless. The kernel of art is nowhere easy to explain. It is easy to teach that short shots communicate excitement, long shots communicate deliberation, and that a perfectly timed rhythm will enable the artist to engross the spectator completely and hold the nature and intensity of the spectator's emotions in the hollow of his hand. But how? The rudiments of design may be taught in art school, but no amount of teaching will guarantee the production of Raphaels, Leonardos, Rembrandts. Nevertheless, it is still worthwhile to indicate and teach, even if, for most of us mortals, the solution on studio floor and cutting-room bench remains a mystery still. The point is that, in cinema, the rhythm *is capable* of infinite precision of control. To achieve what you want, you have to think it out, to direct and shoot, or select and shoot, your material with a knowledge of all the factors that may be involved in achieving what you want; to assemble it, arrange it, join it, view it, react to it, trying to imagine yourself always not yourself but a fresh eye coming to it; rearrange it, trim it, try and try again till you feel it is right. And it will not be *right*, unless you are a Leonardo, but it will probably be a great deal better than if you had just stuck the camera in front of it, let come what will come, and slung it all into one.

Film World, 1964

[7] Such contrasts, with a depth of focus achieved by the 28 mm. lens, are mentioned by Eisenstein as his favorites.

IV. COLOR

The Mobility of Color

LEWIS JACOBS

*B*ecause of the personal associations and age-
old connotations of color, its capacity to
arouse subjective responses makes it a highly important cinematic
resource. Some colors make people feel gay; others, depressed.
Some irritate; others have a calming effect. People get "the blues,"
fall into a "brown funk," "see red," or feel "green with envy."
There are beautiful colors, oppressive colors, voluptuous colors,
garish, gentle, and lifeless colors. Color stirs the mind and feelings
and amplifies responses that would be toned down or be nonexistent without color.

In addition to its inherent emotional, symbolical, and psychological appeal, color provides an opportunity to utilize its spectrum
in another way, more unique and organic to film. This involves
using color to promote movement from one part of the film to another. Properly arranged and composed to flow from shot to shot
as an integral element of mood and story values, color, in addition
to its decorative value, affects the deeper overtones of structural relationships. In this form, instead of serving a random collection of
pictures, color takes on the quality of shifting harmonies, discords,
and rhythms in support of propelling and enhancing dramatic action, and therefore becomes an expressive part of film structure itself.

This special emphasis on the mobility of color was not always recognized. When color was first available on a practical basis in the early thirties, its manipulation for dramatic purposes was limited, and technical and artistic principles for its use were still unformed. Technological secrecy and a lack of industry-wide cooperation kept color cameras, laboratory and studio practices, as well as research, in the hands of a few, discouraging experimentation, curtailing directors' imaginations, and restricting artistic progress. Color pictures of this period were crude and had little appeal and for a while it looked as though color might be abandoned.

And then a comparatively unknown and fledgling producer, Walt Disney, working a field that was generally disdained—short animated cartoons—made a picture called *Three Little Pigs* (1932) in an inimitable color style that immediately won the plaudits of viewers and filmmakers alike. The color in this picture and many that followed, particularly the *Silly Symphony* series, revealed little artistic self-consciousness and a fertile imagination. Color was not something added merely for the sake of novelty, but found its motivation in humor, sentiment, violence, and movement. As Disney's animal characters flew, danced, ran, and changed shapes, so the film's color became animated, changing hues with each of the dramatic developments—becoming gay, sinister, cold, warm, or extravagantly varicolored in an unswerving disregard for reality and a delightful flair for mobility that matched the unbroken rhythm of the sound.

The Four Seasons (1933) used a wild extravaganza of the spectrum to express the seasonal color changes in nature. When the North Wind blows, the entire tonal scheme of the forest changes from golden red to icy blue. In another film, when Pluto the dog, lost in the Alps, gradually freezes, his color sinks into a deep blue. But a Saint Bernard finds him and forces whiskey down his throat. A warm color seeps back into Pluto's body as the liquor thaws him out. The wolf trying to blow down the house in *Three Little Pigs* literally blows himself blue in the face. In *Snow White and the Seven Dwarfs* (1938), Snow White's frenzied flight through the forest is expressed through a sinister medley of changing hues that develops into a fantasy of terror not unlike the twisted imagery of *The Cabinet of Dr. Caligari*.

The elasticity of color Disney achieved in his animated world of cartoons—flowing like a kind of visual melody—awakened some producers of dramatic films to look at color with a new hope. The eminent New York stage designer Robert Edmond Jones was engaged as a "colorist" to explore the Technicolor process—a three-color negative system—in order to advance the creative directions of color in feature films using real people and real settings. At that time, color films had been imitating the worst aspects of nineteenth-century naturalistic painting in an effort to be realistic. The general industry policy had been to use color as "natural color" and to keep it as unobtrusive as possible, so that "the audience's eyes would not tire."

After some months it became apparent to Jones, as it had to Disney, that if color was to become an important component of motion pictures, there would have to be a complete change in film technique "as radical in its own way as when sound was added to silent film," according to a statement of his at that time. "Color is an integral element of a picture. Its use means much more than the mechanical recording of colors which the camera has heretofore blotted out. Just as music flows from movement to movement, color on the screen . . . flowing from sequence to sequence, is really a kind of music."

To prove his theories, Jones designed two color films: *La Cucaracha* (1934), a two-reel musical; and the full-length dramatic feature, *Becky Sharp* (1935). Instead of playing down color in these pictures, Jones emphasized it and made color cinematically expressive.

The brilliant rendition of color in *La Cucaracha* heightened reality at every point and gave the picture a chromatic sensuality that sharpened the hedonism of the plot. Luminous harmonies of blue-greens underwent subtle changes from scene to scene in an association intimately bound up with the music's titillating rhythms. The original conception proved an impressive demonstration of the emotional power of color.

Becky Sharp, on which Jones worked under the direction of Rouben Mamoulian, turned out to be the first full-length color film to excite the public and evoke enormous praise in the press. "It is a gallant and distinguished outpost in an almost uncharted domain, and it is probably the most significant event of 1935 cinema," declared Andre Sennwald in *The New York Times* (June 14, 1935).

Chromatically, *Becky Sharp* encompassed a broad spectrum of color patterns, ranging from icy grays to hues of luxuriant crimsons. Every set, every costume, and every action was given its own color style, keyed to the various moods and spirit of the subject. The highlight of the picture was the scene of the great ball on the evening before the battle of Waterloo. It began with a pastel serenity—subtle variations of cool blues. Then, as news of Napoleon's battle preparations reach the guests, the color deepens and builds in intensity. With the rumble of distant cannon, apprehension strikes the various groups; as they hurriedly depart, there are quick cuts of them patterned in yellows, oranges, and dull reds. Finally the sounds of battle are heard and vivid scarlet becomes the predominant color as officers dash wildly across the screen frame, their brilliant red cloaks flashing crimson linings in a striking emblematic color climax that coincides with the dramatic climax of the subject.

At its best, *Becky Sharp* carried with it the feeling of authentic creative pioneering. Its design and dynamic approach to color became a promise of the future and forced the industry to recognize the new element as an integral attribute of the motion-picture medium.

During the next years the proportion of color films gradually increased; language and technology of color steadily improved. With the widespread competition between movies and television in the early fifties and the invention of the wide screen, color was propelled into greater importance than ever before, resulting in a preponderance of color movies over black and white. Few filmmakers, however, made any imaginative use of color other than as an additive or for decorative value. Jones's sharp break with "tradition" and his special emphasis on the mobility of color—sequences keyed to dominant harmonies and discords in a chromatic flow—were generally overlooked.

The single exception was a Japanese picture, *Gate of Hell* (1953). Responding chromatically to the heroic atmosphere of ancient Japan, Kinugasa designed dominant but subtle tonal patterns to model the mood of the scenes and underscore the character of the action. The color was not supplementary but an essential element of the structure, flowing smoothly and gracefully with a special kind of élan and radiance from part to part in contrapuntal relationships. From the opening red-orange harmonies depicting the chaos in the Imperial palace to the steely blues of the assassination scene—the story's climax—the picture was a seamless tissue of color music with delicate psychological stresses and elegant harmonic rhythms.

Failure to merge color with the elasticity and dramatic flow of the subject accounts in great part for the weakness of *Moulin Rouge* (1953) and *Lust for Life* (1956), whose color design stemmed from the palettes of Toulouse Lautrec and Vincent Van Gogh. Because the directors of these movies failed to realize that, on the screen, color can be structured in time and not just in space as in painting, they neglected to use color for more than its emblematic associations. The predominant color scheme of *Moulin Rouge* was blue-greens. These were keyed to suggest the tonal quality of Lautrec's paintings, but there was no color progression from shot to shot or within a sequence. The few attempts to utilize the emotion-arousing quality of color—green gelatins to dramatize Lautrec's effort to drink himself into insensibility, and when he tried to commit suicide; and a shaft of icy blue to punctuate the accident that made the painter a cripple—stood out as mere effects.

Yellows, oranges, reds, and black keyed the visual style of *Lust for Life*. But only toward the end of the film was the color pattern extended beyond individual shots to a succession that underlined the dramatic situation. As Van Gogh's mind begins to falter and he becomes increasingly mad, the color progressively changes from shot to shot; the reds and browns appear less and less until there is only the pale yellow of a wheat field, which provokes an uncanny sense of foreboding and approaching death. When the artist finally dies, the yellow of the field is suddenly torn apart by the swift inundation of a flock of black crows. The impact of the abrupt contrast between yellow and black was striking and both dramatically and psychologically expressive. The scene gained an added overtone from the fact that the color scheme and composition which inspired it came from the artist's own painting of a wheat field and crows, made at the very time of his own approaching madness and death.

Recent color films, styled from the painter's palette, emphasize the sensual qualities of color to serve the foundation of film. The aim is to keep the spectator at a high pitch of involvement by an exuberant variety and richness of color, whose emotional effect springs from the intrinsic quality of color, independent of other film constituents. Here the specific sensation of color itself, pitched directly at the senses of the viewer, gives the image an ambience that has as much to do with the film's appeal as the story, actors, or direction.

The brash, sugar-sweet musical *The Umbrellas of Cherbourg* (1964) demonstrates an artful stylization of bright, bold, flat colors that suggests billboard posters, comic strips, and pop art. Its hard-edge, vivid, and often garish color patterns bluntly attack the senses in a way that is more visceral than intellectual, lending vivacity to a picture that is essentially a simplistic adolescent fantasy.

A Man and a Woman (1966), frankly romantic, employs another kind of stylization. Its striking color progression is keyed to switching from scenes in full realistic color to monochrome scenes in sepia, blue, green, and other shades intended to reflect and deepen the currents of feeling between the two main characters and to heighten the viewer's reaction by the multiplicity of hues and tints.

More lyrical in style are the sensuous color explorations of *Le Bonheur* (1965) and *Elvira Madigan* (1967), both bittersweet romantic stories of love. Virtually every shot in these films—one French, the other Swedish—pays homage to the French school of Impressionist painters, who employ colors intrinsically pleasing and harmonized to yield effects of light and simple physical charm. The use of delicate pastel shades to render the shimmering atmosphere of parks, fields, and flower-blown meadows, tenderly blurred out of focus to accentuate the unity of man and nature, emotionalizes for the viewer the romantic dreams and reveries of unhappy lovers. Ethereal and delicate tonalities of imagery in great measure intensify the poignancy of the sentimental situations but give little recognition to color progression from scene to scene.

Attempts at a radically new and more complex use of color beyond that obtained from painting styles or glamorized or subdued naturalism (all of which can work in time as well as space) distinguish two films that address themselves to interpreting the psychological state of mind of two women through a style that employs color subjectively. *Juliet of the Spirits* (1965) turns the color camera inward to paint the fantasy world of a repressed wife whose psychic probing is incited by the unfaithfulness of her husband. Michelangelo Antonioni in *Red Desert* (1964) turns the color camera outward to depict the drab environment of a neurotic wife whose mental turmoil is brought about by an accident and the neglect of her self-centered husband.

As different as these two directors' ways of approaching their subject is the range of color each uses to express his individual vision. Fellini employs bright hues and tints, highly decorative and visually stimulating, to paint a psychic wonderland that captures the sensations, fantasies, and exaggerations of the inhibited woman. His chromatic design is flamboyant and dazzling, emotionalizing the subjective explorations of the heroine's moods and feelings with a kind of baroque splendor and an intrinsically sensual appeal. Freudian fantasies, orgiastic visions, childhood fears, and epicene grotesques are transfigured in rich, glowing, color combinations and rococo settings that transcend the merely psychoanalytical and dazzle the senses with their extravagant effects and compositions. From the infinitely diversified blue-gray nocturnes in which the wife's grandfather is seduced by a lady bareback rider, to the high-fashion art-nouveau tree house where every hue and tint is designed for impromptu lovemaking, the physical presence of color dynamizes this "fairy tale for adults," as Fellini calls his picture, by serving as the artful device of erotic stimuli.

In contrast, Antonioni shows a relative barrenness of color. He calls upon a more rigorous, grayed-down palette to compose a somber wasteland that reflects the emptiness and morbidity of his character's neurosis. His color style is directed at portraying not so much an individual's personality but a particular relationship with the world.

Antonioni describes his subjective use of color as an attempt to take away "the usual reality and replace it with a reality of the moment," so that his color harmonies and dissonances could better capture the turmoil of a woman in crisis. By coloring the physical landscape as an extension of his heroine's mental disturbance, he relates a dislocated mind to a bleak vision of a modern industrial scene. Hues and shades of actual reality are altered; streets and machines painted; houses, trees, and grass sprayed with an aberrant grayness of alienation, in tones that shroud the real world and reveal it as a wasteland that is symbolic of the wife's anxieties.

A giant chemical plant with red and green condensers and the geometry of multicolored pipes and smokestacks ejecting billows of white steam and yellow smoke is made to look like some ominous technological monster. Streets and surroundings through which the woman wanders are weather-toned a ravaged, mineral gray that suggests a nightmarish fragment of a surreal world. An oppressive grayness also clouds the strange freighters and tankers that drift through a desolate canal flanked with barren pines trapped in a vise of petrified time and space. The foliage in a hotel lobby is modulated into a murky grayness to underline the barrenness of a mind drained of dreams and emotions.

Perhaps the stark, symbolic resonance of Antonioni's color asserts its presence most effectively in the sex-play and near-orgy scene held in an abandoned, slate-blue shack in a shag-polluted marsh. Here a group of husbands and wives, engineers and lonely women, tease and excite one another on a huge nondescript couch enclosed by shaggy-red walls that bluntly accent the emotional poverty and sterility of these victims of a computerized society, groping for human warmth and affection.

Throughout the film, Antonioni's color subtly builds a metaphorical bridge between mental and physical wastelands with an evocative power that reveals a probing and profound approach to the role of color in film.

Color holds a powerful position among the elements of film structure. A kind of universal language, it appeals equally to the illiterate and the sophisticated, to the child and the adult. Its function on the screen is both utilitarian and aesthetic. When made relevant to the picture's subject, color offers an immediate resonance that vivifies mood, delineates character, enhances meaning. When structured to further movement from sequence to sequence, color adds a new richness of film expression that immeasurably deepens the total work.

Color and Color Films

CARL DREYER

Color films have now been on the screens of the world for twenty years. How many of them do we remember for the aesthetic pleasure they gave us? Two—three—four—five?

Possibly five—but probably not more.

Castellani's *Romeo and Juliet* (1953) just manages to be among these—after Olivier's *Henry* V and Kinugasa's *Gate of Hell*. Olivier got his ideas for his color schemes from the illuminated manuscripts of the period. Kinugasa got his from the classical wood engravings of his people.

Except for these three films, there have been only attempts to accomplish things with color. These attempts are best exemplified by *Moulin Rouge*, where the smoke-filled room, right at the beginning, compelled admiration. The rest of the film, so far as color is concerned, was mediocre. Why? In the other scenes the director did not have Toulouse-Lautrec to hold on to. Huston is a great director, but as a painter Toulouse-Lautrec was greater.

So in twenty years' time there have been three or four aesthetically satisfying color films. A modest yield.

Apart from the amusing and surprising color effects that are to be found in film musicals, a rather plain taste has dominated the use of color in motion pictures. This may be due to a fear to depart from the firm fundament of naturalism—firm, but boring. There can be poetry, of course, in the colors of daily life, but color film does not become art by even a sincere imitation of nature's own colors. When a film colorist is merely imitating nature, the audience is merely appraising how well or ill the colors come out.

Indeed, we have so often seen the grass green, and the sky blue, that sometimes we wish we could see a green sky and blue grass— just for a change. Also, there might be the intention of an artist behind it. Let us not forget that color in film can never look exactly like the colors of nature. The reason is simple: in nature, color nuances are endless, and the human eye cannot distinguish them all from one another.

The tiny color differences, the semi-tones, all those nuances the eye receives without discrimination, are missing in color films. To demand that color in color films should be *natural* is to misunderstand all that is involved. Indeed, the spectator can have a much greater aesthetic experience *because* color in film differs from that in nature.

Color is a valuable help to the director. When colors are chosen with due regard for their emotional effect, and selected to match each other, they can add an artistic quality to a film that black and white lacks. But it must always be borne in mind that color composition is as important in color film as composition is in black and white.

In black and white films, light is set against darkness, and line against line. In color films, surface is set against surface, form against form, color against color. What the black and white film expresses in changing light and shade, in the breaking of lines, must, in color films, be expressed by *color constellations*.

There is also the matter of rhythm. To the many other rhythms in films, it is necessary now to add the color rhythm.

While a color film is being made, the problem of how it will be cut—i.e., edited—must be a constant concern. The slightest shift can change the balance between the color planes and cause disharmony.

It must never be forgotten that because persons and objects constantly move in motion pictures, the colors in color films constantly slide from one place to another in changing rhythms, and when the colors collide, or melt together, very surprising effects can occur. The general rule about this is: use the smallest possible number of colors, and use them in conjunction with black and white. Black and white are too little used in color films. They have been forgotten in the childish rapture over the many bright colors in the paintbox.

All this makes the director's task more difficult—and more attractive too. Creating a scene in black and white is a fight, as every director of integrity knows. Colors do not make this fight easier, but they do make the victory, when won, sweeter. And the victory will be much bigger when the director succeeds in breaking the vicious circle that confines color films to naturalistic ideas. The color film can be a really great aesthetic experience—in regard to colors —when it has been freed from the embrace of naturalism. Only then will the colors have a chance of expressing the inexpressible, i.e., of expressing that which can only be perceived. Only then can the motion picture encompass the world of the abstract, which hitherto has been closed to it.

The director must not see his pictures in black and white first and *then* think of color. The colors for the scenes must be in his mind's eye from the beginning. The director must *create* in colors. However, color feeling is not something one can learn. Color is an optical experience, and the capacity to see, think, and feel in colors is a natural gift. We may presume that painters, in general, have that gift.

If there are to be more than just four or five artistic color films in the next twenty years, it will be necessary for the film industry to get assistance from those who can help—that is to say, from painters—just as the film industry has had to get help from authors, composers, and ballet masters. The director of a color film will have to add a painter to his already large staff, and the painter, in cooperation with, and responsible to, the director, must create the color effects of the film. A "color script" should parallel the actual script, and the painter's drawings in this "color script" should abound with details.

People may object: the director has his color technicians. These advisors are, and will undoubtedly remain, immensely useful to the director, for their knowledge of chromatology and color theories can save him from many traps. But, with all due respect to their efficiency and sense of responsibility, a good painter has one important quality they do not: he himself is a creative artist and fetches impulses from his own artistic mind. Incidentally, it will help the color technicians also to have a professional painter at hand.

Let us take a purely suppositious case. Suppose Toulouse-Lautrec were alive and had worked on *Moulin Rouge* from the beginning to the end, not merely during the opening scene, but in all the scenes. Wouldn't these then have been at the same high level as the opening scene, which was based on an actual color composition by Toulouse-Lautrec? And would not *Moulin Rouge*, instead of being a promising attempt, have turned out to be a really great color film? The director would not have been lessened thereby. It is not his job to do everything himself, but to guide everything, and keep it all together and force the parts into an artistic whole.

The wish underlying what I have written here is for the color film to get out of the backwater in which it is and sail forth on its own. As it is now, the color film seems to aim no further than to "look like" something it is not. *Henry* V tried to resemble a medieval illuminated manuscript, and *Gate of Hell* a Japanese print.

It would be ever so beneficial if there were a color film that bore throughout the hallmark of a colorist of today. Then the color film would no longer be mere film with colors, but an alive art.

One Path to Color:
An autobiographical fragment

SERGEI EISENSTEIN

*W*as it fortunate, or merely lucky—everything that led me to my first work in color? In any case, the role of chance is unquestionable. It formed a chain that extended right into the actual work. And it was such a chain of chance and unexpected factors that showed a way toward solutions for the most fundamental problems of color.

It was a very long time ago that color in cinema first captured my attention. I must have seen some of the first examples of color cinema—the *Fairies* of Méliès, tinted by hand. A submarine kingdom, where warriors in bright golden armor were concealed in the jaws of green whales, and blue and pink fairies emerged from sea foam.

Not long after, there were attempts at more natural color. I cannot be sure what system or technique was used, but I recall that it was about 1910 or 1912 that such films began to be shown in Riga. Actually they were exhibited in only one cinema, in Ermann Park, which bore the grand title of "Kino Kultura," notwithstanding the fact that these "scientific" short films were accompanied, week after week, by chapters of *Fantomas* and *Vampires*. The colored short films always seemed to have a pinkish tone, whether they showed the white sails of yachts skimming over an ultramarine sea, or variously colored fruits and flowers being arranged by girls with flaming red or straw-yellow hair.

Our own first trial in the field of screen color was the familiar hand-colored red flag of *Potemkin*, followed by the less well known montage of contrastingly toned short shots in *The General Line*—in the circle watching the milk separator, and in the bull's wedding.

It was not until 1939 that color entered my work as a genuine problem. I planned a film about the Ferghana Canal: its theme was the struggle for water, and it was to have the form of a triptych, beginning with a blossoming Central Asia and the superb irrigation system developed in antiquity. But the power of man over water perished in fratricidal wars and the campaigns of Tamerlane —and the sands of the desert covered everything. Then the misery of sandy deserts under Tsarism, when each stray drop of water had to be squeezed from ditches where the most perfected irrigation system in the world had once flourished. And, finally, the wonder of the first collective victory: the Ferghana Canal, built by the farmers of Uzbekistan, a lasting testimony to brotherhood and socialism.

On the very eve of the beginning of work on the first part of the triptych, production was halted. The composition of the whole was suspended helplessly in mid-air. And soon the entire film was cancelled.

And I went to work on the staging of *Die Walküre* at the Bolshoi Opera. In my treatment of the last scene (the Magic Fire) I searched for means of fusing the elements in Wagner's orchestration with the changing colors of light on the stage.

Almost simultaneously with this work on Wagner, a serious proposal was put to me to enter fully the field of color film. As might be expected, the proposed theme came under the heading of natural "colorfulness." It was in the brightest tones that the Film Administration painted this vivid as well as ideologically interesting and acceptable topic—Giordano Bruno. You see, Italy . . . Renaissance costumes . . . Burning at the stake.

Any other topic would have been presented similarly. The colorful past was inevitably sought on the border between the Middle Ages and the Renaissance. This topic, with its colorful costumes (everyone insisted on these—exactly like the terrier with a slipper in his teeth), was proposed to me by one of the readers of the Film Committee. The subject was the plague. Why the plague, and not cholera? Or smallpox, or typhus?

The idea, however, attracted me (although not for long: it was recorded at the time in a sketch), not for reasons of color, but for exactly the opposite reason. This was the possibility of building the film on the spreading plague's engulfing everything in *blackness*.

It was in another setting, and with other material, that this same idea—of a wonderful (and vivid) richness of life absorbed by an engulfing death—had excited me once before. That was how I had handled the key section of a drama about gold, in a film project (with completed scenario) based on Blaise Cendrars's novel, *Gold*. This romanticized biography of Captain Sutter was to have been made in America, for Paramount. The destructive search for gold on his California land, which brought ruin and ravage to his blossoming estate and to himself, I wanted to express through something I had actually seen, something which left an impression on me that still works with the persistence of a California gold-digger's dredge.

Still to be seen then, as in Sutter's day, were mountains of crushed stone, thrown up from half-exhausted mines, and covering the fields all around. Under a gray, soul-less layer of rock perished blossoming orchards, fields, plowed land, meadows. Inexorably, endlessly, and unrestrainably, a wave of stone advanced over the green land, pitilessly trampling down, for the sake of gold, the living victories of life.

The Gold Rush of 1848 brought thousands of prospectors to California, their number many times exceeding the number whose labors might have extracted the gold with profit. It is now difficult to imagine how these people, crazed by the gold fever, could have been induced to go through what they did.

Now, however, by means of a small image from my own experience, I can easily imagine the typhoon of mad passions that burst out in this elemental pursuit of gold. It was considerably later, in the Kabardino-Balkarian Republic, that I happened to be traveling in the mountains at a place where gold had recently been discovered. My companion and guide stooped down and scraped to-

gether a few handfuls of muddy soil. Then he placed the clods of
soil in a tin vessel like a soup tureen, and the soil was carefully
washed there. And suddenly at the bottom a few grains could be
seen. Gold!

Involuntarily, one had the sensation of the earth moving beneath one's feet, opening its womb, and releasing through its surface, overgrown with clumps of grass, millions upon millions of almost imperceptible grains of golden sand—of gold!

One can easily imagine people throwing themselves on this
earth, people intoxicated by the contact with the riches scattered
beneath the soles of their boots, people ready to murder the own-
ers of any feet that dared step on this sea of gold concealed only
by a dull shroud of soil . . . The feet of thousands of such mad-
men trampled Sutter's land, thousands of hands ripped it open
and pulled it apart, the teeth of thousands of people who had
raced from the ends of the earth were ready to sink into each other's throats for any shred of this land which might conceal in its
bosom a marvelous harvest of pale yellow metal.

The flowering paradise of California gardens and fields culti-
vated by Captain Sutter was invaded and trampled down. And
Sutter was ruined . . . But the proud old man hurled at the invad-
ing hordes thousands of lawsuits, in answer to the arbitrary confis-
cation of his land. Sutter's possessions were vast at that time.

Within a few years, the tiny mission of Saint Francis grew into
the big and noisy city of San Francisco. Contemporary engravings
show how it happened. The bay was choked with barges and ships
that had docked anywhere a mooring rope could be tied. Ships
dropped anchor in the bay and remained there. The space between
ships was bridged with planks and then filled in with sand. Huts
were built on the decks; holds were transformed into basements;
the joined decks became streets and lanes. The invaders swarmed
over the ships as the mountains of crushed stone overflowed into
the green meadows, as the secretly shifting sands covered the
former green paradise of Central Asia's salty deserts.

And suddenly, on to this octopus—sucking in the settlement of
boats and barges, and eating into the surface of shore and surrounding hills—one man, tall and determined, hurls his challenge.
And now another cloud approached California.

This time it was a *black* flock. In the 1850's lawyers wore long frock coats and tall top hats, shaggy like those we see in portraits of Lincoln and his colleagues. Hundreds of black frock coats and top hats—a flock of ravens and ruffled black eagles—alighted on the city of San Francisco. An unprecedented war was engaged: an entire city against one man. This third stratum over the once fruitful lands of Captain Sutter was black and frightful; you could see their silhouettes amid the ships' rigging and against the lamps hung in the coastal fog and blackness of California's night.

This black flock was an image which stood alive and magnetic before me. Perhaps it was also based on something I had actually seen? Where, how, and in what circumstances, now or before the war, could one see tens, even hundreds, of black top hats wandering amid ancient low buildings, vanishing in the dusk and suddenly reappearing in the yellow light of candles filtering down from small latticed windows? Is there really a place, not merely in the lithographs of Daumier, but in life, where one can see such a fantastic sight?

Imagine—there is!

Beneath the top hats, though, you do not see beards or mustaches. Not even down on the upper lip—for I don't suppose that the oldest of their wearers is yet twenty. But the mysterious light of dusk conceals exact age in a generalized silhouette, and the silhouettes of young figures, immature wearers of top hats, moving through these lanes and half lights, further aggravate the fantasy. These might be gnomes escaped from the brain of a Hoffmann, or the peculiar inhabitants of a frightening tale by Poe.

Actually, they are—boys. Not boys, really, but lads—the sons of privileged English families who are able to send their offspring to be educated at Eton. I refrained from mentioning the vicinity of Windsor Castle, or the white, round, turned-down collars and striped trousers, just to keep you from guessing whom I was hinting at.

After a tour of Windsor Castle, with its collection of Leonardo notebooks and Holbein drawings, I was taken by my friend Professor Isaacs—in red whiskers and bowler, with the inevitable rolled umbrella on his arm—to visit nearby Eton. Here was the first link in an English educational system that forged fragile and degenerate or overfed and spoiled boys into stern and implacable, harsh and heartless gentlemen, who never shout that they have been placed in charge of the globe, as do the less prudent Germans, but firmly believe that that is their mission, appointed for the glory of Britain, Queen of the Seas . . .

An avalanche of blackness, devouring all color before it—this image has long waited in the circle of ideas dear to me. From time to time new impressions nourish it: the trip to Windsor, a page from Cendrars's novel, the mountains of crushed stone near Sacramento, even a flock of black eagles settling on the corpses of horses dragged from a Mexican bullfight arena. How sedately the black eagles sit on the walls around the real courtyards of the arena in Mérida, capital of Yucatán. Waiting . . .

However, in the agenda of my creative plans both Giordano Bruno and the plague swiftly gave way to another candidate, a hero almost mathematically calculable—just as, through observation of the orbit of various heavenly bodies, the planet Uranus was computed a priori, long before it was actually seen by a high-powered telescopic lens.

When sound came to films, what subject matter did it bring with it? The biographies of musicians.

And what topics were brought with the coming of color? The biographies of painters.

And color and sound together?

Musicians' and painters' biographies have been exhausted, so we must look for other subject matter. What about the biography of a poet? This is how the idea was born for a film on Pushkin.

And from it rose *Ivan Grozny*.

Then came the war; and then victory. Out of conquered Germany came an avalanche of loathsome German color films—and also a negative in three-color process.

And here, after the war, starts a new chain of chance, adding to a chain of ideas about color that had begun to form before the war.

Of course, a longing for color grows directly from work on audiovisual counterpoint. For it is color, color and again color to the very end, which can solve the problems of proportion and abduction to produce a general unity of sound and visual factors.

Once upon a time, enthusiastically greeting the arrival of sound in films (Pudovkin and Alexandrov signed, with me, a statement "on the sound film"), I wrote about color (in "The Third Dimension in Cinema") that it could bring nothing new in principle to film form. At that time we had only a hint of the possibilities for audiovisual counterpoint. The image had only begun to be torn apart by its growth into sound film.

Today, practical work in audiovisual cinema is a concrete investment in the business of developing cinema. And sound, seeking to be embodied in the visual image, powerfully beats against its black and white limitations, shrinking the passions that require full fusion with the image. The higher forms of organic relationship between the melodic outline of music and the tonal structure of systematically blended color shots are possible only with the appearance of color in the cinema.

However—from generalities, to business. From a tirade to a history of the comic and the sad, the consoling and depressing, exciting and optimistic (but more often distressing) soarings and downfalls on the road to practical work in color film, in two sequences of *Ivan the Terrible*, Part Two.

What *didn't* happen there!

There was the fact that Prokofiev left Alma-Ata before I did. But Ivan's feast and the dances of the *oprichniki* could not be filmed without the music being written and recorded in advance. This obliged us to transfer the filming of the feast and dance to Moscow.

And that wasn't all. Prokofiev fell ill, and amid his obligations to both *War and Peace* and *Cinderella* he could not find time that summer to give me the needed orchestrations. Autumn came and winter approached. The finished set had been ready and waiting since summer. The orchestration was delayed.

Just then a conference on color was organized at the Dom Kino. Not so much on the desolate spectacle before us, as it was a discussion of something none of us had yet had a chance to work on. The emptiness of the discussion was irritating. Most irritating of all, though, was the free supplement to the discussion: the screening of examples of the color creations of the American and German industries, along with a few significant attempts of our own (pre-war) to use two- and three-color-negative systems—attempts much vaunted and boasted of. Now on our screens we also could show "a miserable splendor of costume" and "an imitation painted cheek." Irritation is an excellent creative stimulus.

Suddenly, amid all this imported vulgarity, a film document in color appeared on the screen: *The Potsdam Conference*. Some parts of this film, as color, were horrible. But then came a series of interiors in the palace of Cecilienhof. In one room, a blindingly red carpet covered the whole of the screen. Cutting diagonally across it was a row of white armchairs upholstered in red. Color was functioning!

Furthermore, the Chinese Pavilion at Sans Souci was shown in a few shots—and the gilded Chinese figures also came off well. Of even greater importance, we could also see on these figures highlighted reflections from the surrounding greenery and from the white marble stairs.

So . . . the red works. The gold also looks right. And, of course, the black does, too. Blue might also work. Perhaps it's worth trying.

The set for Ivan's feast had been ready since summer. The feast must burst like an explosion between the dark scene of the conspiracy against the Tsar and the gloomy scene of the attempt to kill him. Why couldn't this explosion be—in color? Color would be a part of the explosion of the dance. And then, at the end of the feast, imperceptibly flowing back into black and white photography, the tragic tone of the accidental death of Prince Vladimir Andreyevich, killed by the murderer sent by his mother to kill the Tsar . . .

But how to blend from the preceding color sequence—and in my style and spirit—the black of the cassocks with the golden caftans of the *oprichniki*, and then the blacks in the cassocks of the *oprichniki* with the gold in Vladimir's velvets, and, most of all, the whole mass of black-gowned *oprichniki* with the blackness that floods the interior of the cathedral, where the blacker blacks of their shadows, mingled with a scarcely audible moan, are swallowed up in the belly of the night of the cathedral's darkness, along with the helpless, pathetic, yet appealing Vladimir . . .

Color: clean, bright, resounding, ringing. When did I fall in love with it? Where?

I feel dull when I do not see on my desk, shining side by side, the blue and yellow pencils, or when the red pillow with the green stripes is not lying on the blue divan. When my motley dressing gown isn't there to dazzle . . . And how pleased I am when the striped ribbon of Filipino lace curls about and lies across the bright Uzbek bedspread. Or the embroidered Mongolian pattern stretches across the dark crimson background of the wall that is so effectively punctuated by the Mexican white paper emblem of All Soul's Day, and the other black mask with its bloody wounds, unexpectedly found this far from the semi-ritual world of the Mexican Indians.

Literaturnaya Gazeta, July 1960
Translated by Jay Leyda

Coming to Terms with Color

WILLIAM JOHNSON

> *"Glorious Technicolor!"—typical movie ad,*
> *1940's*
> *"Glorious Technicolor!"—typical term of criti-*
> *cal irony, 1940's*
> *"Shocking Eastmancolor!"—nudie theater*
> *poster, 1960's*
> *"I have rarely seen such a blaze of irrelevant*
> *color."—Kenneth Tynan, on* The Umbrellas of
> Cherbourg
> *"One of the most breathtakingly lovely films*
> *ever made."—*Life, *on* Red Desert
> *"*Red Desert *only confirms my feeling that*
> *color is a drawback."—Arne Sucksdorff*
> *". . . these blear'd eyes*
> *Have waked to read your several colours, sir,*
> *Of the pale citron, the green lion, the crow,*
> *The peacock's tail, the plumed swan."*
> —Ben Jonson, The Alchemist

*E*ver since the modern alchemist learned how to transmute different wavelengths of light into a film image composed of equivalent dyes, there has been wide disagreement about the role of color on the screen. Until the early 1950's, the chief disagreement was between the public, which generally flocked to color movies, and the critics, who generally dismissed color movies as garish, pretty-pretty, or otherwise inartistic. During that period, of course, only a handful of critically respectable directors—Ford, Hitchcock, Olivier, among others—had made films in color.[1]

But in the past decade or so the picture has changed. Not only has the proportion of color films increased—overwhelmingly so in America—but the number of critically respectable directors who have worked or are working in color may by now form a majority. The list includes Antonioni, Bergman, Buñuel, Chabrol, Chaplin, Demy, Fellini, Godard, Huston, Ichikawa, Kazan, Kozintsev, Kubrick, Kurosawa, Lean, Losey, Malle, Renoir, Resnais, Richardson, Rosi, Truffaut, Varda, Visconti, Wajda, Welles, and Zinnemann, as well as the late Max Ophüls and Ozu. No critic can dismiss this entire group with "glorious Technicolor" irony, or claim that they are all exceptions which prove the rule.

Thus disagreement today about the role of color on the screen arises chiefly among critics when they try to assess the color films of these directors. (The public, of course, no longer flocks to color as in the past; it merely stays away more from black and white.) The disagreement stems partly from perplexity. Recent color films have undermined many accepted "facts" about screen color—that it is more realistic than black and white (Does *Juliet of the Spirits* look more realistic than *8½*?), that it is more sensuous (Is *Muriel* more sensuous than *Last Year at Marienbad*?) and that it is slower (Does *Help!* move more slowly than *A Hard Day's Night*?). And it isn't easy to discern any more deplorable rules of thumb about color in the recent films. What common denominator does the color have in *Muriel, The Umbrellas of Cherbourg, Red Desert,* and *Juliet of the Spirits*? Not surprisingly, in appraising the use of color in these new films, critics have tended to take refuge in generalities, accepting or rejecting the color as a whole.

One obstacle to any deeper study is the sheer elusiveness of screen color. There is no durable record of the flickering images except on the film strip itself. While a black and white still can record the form of the screen image accurately enough, a color still is bound to distort the original colors, if only because of the physi-

---

[1] This article is concerned with the photographed film and not the animated film. The two differ widely both in their approaches to color and in the problems they face, and it would be confusing to deal with them concurrently. Of course, many of the general statements about screen color will also apply to the animated film.

cal difference between a projected image and printed inks. One's memory may be even less reliable: I have clearly "remembered" colors which a re-viewing of the film showed to be nonexistent. For that reason I've limited my examples of screen color to those which I noted while viewing the film; and in most cases I've checked my notes against a further viewing.

A second obstacle to critical study of screen color is the difficulty of attributing credit (or blame). If a director paints the grass, of course, the critics know where they are; but if he doesn't, do they praise the local weather, the photographic lab workers, or who or what? A similar doubt exists about effects in a black and white film, but it seems much more acute where the fragile and elusive phenomenon of color is concerned.

Probably the reddest of herrings that confronts a critic examining screen color is the fact that the history of photography runs back to front. If Niepce, Talbot, Daguerre, and the other pioneers of photography had found a chemical that distinguished among different wavelengths of light, they would surely not have rejected it in favor of the silver salts that distinguish only between bright and dark. And in that case, black and white would have been the later and more sophisticated development—in both still and movie photography—that it is in the other visual arts. But because color came later, many people saw it as an additive to black and white instead of a medium in its own right. Those in favor of screen color welcomed it for its decorative value; those in opposition condemned it for painting the lily.

This view of screen color as a mere additive was supported by the earliest attempts to introduce color into films. Before the end of the nineteenth century, color films were being produced by two methods, both of which consisted of adding color to black and white. Some filmmakers almost literally painted the lily by having their films hand-colored, frame by frame. The far more widespread and longer-lived method was to tint the film, bathing entire scenes in a single color. Often the tinting was little more than functional: yellow for sunlight, blue for night. Sometimes it was used for dramatic or expressionistic effects, like the red-tinted shot of gleaming swords, expressing the husband's violent jealousy, in Arthur Robison's *Warning Shadows*. Sometimes the functional and dramatic uses were combined, as in the impressive red-tinted night scene of

Babylon under attack by fire in Griffith's *Intolerance*. While tinting was more aesthetic—and certainly more practical—than hand-coloring, its expressive possibilities were obviously limited by the fact that everything in a scene had to be the same color.

Attempts to record "natural" color on film date back more than half a century. But the earliest successful color film process was three-strip Technicolor,[2] first used for a feature in 1935 (Mamoulian's *Becky Sharp*). This process dominated color filmmaking until the early 1950's.[3]

Naturally, the standard of success in the quest for a color film process was the ability to reproduce colors as closely as possible. There is an analogy here with painting, since art students must usually learn to imitate nature before achieving independence. But the prentice years of color filmmaking dragged on and on, occupying a longer stretch of the cinema's short history than the prentice years of sound or the wide screen.

One reason was technical. Since color was *not* an addition (like sound) or a simple modification (like the wide screen), the color images had to be clear and legible or the whole movie would collapse. Technicolor was a less flexible medium than the black and white films that directors were used to: it was slower (that is, it needed brighter lighting) and it had a narrower latitude (shadow areas were more liable to black out and highlighted areas were more liable to white out). In addition, color was relatively more expensive than it has become since. So directors were not encouraged to take chances.

Indeed, they were actively *dis*couraged. The Technicolor Corporation exercised tight control over the way its film was used. The earlier two-strip film had been widely condemned as crude and garish, which the corporation blamed largely on the filmmakers' choice of colors. So now the corporation insisted on leasing (not selling) the special cameras required, on doing all the developing

[2] Three-strip Technicolor in effect breaks down every tone into a combination of three primary colors, which are recorded on three different strips of film. An earlier version of Technicolor used only two strips and two primaries; a number of films were made with this process in the 1920's and early 1930's.

[3] The second successful color process was Agfacolor, developed in Germany during World War II and subsequently taken over by the Russians. It, too, used a three-primary system but combined the three color layers on a single strip of film.

and printing, and—most important of all—on supervising the choice of colors for sets, costumes, and so on. Technicolor was anxious to display the range and subtlety—indeed, the *ungarish-ness*—of its process. But, in so doing, it fell into a different trap: too many of the early color films contain scene after scene of finely modulated, tasteful, and utterly cloying harmonies. A typical example is Norman Taurog's *Words and Music* (1948), whose interiors are a genteel riot of beiges, oaks, olives, lavenders, and other modest shades. Not surprisingly, some of the most exciting color effects in any Technicolor film occurred in Huston's *Moulin Rouge* (1953), which broke the corporation's ban on using filters.

By the time *Moulin Rouge* was made, however, Technicolor's preeminence in the Western world was being challenged by several new color film processes, of which by far the most important was—and is—Eastmancolor.[4] Unlike Technicolor, Eastmancolor could be used in a conventional camera, and Eastman Kodak did not impose control on either its use or its developing and printing.[5] Before long, Technicolor was dethroned.

At first, films made with Eastmancolor were generally inferior in color quality to those made with Technicolor. Hitchcock's *To Catch a Thief*, which was made with Eastmancolor in 1954—and won an Oscar for its color photography—contains scenes of the Riviera which are coarse and unpleasing compared to the delicately nuanced Riviera scenes in Powell and Pressburger's *The Red Shoes*, made with Technicolor in 1948. Of course, Eastmancolor was a new product, starting from scratch, and the absence of any central control over the prints meant that they could fall far short of the film's capabilities. It took years of improvements in Eastmancolor itself and in the processing of it to raise the color-recording quality of the general run of color movies to the late-1940's level.

This may partly account for the fact that few filmmakers in the 1950's made imaginative use of the freedom which Eastmancolor brought them. The earliest and almost lone exception was Kinu-

---

[4] All the new processes used a single-strip, three-color system. Today by far the greatest number of color films produced outside the Communist countries are made with Eastmancolor.

[5] Eastmancolor goes under many different names according to the studio or laboratory that controls the developing and printing; e.g., Metrocolor, De Luxe, and Technicolor (which still thrives on its distinctive printing process).

gasa's *Gate of Hell* (1953).[6] In general, the old habits of decorative color persisted—and still persist in many filmmakers today. Fussily conceived harmonies, "tasteful" to the point of nausea, abound even in colorful-sounding films like *The Pleasure Seekers* or *How to Murder Your Wife*.

One spur to a freer use of color was the spread of location shooting. Even the glossiest Hollywood production, like a high-fashion model revealing a human blemish, admitted to scenes with heavy shadows, silhouettes, twilight, real mist, and other "imperfect" lighting conditions. Theoretically, of course, these conditions led to increased naturalism; but in fact they presented audiences with unfamiliar, somewhat distorted color effects (as I shall explain later). The unrealism of such "naturalism" becomes obvious in films like *The Umbrellas of Cherbourg* and Godard's *Contempt*, in which daylit areas are included in scenes filmed in artificial light and thus appear an unearthly blue.[7]

Meanwhile, the extra cost of using color rather than black and white was no longer big enough to exclude directors with modest-sized budgets and audiences. The important thing was not that these directors used color well (which many did not: Baratier's *La Poupée* was messy; Malle's *Zazie* incoherent; Bergman's *All These Women* insipid, among others)—but that they used color primarily because they wanted to, not because they would suffer at the box office with black and white.

Ever since the first Technicolor film, some directors had tried to do more with color than soothe or dazzle the eye.[8] But only in the 1960's did that "some" become "many."

What exactly are these directors trying to do? To answer this

[6] I have not seen the film again since it first appeared, but if my memory is at all accurate there was a sharp break with the "tradition" of lush landscapes and multi-tinted interiors, and different sequences were keyed to dominant tones.

[7] The eye adapts easily to the difference between bluish daylight and yellowish tungsten light, but film cannot.

[8] At the beginning of *Becky Sharp*, Becky and the headmistress of her girls' school are parting company with expressions of relief and mutual dislike. The headmistress wears an austere black and white dress, while Becky and the other girls are dressed in pastels. Later, an English ball in Brussels is interrupted by the sound of gunfire from Napoleon's army. As everyone runs out, the atmosphere of excitement and danger is heightened by a shot of English redcoats dashing along beneath a red lamp.

with any clarity, I must first deal (as briefly as possible) with three more basic questions: (1) How do colors affect us in real life? (2) How do colors affect us aesthetically?(3) How do colors affect us on the screen, where aesthetic experience and a representation of real life are combined?

1. Unlike shape or mass or even sound, color is not an attribute of the object; [9] it is a subjective experience. Color is the brain's response to a particular wavelength of light emitted, reflected, or refracted by the object.

For physical and physiological reasons, colors form complementaries, contrasts, harmonies, and clashes. That is, colors interact to enhance or diminish one another's effectiveness, with results that strike the viewer as more or less pleasing.

Colors stimulate various psychological responses. Many attempts have been made to codify these responses, and the dicta of color engineers and theoreticians today exert a considerable influence in fields ranging from fashion to packaging. But, as a recent survey of color [10] points out, there has so far been very little *scientific* investigation of human response to color. There is some doubt about even the simplest responses. For example, red is generally considered an "advancing" color and blue a "receding" color, the physical reason being that these wavelengths of light are refracted differently by the eye's lens and do not focus at the same point; but some scientists believe that a bright color "advances" more than a dim one, irrespective of hue.[11]

One series of scientific tests has shown that the color adults tend to like best is blue; the one they tend to like least, yellow. But a preference expressed about swatches of single colors displayed against a neutral background has little bearing on the interplay of colors in real life—or else few women would ever wear yellow.

Emotional responses to particular colors in real life probably depend to a great extent on associations. Thus, red is felt to be

[9] If grass, for example, could be said to possess a color, it would be a combination of everything in the spectrum *except* green, which is the one color that grass does not absorb.

[10] Robert W. Burnham, Randall M. Hanes, and C. James Bartelson, *Color: A Guide to Basic Facts and Concepts* (N.Y.: Wiley, 1963).

[11] *Ibid.*

warm and blue to be cool because of the associations with fire and blood on the one hand, water and ice on the other. But such responses don't necessarily work in the abstract, and may not work at all if the colors are attached to objects with associations of their own. Green may be restful so long as it can conceivably be associated with summer foliage, but not if it suggests moldy bread or Ben Jonson's lion!

2. All the visual arts which involve color make use of the relationships and associations described above. Although architecture and sculpture do not usually involve so much variety of color as the stage arts and, above all, painting, the artist in every one of these media has an extremely free choice of colors and modes of using them. Even in a strictly representational painting, the artist can modify the color of any or every object within wide limits.

The painter's control over his color effects can be very precise indeed. He can choose colors solely for their harmonies, solely for their expressionistic value, or in varying combinations of the two modes. At the same time, he can determine the strength of any color associations by the degree of realism in his painting. Thus certain colors in an op-art painting may evoke virtually no associations; the same colors in an abstract expressionist painting, in which forms are on the threshold of recognizability, may evoke an emotional response through the association of color with form; while the same colors in a pop-art painting may evoke an entirely different emotional response because they are *not* usually associated with the all-too-recognizable forms.

3. The filmmaker is in an equivocal position. On the one hand, he can exercise a much wider control over the colors in his film than many people realize. As far as interiors are concerned, the colors of virtually everything that appears in front of the camera— sets, costumes, props, make-up—may be chosen or modified at will.[12] This control is readily recognized in Hollywood musicals, especially in set pieces which are colored with a non-realistic pal-

---

[12] I'm not suggesting that such complete control is the general rule. Budget considerations will often preclude much trial and error. And, in any case, the filmmaker (director or producer) may not be interested in exercising his freedom of choice, which may be delegated partly to someone else and partly to happenstance.

ette—the dream sequence in *Singin' in the Rain,* where Cyd Charisse's long white gauzy stole floats against a surrealistic, lavender-
lighted void; or the Mickey Spillane spoof in Minnelli's *Band
Wagon,* which metamorphoses a New York subway station into
pale clinical green, a bar into misty pink and powder blue, and so
on.

But it's a mistake to assume that creative screen color must
begin and end with fantasy. In natural exteriors, the filmmaker can
still choose the settings—and therefore the colors—he wants.
Whether Terence Young knew it or not, filming parts of *Thun-
derball* under water constituted a choice of blue-green tones just as
much as Roger Corman's deliberate blue-green tinting of the
dream sequence in *The Premature Burial.*

The filmmaker can also control the colors of an exterior scene
by deciding what season of the year, what time of day, and what
weather conditions to shoot in. For both exteriors and interiors he
can exercise still further control by means of lighting, exposure, filters, and adjustments in printing the film.

Perhaps the most important—and most easily overlooked—of all
the filmmaker's tools for controlling color is the camera itself. By
changing the camera angle, the filmmaker can include or exclude a
particular color in the setting. By moving the camera back for a
long shot or forward for a close-up, he can minimize or emphasize
a particular color in the scene—just as Hitchcock keeps us detached from the mysterious spots of red that disturb Marnie until
the denouement, when he moves in for a screen-filling close-up of
blood.

So the filmmaker does have considerable control over color; but,
on the other hand, it is impossible for him to determine all the
colors in a scene independently of one another, as a painter can.
Unlike a painting, the screen image is not completely autonomous
but is linked closely to the objects filmed. Except in the extreme
case of *trompe-l'oeil,* a painting is seen and accepted as a two-dimensional image, distinct from reality; but a film is seen partly,
perhaps chiefly, as a window on a three-dimensional reality "behind the screen." Thus a green lion in an otherwise representational painting may be mystifying, but the spectator doesn't seek a
physical explanation for its greenness. On the screen, however, a

green lion in an otherwise realistic setting is automatically set apart, since the viewer consciously or unconsciously wonders *how* the lion is made green as well as why. He expects screen colors to obey the same rules of cause and effect as operate in real life.

Yet, in spite of this, screen colors *always appear different from reality*. For one thing, they almost certainly *are* different to a slight degree, because of the nature of the film process.[13] More important is the equivocal nature of the screen image; although the viewer sees it primarily as a representation of real objects, it is also an object in its own right—an object unified by its isolation amid darkness and by its dependence on a single light source, the projector.

In real life, one's perceptual mechanism takes all sorts of liberties with colors. Often it tones them down: one doesn't normally much notice colors unless they are unfamiliar or unexpected. Even colors that must be noticed—functional colors like traffic lights— are seen in a generalized way: one doesn't observe whether the red tends to orange or crimson, or the green to lemon or turquoise; one simply registers red and green. At other times the brain changes the colors reported by the eyes, or even creates colors where none is reported. For example, an object will take on different colors in daylight, lamplight, sunlight filtering through foliage, etc., but the brain sees it as its "normal" color at nearly all times. Moreover, the brain grasps a black and white image of a familiar object as if it were in color; so that, even with an effort of will, it is almost impossible to see a black and white portrait as a faithful record of an ashen face! In real life, one generally sees the colors one expects to see.

But the color film offers no scope for this subjective vision. The brightness and isolation of the screen image compel attention; and because the image is a single object, it compels observation of all the colors on the same terms. In short, the viewer is made to see specific colors which differ from those he's accustomed to seeing.

---

[13] Color film contains the equivalent of three layers of black and white film, which record the amount of red, blue, and green in each object color. In the final print, the monochromatic tones in each layer are replaced by red, blue, and green dyes. Thus, there is only the most indirect relationship between object colors and print colors.

By objectifying the deeply subjective experience of color vision, the color film can work for (or against) the filmmaker in three broad areas:

Color sharpens the viewer's perception of the screen image—or, more simply, it brings out details.

Explaining how *Neighbours* was made, Norman McLaren says: [14] "We selected color: there was going to be speeded-up action and moments of very fast cutting, and I think it's possible to sort out an image more quickly, grasp it sooner in color than black-and-white, especially if the image is at all complex and the movement fast."

Obviously there can be a greater variety of visual contrasts among colors than among gradations of black and white. This is a functional effect—but it can also enhance any emotional or dramatic content in the film. In Alexander Ford's *Five from Barska Street*, for example, there are several long shots of the heroine playing a kind of hide-and-seek with her boyfriend at dusk amid the ruins of Warsaw, and her gleaming blond hair stands out vividly, even at a distance, against the predominantly bluish surroundings. The visual contrast, keener than anything possible in black and white, heightens the emotional contrast between love and destruction.

But color is not a wonder detergent, making every script situation automatically more sparkling than with Brand X. In *Five from Barska Street*, the girl's hair is one bright spot against a background of near-complementary tones. In *Neighbours*, the setting —grass and shrubbery—forms an almost uniformly green background which contrasts well both with the warmish colors of the neighbors and with the white of their "houses." If a filmmaker lets his colors get out of hand, the accumulation of detail may lead not to clarity but to confusion. There's a striking example in Minnelli's *Meet Me in St. Louis*—striking because the use of color in this film is otherwise careful and imaginative. But the color literally falls to pieces in the ballroom scenes toward the end, where the variegated dresses of the dancers and the Christmasy décor collapse into a formless jumble.

The ability of color to emphasize detail carries with it another

[14] In an interview reported in *Film: Book Two*, ed. Robert Hughes (N.Y.: Grove Press, 1963).

disadvantage: fakery of any kind is far more obvious and jarring than in black and white. Painted backcloths and models do not have the minuteness of detail that color film can reveal in landscapes or large-scale objects; in back-projection or process shots, the colors in one part of the image may be in a different key from those elsewhere.

Most of the earlier color films escaped the worst of these flaws because they were either action pictures shot outdoors or frankly artificial musicals. But directors who turned to color after many years of working with black and white often did not allow for this difference—hence the glaring fabrications in Hitchcock's color films, the poor process shots in Wyler's *Ben-Hur,* and the ill-fitting patchwork of such De Mille stunts as the parting of the Red Sea in *The Ten Commandments* and the collapse of the temple in *Samson and Delilah.*

In watching a color film, the viewer has a heightened awareness not only of details but of colorfulness in general.

This probably accounts for the fact that many people found the early Technicolor films garish. (Some films actually were garish, of course, but far more were bland.) Viewers were simply not accustomed to seeing colors as the objective screen image compelled them to. Now that audiences *have* become so accustomed, the blanket charge of garishness is rare—even though recent films like *The Umbrellas of Cherbourg* and *Juliet of the Spirits* use bright colors far more freely than almost any film of the Technicolor era.

Instead of balking at this heightened awareness of colors, many viewers reveled in it for its own sake. And if theater managers are to be believed,[15] a majority of moviegoers in America today look upon color as a decorative wrapping that adds pleasure to any film.

A filmmaker who doesn't want his colors to be taken for mere decoration can of course tone them down. One of the most rigorous examples of toning down is *Red Desert:* in most scenes, Antonioni chooses settings and lighting conditions which make all colors tend toward gray. A milder case is *The Bible,* in which Huston carefully avoids any chromatic resemblance to other films based on the same book.

But it would be self-defeating to try to eliminate all sensuous color—even Antonioni doesn't try that. It would certainly be out

[15] See the exhibitors' comments in almost any issue of *Box Office.*

of character for a musical not to make some of its colors as sensuous as possible—like the stunning set, all of luminous rose madder, in the Mickey Spillane spoof in *Band Wagon*. And recently there have been successful attempts to use sensuous color as a dramatic foundation of the entire film. I shall have more to say about this later, in discussing *The Umbrellas of Cherbourg* and *Le Bonheur*.

The viewer responds more keenly to specific colors on the screen than in real life.

Let's look deeper into the case of the "restful green." In real life, people are of course well aware of the difference between a dirty olive and a brilliant chartreuse, and wouldn't insist that either is restful; but within these extremes they tend not to notice a particular shade of green (or any other hue) unless compelled to in some way (e.g., by being in a room decorated entirely in that shade). Normally, they can just look away. But the hypnotic screen image, filled with objectified, not-quite-familiar colors, forces them to see the specific shade of green, its relationship to other specific colors around it, and its relevance (if any) to the dramatic context.

Under these conditions, a green *may* still be restful, as in Resnais's *Muriel:* the foliage seen through the window when Hélène visits her quiet acquaintances, Antoine and Angèle, suits this haven of contentment. But green may also be:

Oppressive—Hitchcock's *Dial M for Murder:* the dark green of the large window curtain behind which the would-be murderer is to hide.

Nauseating—*Red Desert:* the blotchy wall cut in after Giuliana reluctantly submits to her husband's embrace.

Nostalgic—Rosi's *Moment of Truth:* the ochreous greens of olive trees and fields when Miguelín revisits his home village.

Stimulating—*Singin' in the Rain:* the sleek lime-green dress worn by Cyd Charisse for her first dance number.

Tense—Fritz Lang's *Rancho Notorious:* the bright pea-green lampshade in the sheriff's office when Arthur Kennedy and Mel Ferrer make their jailbreak—green for danger!

For all I know, none of these color effects was intentional. In any case, I'm certainly not implying that each shade of green denotes the corresponding state of mind. Working through the relationships and associations described earlier, the color acts as a kind of servo-mechanism, amplifying a mood that would still exist without color. The "green for danger" effect in *Rancho Notorious*, for example, derives partly from the fact that the green is an eye-catching tone (by far the purest and brightest color in the scene) and partly from the viewer's realization that its light might expose the jailbreakers. If the scene were in black and white, the mere brightness of the lamp would convey some of the tension. Just as the greater visual range of colors can make details more legible than in black and white, so it can bring out moods and emotional reactions more sharply.

But color is more than a heightened black and white, as some less casual examples will show. In *The Umbrellas of Cherbourg*, color reinforces the mood directly in the scene where Guy decides to ask the quiet Madeleine to marry him. The setting is a sidewalk café painted a brilliant orange—a vibrant color generating a sense of energy and radiance that would be absent from its equivalent in black and white.

In the high-school commencement scenes in Robson's *Peyton Place*, color reinforces the mood by contrast. Amid the general excitement and optimism, Hope Lange is gloomy at the thought of her prospects. The cheerful crimson of caps and gowns which dominates the screen forms a striking dissonant setting for her downcast face.

There is a subtler example of this kind of contrast, the coloring of the face being as important as that of the setting, in Peckinpah's *Ride the High Country*. During the wedding ceremony in the saloon-*cum*-brothel of the mining camp, Elsa's freckled face and golden hair shine out against the darker, viscid colors of the décor. Black and white could easily convey the visual contrast between light and dark, but not between the freshness of over-innocence and the staleness of over-experience.

A special form of contrast with no counterpart in black and white is the color clash. Usually, of course, the filmmaker tries to avoid this effect, regarding it as one of the additional possibilities for error with which he has to pay for the additional expressiveness of color. But it can also be an asset. In the middle episode of Asquith's *The Yellow Rolls-Royce* (a film not otherwise distinguished for its use of color) the disarming uncouthness of the

gangster's moll (Shirley MacLaine) is neatly suggested by the juxtaposition of her shocking-pink dress and the yellow Rolls itself.
And in *The Battle of the Villa Fiorita*, Delmer Daves uses a color
clash to editorialize on Moira's decision to leave her husband and
live with Lorenzo: for a shot of the two relaxing quite innocently
in the villa, he arranges the décor and lighting to produce a color
scheme of bilious greens and blues.

By far the most common type of contrast is the one that usually
occurs in exterior long shots—between the blue of the sky and the
generally warmer colors of landscapes or buildings. Whether because of the contrast alone, or because blue recedes and warmer
colors advance, such exterior shots tend to give a stronger impression of spaciousness than black and white. The color-film maker
can modify this sense of spaciousness by shooting in different atmospheric conditions. One example (which may or may not be intentional) occurs in the early scenes of Hathaway's *Nevada Smith*
when the callow young hero sets out in pursuit of the men who
killed his parents: the sky here is a particularly limpid and distant
blue, and its extra spaciousness suggests the long way Nevada must
go to attain his goal.

The finest use of this outdoor contrast I've ever seen is also one
of the earliest. In Henry King's *Jesse James* (1939) the James gang
holds up a railroad train at dusk. Jesse leaps onto the train and
runs along the top while it is still moving: he is silhouetted against
the deepening blue of the sky, while the car windows below him
glow with orange lamplight. Thanks to the bold silhouetting,
which eliminates virtually all colors except those of the sky and
the windows, the scene conveys a striking and economical contrast
between the cold, dangerous world of the outlaw and the warm,
comfortable world of the law-abiding passengers.

All the examples I have cited so far merely scratch the surface of
screen color, since they do not involve one of the most important
attributes of the film—duration.

A good color film must consist of more than individually effective scenes. Failure to relate color to duration accounts partly for
the weakness of Satyajit Ray's first color film, *Kanchenjungha*.
While many individual images show a perceptive use of color, the
effect is frequently annulled by movement within the scene or by
the transition to the following scene. These continual shifts in

color keys are particularly unfortunate because the action of the film leaps to and fro among six or seven members of a family: instead of helping the different sections to cohere, the color only increases their dislocation.

Thus a whole new area of possibilities—for good or ill—is opened up by the fact that *all the foregoing effects of screen color work in time as well as space, tend to work more powerfully in time than in space.*

There are some obvious similarities here between film and stage. In plays, especially costume plays, colors are often chosen for what might be called emblematic purposes, so that the characters are easy to identify when they appear on stage or intermingle with others. The costumes in Olivier's film of *Henry* V are emblematic in this way: warm reds and golds for the English; cold blues and silvers for the French. The fact that *Henry* V is adapted from a stage play doesn't mean that this kind of color effect is uncinematic. It can also be put to good use in unstagelike films such as Terence Fisher's *Horror of Dracula*, where Dracula's castle and all the vampires appear in bluish tones, while the humans are keyed to warm tones. However, the flexibility of the film medium—its power of showing both the wood and the trees, of controlling transitions from one scene to another—enables it to go far beyond the simple use of color to which the stage is largely limited. Indeed, as was implied earlier in the discussion of responses to specific colors, this flexibility even enables the film to override or reverse such emblematic associations. Silver and blue may stand for coldness and lack of vigor in *Henry* V; but in the context of Varda's *Le Bonheur* a silvery statue and a blurred background of silver birches can become lively; and because nearly all the other colors in *Ben-Hur* are drab, the blue scarf that Charlton Heston wears for the chariot race can become vibrant and exciting.

Another stage device for organizing colors in time is a change in the lighting. Here again the film is far more flexible, since it can move at will from day to night, sunlight to mist, and into any kind of artificial light. Insofar as these conditions are naturalistic, they are means of controlling color effects rather than effects in themselves, and do not need separate discussion. But artificial lighting on the stage is sometimes emblematic in color, and a few films have borrowed this device.

When the situation as well as the lighting is artificial—as in the ballet sequence of *An American in Paris*—the device can be successful on the screen. But attempts to bathe naturalistic scenes with mood colors—like the rose-tinted scene between the Norman knight and the peasant girl in Schaffner's *The War Lord,* or the variety of pastel-lighted interiors in Bergman's *All These Women* —are unsatisfactory. The mixture of naturalism and artifice is as basic an element of the image as its lighting is disruptive; and as with our old friend the green lion, the viewer is distracted into wondering about the how as well as the why of the color.[16]

While stage colors can be varied in time but have little flexibility, colors in painting have great flexibility but cannot be varied in time. As Egbert Jackson writes in his book *Basic Color*: "Although discord is often carefully written into music, it is not so common in painting, where there is no time element to resolve it; a color juxtaposition on canvas, once established, remains." For "music" one can read "movies."

Some painters argue that painting does have a time element because the viewer rarely takes in the whole canvas at a glance but lets his eye travel over it. But a painting is not *organized* in time like a film. A series of paintings—such as Monet's studies of Rouen Cathedral—may be very loosely organized in time if hung side by side; but only when a painting becomes the subject of a film can it be fully organized in time. The director then transposes space into time by the use of close-ups, long shots, movements, etc.—or, in a rare instance like Clouzot's *Le Mystère Picasso,* by recording the actual process of creation.

Attempts to return the compliment and give individual film scenes the balanced, finished look of paintings are successful only insofar as they respect the time element—that is, insofar as they fit into the succession of scenes. In *Meet Me in St. Louis* the two older sisters are shown singing at the piano in a scene which, in its composition and soft coloring, calls to mind Renoir's painting *Jeunes Filles au Piano.* The similarity is justified because the scene

---

16 This article is not meant to be prescriptive. The failure of colored lighting in *The War Lord* and *All These Women* is undoubtedly linked with the fact that these aren't very good films anyway. In a really imaginative film, a similar use of colored lighting—or any other effect termed unsatisfactory in this article—might be fully justified. There is hardly any device that the film *can* use which it cannot occasionally use well.

fits both visually and dramatically with what precedes and follows; otherwise, it would stand out as a mere effect. Ironically, Jean Renoir runs afoul of the time element in *French Cancan*, which he tries to imbue with the sensuousness of his father's paintings by the systematic use of soft, pale pastels; but being repeated in scene after scene, this coloring quickly cloys. Minnelli avoids this trap (if not others!) in *Lust for Life*. Here the colors—predominantly yellow-orange-red-brown-black—are reminiscent of Van Gogh's own vivid sunlight-and-shadow palette; but instead of repeating them totally in scene after scene, Minnelli extends them through time. As Van Gogh approaches death, for example, the colors are progressively withdrawn until there is virtually nothing left but the black of the crows and the straw-yellow of the wheat field in which he dies.

The principle that color effects in time are more telling on the screen than static effects applies just as strongly when there is no allusion to painting. In Corman's *Masque of the Red Death* the demonic scenes in Prince Prospero's sanctum—lighted throughout by the glow of a red window—are far less striking than the sequence in which the victims of the red death swarm around the prince, filling the screen with more and more redness. The relative effectiveness of the two sequences is in no way altered by the fact that the sanctum set is elaborately designed while the climactic red death obviously comes straight out of the make-up box.

All the color effects described earlier can be developed in time as well as space. For convenience, I will discuss the ways of developing them under three broad headings:

1. A *color progression within a scene.* Moving objects are more eye-catching than static ones; moving colored objects, or the movement of the camera among static colored objects, can form the basis of striking color effects.

In Donen's *Funny Face*, when the fashion-magazine crew have left the somber bookstore which they invaded to take photos, the young salesgirl (Audrey Hepburn) finds a hat they overlooked. She begins to sing "How Long Has This Been Going On?" and at the same time slowly unfurls the hat's gauzy chartreuse veil, which gradually brightens up the whole scene with its romantic coloring —a visual equivalent of the romantic awakening of the girl herself.

In *Le Bonheur*, François and his wife are picnicking in a wheat field when he announces that he has a mistress, assuring her that this does not diminish but increases his marital love. When the wife, submissive, says that she too now loves him more than before, he joyfully stands up and pulls her to her feet. As the camera follows them, the background changes from the pale yellow of the wheat to the luminous green of distant trees. The color change is ambiguous: it takes François's view of his wife's reaction as a joyful cadence, but it also presages the green setting in which she drowns herself.

2. *A color progression from scene to scene.* The climax of *The Masque of the Red Death,* described above, is a simple dramatic example of this. A simple atmospheric example occurs in the scenes of the Seville Holy Week with which *The Moment of Truth* opens: blue-black silhouettes against a pallid dawn sky; then the yellow of lighted candles; and finally the brightly colored processional altar.

There is a subtler use of a color progression in Abram Room's *The Garnet Bracelet.* The action of the film is set in Tsarist Russia: the Princess Vera is loved from a distance by a government clerk, who sends her letters and a bracelet but hopes for nothing in return. In one scene Vera stands pensively in a room furnished richly with reds and mahoganies. In the next scene the admirer is entering a cellar café whose walls are a pallid green. The extreme change—between complementary colors—obviously suggests the gulf between the princess's circumstances and the clerk's; but Room adds overtones to the contrast by means of the sound track, which leaps from near-silence to a vigorous saltarella played by the café violinist. Thus the green setting creates an impression not only of poverty after luxury but also of liveliness after languor.

An even more complex color progression occurs in *The Umbrellas of Cherbourg* when Guy makes love to Geneviève for the first and last time. After showing them together in Guy's room, Demy inserts four transitional scenes, each cut in rhythmically on a beat of music, which on the surface merely indicate Geneviève's homeward journey. But the scenes do more than that. Each is keyed to different colors—the rather sickly green of the entrance to Guy's apartment building; the crimson, pink, and yellow of a poster across the street; the blue light in which the street itself is bathed; the pale green and pink of the striped wallpaper in Geneviève's living room—and these rapid contrasts mark out Geneviève's inner journey through a turmoil of emotions until, at the end of the fourth scene, she buries her head in her mother's lap.[17]

This kind of transition is made even more abstract by Agnès Varda (Demy's wife) in Le Bonheur. Taken out of context, her rapidly cut sequences of colored façades, sunsets, and colored fade-outs might seem to consist of manner without matter. I will discuss their context later; I mention them here as a reminder that a good color film does not present a simple series of color effects but an intricate skein, and even an entire sequence may make little sense if the rest of the film is ignored. That's why the third basic way of developing colors in time, namely

3. *A combination of color progression within a scene and from scene to scene*, is necessarily a catchall. Endless variations are possible, and it would be ludicrous to try to offer even a representative sample. One example is enough to show how screen colors can enhance a film by ramifying and intertwining through time.

In the first episode of Kobayashi's *Kwaidan* the ambitious samurai leaves his humble weaver wife and marries a well-connected but selfish woman. The newly married couple wander around a street market, where the wife sees a roll of blue-violet fabric that seizes her fancy. She picks it up, almost embracing it, and the sight of this reminds the samurai of his first wife at her loom. Time passes, and the marriage deteriorates. One afternoon, as the samurai is taking a nap, his second wife comes into the room wearing a dress made of the blue-violet fabric, which looks more somber in the shuttered half light. Irritated by his sleeping, the wife wakes him by slapping his face with her fan, and they quarrel. As the wife turns to storm out, there is a brief flash of white from the petticoat beneath her dress. Here, the change in the appearance of the blue-violet fabric between the two scenes reflects the change in the marriage; and the sharp flash of white amid darker tones creates a visual sensation of bitterness.

In my attempts to describe complex uses of color as succinctly as possible, I may seem to have implied that a specific color can have a specific absolute meaning. Let me repeat that the context is all-important. As Eisenstein writes in *Film Sense*: "In general the

---

[17] It's also possible to react to the sequence as suggesting stages of the lovemaking itself.

'psychological' interpretation of color is a very slippery business.
. . . In art it is not the *absolute* relationships [associations] that
are decisive, but those *arbitrary* relationships within a system of
images dictated by the particular work of art."

In considering particular works of screen art in their entirety, it's
easiest to begin with the most elementary form of color system—
the insertion of a brief color passage into an otherwise black and
white film. The 1925 *Phantom of the Opera* and Lewin's *Picture
of Dorian Gray* reserve color for their dramatic peaks: the unmask-
ing of the Phantom in the former, the portrait and the corrupted
corpse of Dorian in the latter.[18] The "arbitrary relationship" here
is a simple one between black and white on the one hand and the
totality of the colors on the other—a stark contrast in which the
individual colors play an unimportant role.

These examples are crude but successful. The device of interpo-
lating color into a black and white film originated at a time when
the available film processes were themselves crude, since it set
them off to best advantage. Yet even today, when film processes
have evolved from Eliza Doolittles into My Fair Ladies, color and
black-and-white are still used together from time to time.

Ironically, the contrast that enhanced the crude color of the
1920's can easily degrade the subtle color of today. It depends
largely on whether black-and-white or color dominates the film. In
all the examples I can think of which follow the *Phantom of the
Opera* practice, the injection of color has a melodramatic and stri-
dent effect. This is true even of a documentary like Joris Ivens's *A
Valparaiso*, which leaps into color for an impression of the Valpa-
raisano's streak of violence. While the sequence is obviously intended to contain some melodrama, color amplifies it out of all
proportion: it is much as if Segovia's guitar were suddenly electri-
fied in mid-performance.

On the other hand, there's nothing inherently melodramatic
about injecting black and white scenes into a color film, and nearly
all the examples I can think of are subtle and effective.[19] A survey

[18] These color scenes were in the early two-strip Technicolor. The prints
I have seen are entirely in black and white, and I don't know whether any
survive with the original color.

[19] The one exception is Vadim's *Blood and Roses*, and here the black and
white scenes have color running into them.

of a few of these examples will show how color and black-and-white can set each other off to both visual and dramatic advantage.

The role of black and white in *Meet Me in St. Louis* is brief but typical. The film is divided into sections according to the season of the year, and each section is preceded by an album-style black and white still picture of the Smiths' house at that particular season. The still then comes to life in color. These touches of black and white add poignancy to the film's gentle nostalgia, reminding the viewer that the action he is watching is set in a past which has long since been fixed and drained of color. He is all the more delighted when, in a casual cinematic miracle, color and movement return and the past is resurrected.

Black and white can add poignancy even to a color film as ungentle as *Peeping Tom*—the story of a photographer who kills women with a sharpened tripod leg because, as a child, he was used by his psychologist father as a guinea pig for the study of fear. If Michael Powell had followed the *Phantom of the Opera* practice in this film, reserving color for the killings and leaving the rest in black and white, the film would probably have been as melodramatic as my brief description makes it sound. Instead, everything is in color except the films projected by Mark Lewis: those taken of Mark as a child by his father, and those taken by Mark himself while killing. The former are poignant because they juxtapose the doomed innocence of the past with the terrible experience of the present. At one point, for example, the black and white film-within-the-film shows the father giving Mark his first movie camera; the scene is interrupted by a brief color shot, in the film's present, of the same camera perched on a shelf above Mark and his projector. Like a spark leaping between electrodes, this alternation of black-and-white and color lights up the gap between a wonderful novelty and the deadly obsession to which it led. When Mark screens his own films, the sharply delineated black and white frame within the color frame rivets the viewer's attention like Mark's, and the viewer shares Mark's disappointment that the image of each killing (black and white) falls short of the "actuality" (color). Here too, black and white represents the past—though a much more recent one—and underlines the fact that Mark is too deeply enmeshed in the past to be able to grasp the present. All in all, the use of black and white helps to make the viewer sympathize with Mark, and thus to elevate the film from Grand Guignol into something approaching tragedy.

Perhaps the simplest and most powerful use of the contrast between black-and-white and color is in *Night and Fog*, Resnais's documentary about a Nazi concentration camp. Here there is a complete reversal of the *Phantom of the Opera* practice. Black and white is used for the flashbacks of the horrors of the camp during the war and at its liberation,[20] while color is used for the post-war views of the camp, now in ruins and overgrown with weeds, and looking serene and innocuous in the sunlight. The contrast strengthens the film in several ways. It serves the practical purpose of distinguishing past and present. (One weakness of Rossif's all-black-and-white documentary about the Spanish Civil War, *To Die in Madrid*, is that one can't be sure where the archive scenes end and the specially photographed scenes begin—a doubt which tends to compromise the entire film.) Second, the transition from pleasant color to black and white throws the horrors into stark relief. Most important of all, it emphasizes the remoteness of those horrors, drained as they are of the colorful detail of the post-war scenes. The contrast between black-and-white and color thus crystallizes the way in which time swiftly buries all events, no matter how terrifying or how worthy of remembrance.

The foregoing examples make it clear that when black-and-white and color are juxtaposed there is only one fundamental difference between them. Neither is necessarily more dramatic, more realistic, or more sensuous. But color, being more specific, has more immediacy than black and white—the scenes in color appear closer in time and space. This doesn't mean that black and white must always represent the past when used with color. In *A Man and a Woman*, Lelouch uses black and white for the "present" scenes in which Jean-Louis Duroc first meets Anne Gauthier and drives her home to Paris. Then, when Anne talks about her dead husband, there are brief color inserts of her memories of them together. The point here is that Anne finds it difficult to accept Jean-Louis's love

---

[20] It doesn't lessen Resnais's achievement to point out that he had to use monochrome for these scenes, since none of the archive material was in color. In films it's rarely possible to distinguish between what was intentional, what was accidental, and what was unavoidable; but the good director manages to work with the grain of those elements he can't control.

because her husband is still so alive within her, so much closer to her than the reality of his death.

Used by itself, of course, black and white no longer lacks immediacy. Indeed, it is a protean medium which can seem to take on nearly all the qualities of color. This adaptability is one reason why black and white can be used in color films with little risk of a jarring effect. But there is a much greater risk when a single-color tint or tone [21] is inserted into a full-color film. The stronger and more assertive the single color, the more likely it is to clash with the full-color scenes that surround it—no matter how "realistic" the tint or tone may be. For example, the red and blue tints in Bert Stern's *Jazz on a Summer's Day,* intended to represent sunset and nightfall, are just as jarring as the symbolic red and blue tints at the beginning of Godard's *Contempt.* On the other hand, a paler or more neutral color may be successful even when it is "unrealistic," as in the blue-green nightmare in *The Premature Burial.* Just on the borderline are the orange-yellow-toned scenes in *A Man and a Woman* in which Jean-Louis tries to make love to Anne and she keeps remembering her husband (in full color). Though not so strong as to ruin the transitions, the tone is strong enough to make them visually irritating.

There is a subtle use of a neutral tint in Wajda's *Lotna,* in which color is reserved for the daytime scenes and sepia for the night. At first the distinction seems purely practical: monochrome requires less lighting than color, and it conveys the real-life neutralization of colors at night in a way that is almost impossible with the highly specific screen colors. But there is more to *Lotna's* use of sepia than that. The film is concerned with the experiences of a Polish cavalry regiment during the Nazi invasion of 1939, and the contrast between color and sepia reflects the contrast between the romantic traditions of the cavalry and the somber reality of mechanized warfare. The film ends at night with the death of Lotna, the regiment's prize mount, as the few surviving men scat-

---

[21] Tinting was achieved in earlier times by literally dipping black and white film in a dye. The gradations of grays thus seemed to be transformed into variations of the dye color; areas which were white in the original film took on the overall dye color also. In toning, which is usually achieved by printing black and white footage on color stock with a filter interposed, the gradations of grays are replaced by varying tones of the color, and white areas remain white. Thus, toning usually has a more delicate effect than tinting.

ter across a bleak landscape that looks all the more bleak for being in sepia.

When it comes to films entirely in color, the possibilities for what Eisenstein calls "arbitrary relationships within a system of images" multiply tremendously. In recent years more and more color-film makers have gone beyond mere decoration or disconnected effects and have attempted, for good or ill, to create a coherent color system for the film as a whole.

These attempts have as yet explored only a tiny fraction of all the possible worlds of color, and it would be ludicrous to classify them in any rigid way. Purely for convenience, I have divided them into four main groups, roughly arranged in order of increasing complexity. But the groups overlap, and the differences between films within a group are often wider than those between films in different groups. These are indeed worlds of color, belonging to a universe that has still to be charted.

1. The simplest color scheme is one in which a single hue or palette dominates the entire film. At the very least, such a scheme helps to give unity to the film and save it from a succession of "tasteful" harmonies. Often the dominant color is determined by the choice of a natural setting. For example, the Arctic setting of Nicholas Ray's *The Savage Innocents* establishes the unusual keynote of white: even though the use of other colors is mediocre, the film retains a visual distinction. Similarly, the Antarctic setting in which much of Delbert Mann's *Quick Before It Melts!* takes place gives a visual lift to this otherwise pedestrian comedy. Lean uses the blue-white of snow and ice as the keynote of *Doctor Zhivago*, just as he used the orange-yellows of the desert for *Lawrence of Arabia* and the yellow-greens of the jungle for *The Bridge on the River Kwai*—which partly explains why Lean's spectaculars are more impressive-looking than most.

In *The Trouble with Harry*, Hitchcock adds piquancy to this kind of natural keynote by choosing a setting—Vermont in the fall —whose picturesqueness makes a sharp contrast with the macabre comedy of the action. Clement uses a similar contrast in *Purple Noon*, where an almost-perfect murder is enacted against a dazzling Mediterranean setting of white, aquamarines, and oranges— colors that are carefully reflected in the interior sets as well.

In a few films it is the sets which determine the dominant color scheme: in other words, the filmmaker uses an artificial keynote. The first film I saw that attempted this was *My Uncle* (1958), in which Tati uses soft pastels for the uncle's environment and aseptic whites and tints for the modernistic house. With this limited range of pale colors, Tati creates a kind of distilled reality that suits his cool fable. Unfortunately, the location scenes fail to mesh with this color scheme, in rather the same way that the comedy itself frequently slips gear from quiet subtlety to sheer boredom. A more successful use of an artificial keynote is found in Petri's *Tenth Victim*, the story of a future society in which people are licensed to hunt one another to death. Here the sets are predominantly neutral or bluish, and the location scenes are chosen and filmed in the right conditions to match. Touches of warmer colors, especially golden browns, appear in unexpected places and sometimes in unexpected combinations, as when the American "huntress" wears a shocking-pink dress in a golden décor. The mixture of the dehumanized and the casually bizarre helps to create a convincing impression of what the world *could* be like in the future.

2. Probably the commonest type of color scheme is what might be called organized realism: the coloring in each scene looks natural, but the sequences are organized to contrast with one another and form a dramatic progression.

A simple but effective example is Gilbert's *Loss of Innocence*, a romantic melodrama about English schoolgirls stranded on their own at a country inn in France. The exteriors are all airy sunlight, clear blue skies, and luminous green foliage; the interiors are keyed to warm colors—rich wooden paneling, rows of wine bottles, and close-ups of Susannah York's golden hair and Jane Asher's red hair. As the film alternates between outdoors and indoors, these two complementary palettes continually enhance each other. Thus the colors take on an apparent glow that reflects the schoolgirls' glamorized view of their surroundings.

Hitchcock uses a similar basic contrast between interiors and exteriors in *Vertigo*, but he creates some striking variations. The exteriors are in subdued greens and blues, while the interiors—such as the apartments of Scottie and Midge—are keyed to soft browns, oranges, and yellows. But for high points in the film Hitchcock intensifies the contrast by modulating to bright colors. Among the interiors, for example, there are the gleaming red walls of Ernie's restaurant, where Scottie first sees Madeleine, and the orange fire-light in Scottie's apartment when he brings her back after her attempted "suicide" by drowning. Among the exteriors, there is the brilliant green of the lawn in front of the art museum where Madeleine goes to look at the portrait of Carlotta Valdes, her "past incarnation," and the gauzy luminous blues and greens in the redwood forest where Madeleine weaves her spell of romantic mystification around Scottie. At the climax of the film, in "Judy's" hotel room, when Scottie has finally transformed her into "Madeleine," Hitchcock turns his world of color inside out—he illuminates their embrace with the lurid green glow of the neon sign outside the window. Color helps elevate what might have been just a gimmicky melodrama into a haunting study of obsession and illusion.

It's hard to decide whether Antonioni's *Red Desert* is saved or compromised by its color. The notoriety of the painted grass, the wall that changes color from scene to scene, the care lavished on the release prints, and so on, have tended to divert attention from the film as a whole to the color for color's sake. Certainly the color is the most meticulously planned of any film yet discussed. But, despite all the artifice, the color is organized almost entirely within the bounds of naturalism; more important, it often conveys the meaning of a scene in a direct yet discreet way. (This marks an advance over Antonioni's black and white films, in which the visual signals tend to be either heavy-handed or obscure.) When Corrado drives Giuliana to Ferrara, the sunlit yellows and lime greens that appear in the scene suggest immediately that Giuliana is responding to Corrado's interest in her. Later, when they meet on the mooring tower out at sea, the touches of cheerful red paint again make one feel that Giuliana's neurotic fears are giving way to trust in this relationship. In both cases the signals work because they are unambiguous—being virtually the only cheerful colors that have appeared so far—and yet not so conspicuous that the viewer is forced to take conscious note of them.

These gleams of color are small-scale reflections of the film's overall color scheme—a contrast between the somber and pallid tones of Giuliana's surroundings and the iridescence of her dream island. When she says "I am frightened of everything," one of the items on her list is colors; and throughout the film Antonioni ingeniously uses colors to represent the ebb and flow of all her fears.

Thus the luminous ochers and creamy yellows of the rocks on her dream island refer back to the yellows at Ferrara, where she first began to trust Corrado; but after he betrays that trust, all she can see is the poisonous yellow of the factory smoke, which "the birds learn not to fly through."

3. The films in the first two groups are selective in their use of color, eliminating or playing down many parts of the real-life spectrum. Now come what might be called the kaleidoscopic films, which stress variety and versatility. To do this, most of them rely heavily on artificial colors, as in the costumes of *Juliet of the Spirits* and the wallpaper of *The Umbrellas of Cherbourg.*

In the best kaleidoscopic films, the profuse and scattered colors appear part of an organic whole. But that isn't easy to achieve. "Kaleidoscopic" is more often a euphemism for "messy," as in Losey's *Modesty Blaise.* Here, nearly every scene strives for effect at the expense of its neighbors: high-key Mediterranean exteriors clash with op-art décor; cluttered sets overrun stylish compositions; the delicate and the garish continually stand in each other's light.

It may be argued that *Modesty Blaise* is high camp, not to be taken seriously. But that's just the trouble: the color is little fun to watch. If kaleidoscopic color is to be enjoyable, it can't be as slapdash as it may look. In Lester's *Help!*, for example, each sequence, no matter how brief or how dislocated, usually has its own palette —the whites and dark shadows of the Alps; the greens and khakis of the army maneuvers; the clear browns, whites, and yellows of the pub.

Kaleidoscopic color is still harder to handle in serious films, partly because it gives them a frivolous surface. Fellini's *Juliet of the Spirits*, for example, is visually well organized: rich and varied as they are, the colors enhance rather than detract from one another. But they quickly expose Fellini's tendency to bombast in presenting the bizarre and the orgiastic. Faced with this bombast in his black and white *8½* and *La Dolce Vita*, one can just sit tight and wait for him to move on; but in the fragmented color of *Juliet of the Spirits*, the Bishma sequence and Susy's party become vapid and irritating.

There is also a deeper trap. I'm not sure whether, at the end, Giulietta is supposed to become reconciled to her situation be-

cause she accepts reality or because she's taken refuge in her visions; but, either way, the ending is a letdown. The gorgeously detailed color that Fellini has accumulated in the course of stating
Giulietta's problem simply overwhelms the resolution. Although
8½ has an equally perfunctory ending—the tacked-on circus pro-
cession—it does not seem so much of a letdown because the rest
of the film has been "held in check" by black and white.

Nevertheless, Fellini makes excellent use of color in *Juliet of the
Spirits* to show the interplay of fantasy and reality. At first the two
are distinct: Giulietta's visions are somber (misty greens for the
memory of Grandpa, the vision of the Lord of Justice, the dream
of the shadowy boat at the beach), while her real surroundings are
bright and colorful. Then the visions become increasingly brighter
until they merge into reality (the appearance of the child at the
stake in the garden, of Susy in the bathroom). This transformation involves many subtleties. To give just one example, the shots
of the orange paper flames which represent the burning at the
stake are repeated more and more briefly: since one responds to
color first and to form afterward, the flames seem more and more
real as the shots become briefer.

The finest example of kaleidoscopic color—perhaps of any kind
of color—so far is Demy's *The Umbrellas of Cherbourg*. Like *Juliet of the Spirits*, it takes bright and artificial colors as its norm.
Even the location scenes are dominated by fresh paint, posters,
and colored lighting. But, unlike *Juliet of the Spirits*, the colors
here have nothing to do with fantasy. The wallpaper, the umbrellas, and the rest provide a multicolored background for the most
ordinary incidents, such as Mme Emery's practical concerns with
her store or the waiting period during Guy's absence. Life, says
Demy through his images, does not need "spirits" to make it toler-
able; even at its most banal, it has a colorful texture of wonder
and of hope.[22] Thus the conventional Mme Emery can bubble
over with *joie de vivre* even when Geneviève is pregnant, Guy is
far away, and Geneviève's solid suitor Roland has yet to learn of
her condition.

With variegated colors forming the warp and woof of his characters' lives, Demy opens out into single colors for scenes of unusual

[22] The music, of course, conveys the same idea—every word is sung,
whether it forms part of garage shop-talk or a declaration of love.

emotion or insight. Strong colors are associated with the direct, unsophisticated Guy. The orange-painted café where he proposes to Madeleine has already been mentioned. Red and orange-red also mark out the high points of his relationship with Geneviève: the apricot-red walls of the dance hall where they first declare their love; the fire-truck-red reflection in the garage window behind them when Guy tells Geneviève he's received his draft notice; and, in their final, accidental meeting, the traffic-light-red neon sign behind Guy's head when Geneviève first sees him. But Demy does not try to make any rigid emblematic use of red: bright blue serves just as well for the love between Guy and Geneviève when they go to his blue-walled room. Later, when Guy returns from Algeria to find that Geneviève is married, and he enters the room where they once loved, his pang of loss is made visible in the sudden reappearance of that blue: its unchanged vividness, when what matters most to him is changed beyond repair, comes as a slap in the eye.

For crucial scenes involving the gentle and sophisticated Roland, the dominant colors tend to be neutral, either dark (like the topcoat he wears when he first meets Geneviève) or light (the summer suit he wears when he accepts Geneviève despite her pregnancy). These neutral tones do not merely stand for his dependability: the sharp contrast they make with the basic variegated texture of the film reveals his emotions to be as powerful as Guy's, though far more controlled. Thus, one of the most visually striking scenes in the film is Roland's first sight of Geneviève as she enters the jewelry store. Dressed in white, beside her mother in yellow, and surrounded by spacious, white-framed windows through which the street is outlined in pale and airy blues, Geneviève seems almost to be floating on light.

The stages of Geneviève's separation from Guy and her acceptance of Roland are marked out in progressively more neutral colors. Even before Guy departs, the delirious scene in which they glide through the blue-lighted streets toward Guy's home modulates to a lurid, prophetic pallor at the very moment that he declares "I'll love you to the end of my life!" Later, when Geneviève tells her mother she can hardly remember what Guy looks like, she goes to the window of the umbrella store and looks out sadly at the carnival festivities: as the camera follows her away from the variegated colors of the store's décor, the screen is dominated by the cornflower blue of Geneviève's dress and the blurred pallid blues of the daylit scene outside. And the entire final sequence, when Guy and Geneviève have come to terms with their separate lives, is a resolution of all the film's colors into a firm and simple balance—the black of the night and the white of the snow. Tynan was completely wrong about *The Umbrellas of Cherbourg*: few films have used color with such relevance from start to finish.

4. My last group consists of films which make artificial use of naturalism. This is a wide-ranging group indeed, with the deliberate grittiness of Resnais's *Muriel* at one extreme and the deliberate seductiveness of Varda's *Le Bonheur* at the other.

In between the two is Lelouch's *A Man and a Woman*, probably the most eclectic color film ever made. It dabbles in almost every color device yet tried; and Lelouch seems so preoccupied with these devices that he often lets the film slide into banality (some of the scenes between Anne and Jean-Louis) or preposterousness (many of the scenes involving Anne's late husband, the stunt man, and Jean-Louis's late wife). Yet the artificial manner in which he films reality—there are virtually no studio scenes—often puts it in a significant perspective.

Ironically, while Anne and Jean-Louis agree that Life is more important than Art, the film demonstrates how the Annes and Jean-Louises of today convert their lives into art—or at least artifice. In several scenes the yellow headlights of Jean-Louis's car are likened to the rising sun, manufacture supplanting nature; in other scenes the viewer is unsure for a moment whether Anne is daydreaming about her past or doing her continuity work on a colorful movie set. By systematic use of telescopic lenses and by continually zooming back from close-up to long shot, Lelouch squeezes and stretches space as if it were hot plastic; and he does the same to time with rapid cutting and lengthy holding. In many scenes, such as the nightfall sequence at Deauville, this compressing of time and space transforms a banal event into an exotic series of colored patterns.

In *Muriel* the natural colors are made not exotic but disconcerting. The patterns within many scenes, and in transitions from scene to scene, rarely gratify the eye like the black and white composition of *Marienbad*, for Resnais is using color to reveal a different aspect of time. His characters are all trying in various ways to come to terms with the past. In the course of the film they are forced to realize that the passing of time is not a flow like that of a river, which with heroic engineering might be reversed, but a continual shattering of the present into fragments that cannot be put together again. Resnais achieves this effect partly by his choice of colors and even more by the restless way he cuts from one to another. There are a lot of in-between shades—steely blues, beiges, umbers—and the interiors are often a quiet clutter of middle tones, with here and there a jarring bright color like Hélène's yellow kitchen. The basic color scheme is, in fact, autumnal, though it only takes on a pleasing *Trouble with Harry* aspect in the few exterior scenes by the sea. Elsewhere, by leaping to and fro across this palette—sometimes between day and night—Resnais neutralizes its languor in much the same way as Ernest's breathless, jerky singing of the Déjà song neutralizes *its* nostalgia. The one direct view of the film's past—the movies that Bernard shot in Algeria—are of trivial incidents that reveal nothing of the experience that affected Bernard most deeply: the torturing of the Algerian girl he calls Muriel. Resnais tints the scenes with pallid greens and ochers —like a verdigris—to make it clear that these fragments of the past can no longer be fitted into the present.

Resnais takes a risk in making his color deliberately non-sensuous, since many viewers balk at the film's gritty surface. Varda runs the opposite risk in *Le Bonheur*, since viewers may think that everything in such gorgeous color is to be taken as an ingredient of François's happiness, including his wife's suicide! Here the glowing colors reveal how intensely François lives in the present moment: he is too dazzled by *joie de vivre* to see that other people need a more solid, less colorful foundation for their lives. That's why Varda fades into colors between sequences, instead of black —to convey the invulnerability of François's present moment, his dangerously beautiful Now.

These examples suggest some of the lines along which the use of screen color is developing. There is a certain parallel here with the development of screen music, from simple echo effects to a freer association. In music, of course, the development is easier to grasp because it is not intimately bound up with the image as color is.

Yet often the color is divorced from the image, either by the filmmaker when he tries too hard to make it significant, or by the viewer when faced with an idiosyncratic use of it. Color films today are in a similar situation (though on a different plane) to the first Technicolor films of thirty years ago. Nurtured on black and white, the filmmakers of that era were tempted by garishness, the viewers prone to see garishness where it didn't exist. Today's filmmakers and viewers, nurtured on indifferent color films and those which use color only piecemeal, are not yet at ease with the concerted use of color to shape the film as a whole. But the increasing number of films that do try to use color in this way suggests that the sense of ease will come to us all before long. Meanwhile, we can look forward to the consolidation of recent experiments and to many fascinating surprises.

Film Quarterly, Fall 1966

V. SOUND

Sound as Speech, Noise, Music

LEWIS JACOBS

*T*he addition of sound to motion pictures in 1929 brought a new dimension to screen expression. Sound altered some techniques, modified others, and provided the developing medium with an added sense of reality. But, above all, sound introduced a new approach that was clearly no longer to be confined to the purely visual but rather oriented to the audiovisual. The need for subtitles to clarify and extend visual action was eliminated; the use of broad pantomime and exaggerated gestures by the performers to evoke what the spoken word provided had to be reassessed; a new element, offering depth and substance, was now part of filmmaking. The addition of the audible—the human voice, noises, and music—challenged the criteria of film expression that had become crystallized as established practice over thirty years; helped to raise the level of film content; opened the medium to more varied spheres of human experience and imagination; and subtly deepened the complexity of its expression.

The immediate effect of the introduction of sound was to cause motion-picture technique to retrogress markedly away from its inner logic. Dialogue became the paramount consideration, supplanting the basic visual approach to expression. Early sound movies, even the most outstanding, were static reproductions resembling stage plays. In part, this was due to the mechanical drawbacks as well as the new technical problems presented by the as yet crude apparatus of the unfamiliar aural element. The microphone was immobile and unselective; it picked up all noises indiscriminately, just as the camera lens recorded every detail it focused on. This meant that the shooting of sound films had to be carried out in the strictest silence. While speaking, the actors had to remain comparatively still if their speech was to be recorded clearly —making scenes even more static. Moreover, the spoken word and its apprehension involved actual, real time and played havoc with all other filmic considerations. The duration of shots with people talking was now determined by the length of dialogue rather than by their filmic time as governed by editing needs. Talk supplanted image, movement was forsaken, the camera lost its mobility, the film continuity shrank to a minimum number of scenes with few camera changes. Film technique returned to a rudimentary level of expression—which appalled many intellectually minded film critics and devotees.

Only gradually did filmmakers learn that sound had to be structurally expressive and functional, had to take its proper place in the cinematic scheme. Ways and means had to be found for sound film to be stripped of irrelevancies and freed from dependence on the spoken word. Thus it was discovered that the microphone and the camera need not necessarily focus on the same subject at the same time: sound and image could be separated. This separation enabled the filmmaker to utilize the microphone selectively to pick up just the sounds he needed, in the same way he used his camera to select shots—thus obtaining a similar freedom of audio manipulation and arrangement. A whole world of acoustic experience was opened up which could now make silence itself meaningful. With this knowledge and awareness, the function of the sound track came to be regarded as an adjunct element, an additional plastic asset, extending, enriching, and enlarging the medium's expressive capabilities to embrace nuances of thought, feeling, and emotion through a collaboration of sound and image.

In the real world, sound is ubiquitous—existing all the time, emanating from many sources and from many directions. The audible boundary is greater than the visual one; therefore, all sounds within earshot—including those with no visible cause—compete for our attention. Usually, however, a person "hears"—that is, listens to—only those sounds which are important to him or which are unusual or disturbing. Familiar sounds go unheeded unless a specific effort is made to listen. The brain directs the ear to focus on the sound that is important and to dismiss or shut out the myriad other sounds that surround us. Though sound itself is objective, its reception is subjective, asserting itself in different ways, depending on our aural perception, sensitivity, and state of mind. At a party, for example, we are accustomed to the hum of conversation, the clinking of glasses, the movement of people, and we seldom notice these sounds, unless there is an abrupt change or interruption—the smashing of a bottle, or an unexpected silence. Our attention is jolted away from what we are doing and directed toward the cause of the sudden intrusion.

In motion pictures, sound comes from only one source: the microphone. Every sound is received by the audience with equal attention until its significance is understood. Even the smallest sound—one which might readily be overlooked in real life—can assume extreme importance on the screen. Thus the viewer's aural perception can be directed and controlled with the same freedom as his visual perception. The selection and separation of a sound from its origin, like the selection and separation of a shot from the mass of subject matter, enables the filmmaker to omit what is unimportant and give meaning to what is heard. Sounds, singly or in combination, regardless of their origin, can be placed together with any shot. In this way the audience is forced to hear only what the filmmaker wants it to hear.

The detachment of sound and its reproduction in a film are made possible by the mechanical nature of the recording apparatus and the editing process. Microphone and camera are independent instruments, recording what is seen and heard either together simultaneously or separately at different times. The aural and visual segments can then be assembled in any order. It is standard procedure for sync sound, usually dialogue, to be recorded at the same time as the picture. Non-sync sound, such as narration, noises ("sound effects"), and music, is individually recorded on a separate sound track, either before or after the picture has been photographed, and then later is added to the edited film.

Unwanted sounds can be eliminated by slicing them out of the tracks. Desired sounds can be added, separated, or brought closer together. At any point, sound may be synchronized with the picture, or made to compliment it. When the different individual tracks have been edited to match the final "cut" of the film, they are then rerecorded and "mixed" on a properly balanced master track. It is at this time that dialogue, noises, and music are superimposed, fused, and orchestrated, to give the various sounds the values, intensities, and purposes the film director wishes.

During this mixing period, sounds can be blended, emphasized, subdued, or even made to fade into silence in a meaningful assembly whose effectiveness is limited only by the sensitivity and aim of the director.

The addition of sound brought to film three of the richest, most complex means of communication: speech, noise, and music. Each of these expressions of sound is an important means of transmitting knowledge, thought, impressions, feelings, of awakening awareness of the existence of many matters and experiences. Each has a life and importance of its own, related of course to the expression of the subject matter and to the intention of the film. The choice and manner in which they are used, and their meaningful interaction, expand the medium's capability to heighten the impact of its subject matter and deepen the viewer's experience.

SPEECH: DIALOGUE AND NARRATION

Perhaps the main function of sound in movies is to transmit speech. People speak with each other in real life; the spoken word is the quickest and easiest way to present information on the screen. Dialogue is both essential and economical in developing characterization and dramatic situations and involving the viewer in the excitement and color (or their lack) of a screen personality. In addition to bearing directly or indirectly upon human relationships, the shapes, sounds, and rhythms of the spoken word can also be used to sharpen the expressiveness of the image and carry it beyond the mere unfolding of its visual action.

To continue the visual flow and avoid tedium, filmmakers have learned how to subordinate dialogue, how to make it economical, yet conversational, fresh yet non-literary, and how to match the movement of the performers and the film's action with a casual delivery. They have discovered how to heighten the eloquence and significance of the spoken word through non-synchronization—that is, by detaching the voice from the speaker. Once it has been established who is talking, the camera is free to change and shift about in a kind of independent life of its own. By showing the reaction of a listener, or some other action related to what is being said, or the speaker's immediate surroundings, or a meaningful event elsewhere, or depicting some other image that comments on the words being spoken, the filmmaker can use speech and imagery in a kind of supporting interaction that allows for dramatic intensification, humor, satire, irony, or any other meaningful collaboration.

There is a danger, however, in overdependence on dialogue at the expense of other elements. Too often we see a person talking and hear his voice, without a change of shot, for too long a time. Such synchronized sound and image add little to the effectiveness of a scene unless the dialogue has some special or dramatic value. Long stretches of talk when the verbal and pictorial coincide, or a preponderance of words, which crushes visual variety, cancel interest and thwart movement, so that the film becomes static, monotonous, and fatiguing. In watching the screen, the spectator still seems to be more intent on what he sees than on what he hears, and he tires quickly if there is too much speech and the camera remains fixed on a single speaker.

One of the factors that make Orson Welles's *Citizen Kane* (1941) outstanding is its inventiveness in the use of dialogue. Welles adapted a device from radio that became one of the picture's most vital features, a kind of aural continuity whereby dialogue that begins in one scene is completed in another, thus uniting two or more scenes separated in time and space, and at the same time advancing the continuity of the whole.

A typical and particularly effective example is the sequence in which Leland is speaking to a small group of businessmen in an effort to further Kane's political ambitions. "He entered this campaign . . ." Leland begins. Then Kane's own voice completes the sentence as we see him in a huge auditorium addressing a mass rally: ". . . with one purpose only." Thus, an audio transition is formed which links and advances the visual continuity. Without a break in dialogue, meaning is carried forward in a unity of spoken words, images, and movement that gives the passage a striking virtuosity.

Dialogue is not the only function of speech. There is another, technically known as narration. Generally speaking, film narration is used as a structural device to describe or explain the images, or to point up the pictorial action, or to comment in some way on the film's content. Such narration, or "voice-over," as it is sometimes called, usually represents the disembodied voice of the unseen observer-commentator frequently heard in documentaries and other non-theatrical movies. Here narration ranges from literal description of what is seen, as in the interesting National Film Board of Canada pictures, *Eskimo Artist, Kenojuak* (1964) and *Judoka* (1966), to poetic interpretation and insight as in *Night and Fog* (1955) and *The Eleanor Roosevelt Story* (1965).

Narration can also take the form of the disassociated third-person voice of an actor-observer who is a character in the picture and describes the attitudes, sensations, and behavior of other characters, as for example the stage manager in the film adaptation of Thornton Wilder's play *Our Town* (1940). The first-person narration by a character who is not seen but conveys what he thinks and feels by what his voice tells us, as does the detective in *Lady in the Lake* (1946), or who is seen, as is the artist in *Another Time; Another Voice* (1960), is a more interesting but little-used device that can add to the impact of visual images.

The "off-screen voice" is another category of narration. Generally, off-screen voice takes the form of speech used to reveal a different state of mind, different thoughts, feelings, or memories from what the visual image depicts. Just as it is possible for the camera to identify what the viewer sees with the subjective vision of the screen actor, so it is possible for the off-screen microphone to identify what the viewer hears with different mental states of the performer. In Hitchcock's *Blackmail* (1929), the camera pictures the outward action of a girl preparing breakfast, while the sound track indicates her inner distress. The girl, who in self-defense has stabbed and killed an artist, overhears a neighbor telling her parents about the unsolved crime and the bloodied knife found by the police. As the girl listens with mounting apprehension, the neighbor's droning voice gradually goes out of focus and only the dreaded word "knife . . . knife . . . knife" is heard clearly. By concentrating on the relevant word, the microphone enables us to hear—as though through the girl's ears—only what has penetrated her consciousness like a repeated accusation.

Evoking the past in a kind of aural flashback is another use of the off-screen voice. In John Ford's *The Informer* (1935), Gypo is dreamily studying a model of a steamship in the window of a travel agency, thinking that it might enable him to escape from the political organization he has betrayed. His fears become apparent as he (we) hears the voice of a former comrade warning him that, without his friend, he is lost.

A more imaginative but infrequent application of the off-screen voice is to depict "inner monologue," in a kind of stream-of-consciousness. A brilliant example of this technique occurs in one of Eisenstein's "montage sketches" for his unproduced screenplay of *The American Tragedy*, based on Dreiser's novel. The following extract from the director's essay, "Detective Work in GIK" (*Close Up*, June 1933), vividly captures what Eisenstein described as "internal as opposed to external speech" through a free association and contrast between what is heard and what is seen:

> . . . Now by passionate, incoherent speech . . . Only substantives . . . or only verbs. Then by interjections . . . with zigzags of aimless figures, hurrying along with them synchronously . . .
> Now visual images hurried along in complete silence.
> Now sounds included in a polyphony . . . Now images . . . Then both together . . .
> Now interpolating themselves into external course of events, now interpolating elements of the external events into themselves . . .
> Presenting, as it were, the play of thought within the dramatis personae—the conflict of doubts, the burst of passion, the voice of reason, by quick movement, or slow movement . . . emphasizing the difference in the rhythms of this and that . . . and at the same time contrasting the almost complete absence of outward action with the feverish inward debates—behind the stony mask of the face.

The technique of shaping and blending the minutiae of thoughts, feelings, and emotions through off-screen voices—jagged narration, interior monologue, inchoate sentences, repetition, the speed-up and slowdown of words—sketched by Eisenstein, has in recent years engaged the interest of other distinguished directors. Bergman, Resnais, and Fellini have become involved with stream-of-consciousness devices in an attempt to force the viewer into a psychological identity with screen characters through the sharing of subjective aural as well as visual experiences.

NOISE

Noise, like speech, is an integral part of subject matter and in motion pictures plays an important role in establishing the meaning and effectiveness of the visual image. Technically called "sound effects," noises—whether reproduced from nature or fabricated from mechanical or electronic sounds or produced by light vibrations applied to the track through drawing, mechanical, or electronic devices—assume significance on the screen depending on how they are used.

In real life, every kind of action is accompanied by some kind of sound. When a car starts, we recognize it by its noise. When the subway train approaches the station, we recognize the sound of its wheels on the tracks. But, on the screen, seeing an action and hearing its accompanying sounds adds little but a characteristic "realism" to the import of a scene. When the sound is easily recognizable, we do not have to see the action or object to know what produced the noise. The viewer mentally supplies the thing or kind of action associated with it. If, for example, a person hears a bell toll, he will associate its sound with a church, even though the church is not seen. If a barking dog is heard while a child is seen looking down at the ground, the viewer assumes that the child is staring down at the animal. Paul Rotha, the British film director and historian, noted this fact when he wrote that sound separated from its source "will not only become a symbol of that source, but also a symbol of what that source represents."

This association of ideas has been used by filmmakers to good advantage to create an illusion that tells the viewer more than he sees. In John Ford's *Long Voyage Home* (1940), for example, a cargo ship is carrying explosives through a war zone; we hear the sounds of approaching enemy planes. As the men on the ship dash for safety, we suddenly hear the roar of dive-bomber engines, followed by straffing machine-gun fire. We never see the planes, but the sound of their motors and guns—an aural symbol of attacking planes—tells us the reason for the crew's terror.

Sound effects can play a forceful role in establishing mood and atmosphere to create a particular emotion. In the opening of William Wyler's *The Letter* (1940) the camera moves through a tropical plantation at night, past darkened buildings and lush foliage. We hear the sounds of insects, of rubber sap dripping from trees, the screeching of unfamiliar birds, hushed voices in native tongues, and the sensual twang of exotic stringed instruments. The pictorial imagery is thus imbued with a heightened degree of authentic local color. At the same time the tapestry of sound builds up a mood of strangeness and foreboding, preparing the viewer emotionally for what is to follow.

Divorced from their natural setting, sounds have an evocative power that can change the meaning of an image. In Fritz Lang's *M* (1931), the murderer has a habit of whistling a few bars from Grieg's "Troll Dance" each time he feels the blood lust rising inside him. Whenever we hear this tune—even though the camera shows an empty courtyard or some children playing in the streets —we are reminded of the menace of the deranged killer.

In *Under the Roofs of Paris* (1930), by René Clair, we see some drunken men fighting near the railroad tracks at night. But, instead of the sounds of the fight, we hear the wheezing and whistling of an approaching outmoded train. The scene provides a special kind of humor that derives from the contrast of sound and action, thereby sharpening the whimsical audiovisual style.

A versatile device, sound effects can function as a potent instrument for binding together unrelated images to advance movement and simultaneously serve a metaphorical purpose. In Hitchcock's *39 Steps* (1935), a woman blunders upon a corpse with a knife in its back. She opens her mouth to scream. There is a swift cut to a speeding train. What we hear is its high-pitched wail, which even while expressing the woman's horror—it functions as a kind of aural metaphor—also acts as a sound bridge to carry the viewer into the next sequence.

The ability of sounds to link and sharpen the effect of visual images by a contrast between what is heard and what is seen can also serve to increase tension through a repetition of what is heard, in complement to what is seen. This is graphically underlined in *The Informer* (1935). After Gypo has betrayed his friend Frankie at the police station, we suddenly hear the loud ticking of a clock.

The ticking continues through the next shots of Frankie at home and becomes ever more exaggerated as he talks to his mother and sister. It is then blended with the tapping of a blind man's cane in the next shots as Gypo slinks away from police headquarters, afraid of being seen by his former comrades in the "organization." The continued and persistent ticking and tapping sounds dramatically link the betrayed and the betrayer. Also, the aural transition advances continuity.

Allied to the associative significance of sound effects is the powerful contrast of silence. Even when the movies were mute, the accompanying musical score would stop as a means of emphasizing a particular dramatic moment. The use of silence to build suspense and dramatic tension is vividly exemplified in the British film, *One of Our Aircraft Is Missing* (1941). Several British fliers, befriended by Dutch resistance fighters, are meeting in an old church amid a group of civilians praying in the pews. Suddenly a Nazi officer enters. The church becomes silent and still. The abrupt sharp clap of the Nazi's boots shatters the stillness as he marches down the aisle to inspect the congregation. At the same moment, the organist is heard lightly playing the Dutch national anthem. The Nazi officer stops and listens. The music suddenly stops. The silence becomes eloquent with fear and suspense. The officer starts walking again; the unseen organist matches the movement with another bar or two. Again the officer stops; the organist stops. Again the silence underscores the rising tension.

Another striking example of the tensile use of silence appears in the Soviet film *Gypsies* (1949). A gypsy chief and a tribesman are fighting a duel with whips in the forest. The camera is not on them, however, but on other members of the tribe, who stand at the edge of the woods, following the progress of the unseen combat through the sounds of the slashing whips. Suddenly all sounds stop. There is a deadly silence. It is obvious the battle has ended, but who is the victor? As the silence continues, neither fighter appears. The absence of all sound becomes unbearable, as the suspense mounts. Finally the battered, bleeding chief staggers into view, relieving the tension with the sound of his gasping breath.

In nearly all instances, sound effects score their most powerful impact through their connotations and the psychological reactions they arouse in the viewer. Natural sounds—those reproduced from the real world by the microphone and recording apparatus —are particularly effective in this area because of their specific as well as their implied meanings. Besides natural and artificial sounds, there are those which are "created" but which are unrecognizable for what they are, and as such are used as abstract sounds. These are produced manually—drawn by hand, or mechanically imprinted by machine—to accompany, generally, non-objective, abstract films.

The creators of such fabricated sounds, predominantly experimental filmmakers, are essentially concerned with pure sound appeal, striving for an extension of imaginative reality through a new kind of audiovisual experience. These filmmakers employ synthetic sounds as they employ abstract imagery, color, and rhythm, not to express any thought or idea, but as an end in itself.

Among the most sophisticated and accomplished filmmakers in this idiom are James and John Whitney and Norman McLaren. The Whitney brothers have invented an apparatus that prints black and white patterns directly onto the motion-picture film, reproducing a variety of tones that can be controlled and composed in patterns of rhythmic movement. These sounds are combined with colored non-representational images—geometric shapes that shift, interlace, and intersect in changing waves of color (also synthetically devised by an optical printer)—which the Whitneys call "exercises," or "rehearsals for a species of audiovisual performances." The sounds rise and fall, advance and recede with an aural texture and quality that is unique and suggests wide scope for exploration and development.

Another kind of manufactured sound expression—one that stems from the methods of animation—is manifested by the Canadian filmmaker Norman McLaren. McLaren's technique is to draw or scratch various shapes directly on film; these reproduce as patterns of percussive rhythm. In such pictures as *Pen-Point Percussion, Loops, Two Bagatelles,* and *Rhythmetic,* all executed in the fifties, synthetic sounds, moving together with McLaren's handdrawn images, collaborate in the form of semi-free improvisations that are lively, witty, inventive, and of high cinematic quality.

In the sixties, when all arts were expanding in various forms of mixed-media combines, and artists became more involved with technology, many experimental filmmakers turned to new and enlarged multi-media methods of image expression. These included variable and multiple screen devices, multi-image projections, stroboscopic-kinetic-light presentations, film loops, and computer-generated movies. To match these new hybrid film shows, fabricated sounds burst out of their limited range to become amplified, aggressive, spectacular, often combining with narration, popular and folk songs, and electric music in a montage of multiple channels striving for maximum aural expressiveness. How much this new development in expanded audiovisual technology and sensibility will experience further decisive transformations, and how valuable these will be to the future of creative film expression, is as yet unforeseeable.

MUSIC

Because emotions and mental concepts can be transformed and intensified by aural experiences, music can underscore the illusionary nature of motion pictures and involve the viewer more deeply in the heart of that illusion. Music strikes directly at the emotions of the movie viewer and can bring to bear ideas and feelings not actually present on the screen. Music, as we know, can identify peoples, locales, and historical periods, can tell a story, create a mood, evoke an atmosphere, portray a character, suggest the sounds of nature, and express states of mind. Music can express nostalgia, love and hate, and the pathos of existence. Music can support the mercurial needs of comedy, prodding it from raucous farce to touching sadness or absurd nonsense; music can also invest a scene with terror, or tragedy. In short, music on the screen is a potent link between picture and audience, reaching out to the audience's aural senses and engulfing all in a more persuasive emotional experience.

The evocative power of music was recognized early in movie history. Back in the nickelodeon days a local piano player, with one eye on the screen and the other on a sheet of piano music, accompanied the picture with appropriate extracts from nineteenth-century sentimental pieces and fitting improvisations to complement the excitement of "chases," fights, of falling off cliffs, or to identify the villain and reinforce the romance. Later an organist, with more breadth of sound, replaced the pianist and attempted to bring a wider range of music closer to the material on the screen. After the First World War, during the period of rising affluence, the organist was supplanted by a full, live orchestra, which could provide a still greater richness of sound. A specially arranged overture now often preceded the film, and the picture itself was accompanied by specially arranged passages selected from the classical repertory. Finally, special music was composed to emphasize the picture's changing moods and dramatic action. This was circulated with the film. By the late twenties, an accompanying musical score was regarded as a necessary adjunct of the film, giving musical shape and body to the pictures themselves. Hollywood studios assembled extensive libraries of all kinds of music—popular, folk, classical. These were strung together in all sorts of "arrangements" —as they became known—suitable, and readily available, for any type of picture. Important films had "original" music written by a composer called in for the purpose.

It was the industry-wide acceptance of the sound track in the early thirties that made possible an exact musical score for the film, to be written, recorded, and reproduced so that all audiences in all theaters heard the same performance, of the same quality. Live orchestras were disbanded and "canned music" took their place. Film companies hired musicians to provide the best musical performances possible on a professional level and composed original scores that would be an attraction in themselves for the moviegoers, particularly those with a musical interest, knowledge, or background.

Technical developments in the recording and mixing of sound kept pace with film artistry. When it was discovered that musical sounds and phrases, either singly or in combination, could be recorded in any order and then rerecorded and transferred to one or more tracks for further manipulation, new creative paths were opened; the film composer and picture director became free to shape their material together at will and devote more careful attention to the unity and integration of music and image.

The creative role of music in films came in for closer examination. Should music remain a subsidiary feature whose function was limited to being heard, and never call attention to itself? Could music satisfy the film's needs and still be true to its own nature? Would music unrelated to the imagery cause a danger which increased in proportion to the value of the music as music?

After some skirmishing between composers and filmmakers, efforts began to be made to extend the cinematic role of music. A way was found to depart from the silent-screen method—that is, the literal accompaniment to the background action of a picture's plot. Music could now offer something more valuable and basic to the cohesion of the film as a whole. The score moved away from mere accompaniment—where its function had been largely descriptive—to become linked more directly with the picture's concept.

One of the most notable examples of the collaboration of film director and composer was that of Eisenstein and Prokofiev in the making of *Alexander Nevsky* (1938). In the book *Film Sense*, Eisenstein describes how closely composer and director worked to achieve a structural harmony between picture and sound. First there were lengthy discussions about the intention and construction of each film section. Following these talks, the composer would sometimes rough out and record musical passages for a scene or sequence. The director would then film these sections and try editing them in accordance with the musical construction. At other times, a reverse procedure would be followed. Music would be written after a sequence had been shot and edited, to conform to a rough of the final picture "cut." The aim was to relate music and picture through an identical fluidity of aural and visual structure.

In the famous battle sequence, Eisenstein points out that there is a deliberate similarity in the notation between the movement from dark to light in the composition of his shots and the corresponding development in the melodic line of the score. This kind of relationship—what the director called "inner synchronization" —appears again in a later sequence, this time matching a rising and falling of images on the screen with a similar musical progression on the sound track. Here music and film are locked together as a building is put together. What matters is not the difference in media and materials but the architecture—the way each is related to form an integrated whole. The formal structure which conditions the cohesion gives each element a new coloration that brings to the film greater intensity of design and depth of meaning.

An early successful collaboration of composer and filmmaker, indicating the new direction, was that of Pare Lorentz and Louis Gruenberg in the film *Fight for Life* (1940). Here the music's role was actually written into the screenplay: "For dramatic effect the music must start exactly with the film—from the moment we see 'City Hospital' until the baby is born, the beat of the music must not vary, and there must be no change in instrumentation sufficient enough to be noticeable. The conception is that we have the mother's heartbeat, two beats in one, with the accent on the first one; with the echo exactly 1½ times as fast and without an accent; practically a beat of 100 a minute as against the fetal heartbeat of 150 a minute."

In a subsequent scene, where the intern leaves the delivery room containing the dead mother and walks out of the hospital, Pare Lorentz wanted music rather than dialogue or narration to express the young doctor's tumultuous feelings of the cruelty of life. ". . . We start with one piano under the intern; then we start another piano as he walks out of the hospital . . . and the two pianos play blues." The music thus provokes the spectator's imagination, compelling him to participate in the doctor's despair, rather than remain a passive observer of it. This collaborative approach offered a more logical method for a film's musical structure and for an integrated audiovisual style.

How the sense of the film image could be altered and given other meanings by the astute collaboration of musical idiom and picture was further demonstrated in the early sound films of René Clair, *Under the Roofs of Paris* (1930) and *Le Million* (1931); of Ernst Lubitsch, *The Love Parade* (1929–30); of Rouben Mamoulian, *Love Me Tonight* (1932); and by Walt Disney in the *Silly Symphonies* series (1933–34).

Original musical scores stimulated more variety and greater organic justification in the aural accompaniment. The use of a leitmotiv to represent a character or an idea, as in opera, was extended. Variations of tempo and orchestration were introduced to support and deepen the pictorial development, which was further unified by the melodies constituting the composition. Film music reached such a degree of excellence that critics frequently commented on it. For example, Richard Hageman's rhythmic score for John Ford's *Stagecoach* (1939) achieved the double distinction of being praised for heightening the picture's dramatic impact and being lauded by music critics for its finely textured score.

The role of music continued to be extended further, and music was called upon for many additional values, particularly to evoke psychological and subjective effects that neither words nor pictures alone could obtain. For instance, in *The Third Man* (1950) the musical score played on a zither contributes an intangible overtone that acts like a commentator, influencing the viewer-listener by the emotional and mental associations brought to bear through its irrepressible and haunting rhythms. The zither cries, sings, whispers, growls, cajoles, insinuates—vividly depicting the variety of moods that were the quintessence of post-war Vienna, as the story demands. These moods account in large part for the picture's considerable effectiveness.

The psychosis of an amnesia victim in *Spellbound* (1945) is dramatically embodied in weird melodies of fear and hopelessness that sound as though they were produced electronically.

In a more traditional vein, but with more dramatic nuances and depth of feeling, William Walton's music for Olivier's *Hamlet* (1948) projects a vital part of the film's emotional framework by defining the inner turmoil of the young Prince. The score hauntingly invokes the ghost of Hamlet's father in the pre-dawn mists of Elsinore, then turns and twists agonizingly behind Hamlet's soliloquy, switches to a sudden stabbing cruelty when Hamlet, feigning madness, rejects the distressed Ophelia, slips into sly humor in the masquerade play-within-a-play, to extend and intensify the internal drama of the Prince's anguish and self-realization.

Screen music supplants cumbersome exposition and does much to dramatize and enliven *The Titan* (1950), a film about the life, spirit, and times of Michelangelo. Without ever showing a human actor, the camera moves over and around Renaissance objects, Italian landscapes, the sculpture, paintings, and architecture of the artist, while the score acts as "dialogue," to give immediacy to Michelangelo's story. It "comments" upon the artist's emergence and his work, binds together the papal and princely intrigues, supplies background atmosphere to evoke the turbulence of the age, dramatizes the siege of Florence and the sack of Rome, and continuously propels the story forward at a high pitch of interest.

More recently and in a lighter vein, a score by Michel Legrand for Godard's *A Woman Is a Woman* (1961) pushes to extreme limits music's storytelling capabilities. In this picture, music breaks its link with abstraction and assumes a mimetic form, to satirize what is said and seen in a way that recalls the famed "touch" of Lubistch's best comedies. Legrand's score frequently counterpoints the pictorial action through the satirical use of marches, waltzes, romantic themes, and even "storm" music that mocks and ridicules the situation and dialogue. Heroic tunes reduce speeches to absurdity; musical jokes serve as aural transitions, add a saucy flavor and rhythm to the film's lighthearted, teasing style.

Two later pictures that might not have had as conspicuous a rhythmic style and meaning without the particular kind of music that went with them are *Cat Ballou* (1965) and *Bonnie and Clyde* (1967). Both were conceived on the ballad form. The first, a spoof of Westerns, also mocks the folk-singing craze, using a lugubrious ballad to complement and elaborate the adventures of a young school teacher turned outlaw in the 1890's. The second film is divided into sequences which end, ballad-like, with an exuberant flourish of banjo music twanging out the derring-do exploits of their protagonists, Bonnie Parker and Clyde Barrow, killer bandits of the Depression era. The assertiveness of the rollicking scores in both films becomes a commentary, a counterpoint of humor against drama, and vice versa—forceful musical observations linked with the imagery and movement that implies more than what is heard and seen.

There also exists a whole genre of audio films known as "musicals"—in which the primary and motivating factor that moves the story is the song and dance score. This is a takeover from the musical theater and runs the gamut from canned theatrical presentations like *The Sound of Music* (1964), utilizing little or none of the special properties of the film, to a picture like *The Umbrellas of Cherbourg* (1964), which tries to develop a musical style more indigenous to the screen medium.

Today the music track can be treated with as much freedom and imagination as the dialogue and sound effects can. The creative collaboration of music and other aural and visual elements extends the role of music far beyond its earlier ornamental uses. The best film music is that specifically designed to integrate with the visual structure into a totality whose form provides the medium with a richness of texture and a pervasive power of expression that organizes subject matter into art.

The Acoustic World

" *I* t is the business of the sound film to reveal for us our acoustic environment, the
acoustic landscape in which we live, the speech of things and the
intimate whisperings of nature; all that has speech beyond human
speech, and speaks to us with the vast conversational powers of life
and incessantly influences and directs our thoughts and emotions,
from the muttering of the sea to the din of a great city, from the
roar of machinery to the gentle patter of autumn rain on a windowpane. The meaning of a floorboard creaking in a deserted
room, a bullet whistling past our ear, the deathwatch beetle ticking in old furniture, and the forest spring tinkling over the stones.
Sensitive lyrical poets always could hear these significant sounds of
life and describe them in words. It is for the sound film to let
them speak to us more directly from the screen."

DISCOVERY OF NOISE

"The sounds of our day-to-day life we hitherto perceived merely
as a confused noise, as a formless mass of din, rather as an unmusi-
cal person may listen to a symphony; at best he may be able to distinguish the leading melody, the rest will fuse into a chaotic
clamor. The sound film will teach us to analyze even chaotic noise
with our ear and read the score of life's symphony. Our ear will

hear the different voices in the general babble and distinguish their character as manifestations of individual life. It is an old maxim that art saves us from chaos. The arts differ from each other in the specific kind of chaos which they fight against. The vocation of the sound film is to redeem us from the chaos of shapeless noise by accepting it as expression, as significance, as meaning."

Twenty years have passed since I wrote down these conditions. The sound film has left them unfulfilled to this day. The arts did not accede to my theoretical wishes. During its evolution, the human spirit has had many a fair prospect open up before it which the great highroad of human culture then bypassed and left behind. No art exploits all its possibilities, and not only aesthetic factors influence the choice of the road that is ultimately followed in preference to many possible others. And I would not have repeated this, my old demand, if the sound film had since advanced further along another road. But it has advanced nowhere. What twenty years ago was opportunity and perspective is still perspective and opportunity today. I quote:

"Only when the sound film will have resolved noise into its elements, segregated individual, intimate voices and made them speak to us separately in vocal, acoustic close-ups; when these isolated detail-sounds will be collated again in purposeful order by sound-montage will the sound film have become a new art. When the director will be able to lead our ear as he could once already lead our eye in the silent film and by means of such guidance along a series of close-ups will he be able to emphasize, separate and bring into relation with each other the sounds of life as he has done with its sights, then the rattle and clatter of life will no longer overwhelm us in a lifeless chaos of sound. The sound camera will intervene in this chaos of sound, form it and interpret it and then it will again be man himself who speaks to us from the sound screen."

DRAMATURGY OF SOUND

"The genuine sound film which has a style of its own will not be satisfied with making audible the speech of human beings, which in the past has been only visible, nor will it rest content with an acoustic presentation of events. Sound will not be merely a corollary to the picture, but the subject, source, and mover of the action. In other words, it will become a dramaturgical element in the film. For instance, sounds will not be merely an accompaniment to a duel but possibly its cause as well. The audible clash of blades may be of less importance—because devoid of a dramaturgical function—than perhaps a song heard coming from a garden by the listening rivals and occasioning a quarrel between them. Such sounds would be essential elements of the story. There is no reason why a sound should be less apt to provoke action than a sight would be."

The first sound films were still intent on exploiting these special possibilities of sound. At that time a film operetta was made in Berlin. In it a young composer has to produce a new waltz before the end of the coming day. He racks his brains and can find nothing suitable. Then, through a mistake, an unknown girl comes to his room. The result of the sudden and unexpected adventure is the birth of a waltz. The composer plays it on the piano and the girl sings it. But the musician's unknown muse vanishes as she had come and the composer again forgets the tune, which he had no time to write down. Only the unknown girl might possibly remember it. So the composer puts a want ad in the newspaper: "The young lady who . . ." After some naïve, even inane complications all turning on the melody, the waltz finally brings the lovers together again. Here was a proper plot for a sound film. The found, lost, and recovered waltz had a dramaturgical, action-moving role.

SOUND SPEAKS UP

In the story just mentioned, the lost and found melody was, however, allotted a role such as might have been played by any other object. It was a mere "prop" in the weft of the dramatic plot, no different than a ring or a document which might have been lost and found and around which the plot might have been woven just as well. The waltz in this case is merely presented as a fact; no significance attaches to its specific acoustic quality and effect. For this reason it is the most superficial form in which sound can be given a dramaturgical function in a story.

Deeper and more organic is the dramaturgical role of sound

when its effect determines the course of the action; when sound is not only made to be heard in the course of the story but can intervene to influence its course. I take an instance from an old silent film, or rather I am inventing an instance in order that light might be thrown on still another problem in the same sphere.

In the early days of the silent film, a film was made about Paganini, with Conrad Veidt in the title role. The wizard fiddler is put in prison but he fiddles himself out again. His playing is bewitching—the enchanted turnkeys get out of his path and his violin paralyzes all resistance to his escape. The crowd outside, charmed by his music, opens a path for the fiddler and his fiddle.

In this film the inaudible playing of a violin had a dramaturgical function, because it influenced the hero's fate, freed him from his prison. As a spectacle, it made a fine and convincing scene, precisely because it was silent! The dumbshow of a great actor made us imagine violin playing so enchanting that hardened jailers dropped their weapons. How great a virtuoso would have been required to play the violin in a sound film to achieve this? Visible, inaudible music existing only in the imagination could have a magic effect. The effect of music actually heard would depend on the public's musical sensibility and taste, a quantity susceptible of innumerable variations. But to make it credible that music did actually charm the rough jailers, it would have to have a like effect on the whole of the audience. It is not by chance that the sound film has not yet touched the Paganini theme.

Petersburg Night, made by the Russian Grigori Roshal, also has a musician hero. Here the varying effect on the audience is not due to the quality of the playing but to the nature of the music played. The Russian violinist plays folk songs and the society ladies and gentlemen in the best seats do not like it and boo, while the poorer patrons in the gallery are enthusiastic. Just as the scene in the Paganini film was possible only in a silent film, so the scene from the Russian picture is possible only in a sound film, for we must hear the songs and experience their spirit to know why they delight one part of the audience and infuriate the other. This scene characterizes not only the music but the audience listening to it, and in addition to its dramaturgical function, it also has a profound ideological significance.

SOUNDS AS DRAMATIS PERSONAE

But it is not only music that can have a dramaturgical function in a sound film. For instance: a sailor is saying goodbye to his family. His wife, rocking a cradle, begs him to stay home. But the sea, the great rival for his affections, is visible through the window. The sailor hesitates. Then two sounds are heard, like two rival seducers. A soft lullaby sung by the woman, and the summoning murmur of the sea. In the picture, one now sees only the sailor, and only his face, but it shows the conflict in his mind, the hard struggle within himself, evoked by these two sounds, these two calls. It is a dramatic, fate-deciding scene in which not a word is spoken. The woman's lullaby and the voice of the sea fight a duel for possession of a soul.

INFLUENCE OF ACCOMPANYING MUSIC

Sometimes the dramaturgical role of sound is indirect. A soldier is taking leave of a girl. The battlefield is near and the noise of bursting shells can be heard. The scene of leave-taking might have been shot without acoustic accompaniment. But it would certainly have gone a different way. For the girl, starting at every shellburst and influenced by the pictures conjured up by the danger, makes admissions which she would certainly not have made in a comfortable, safe, cozy room, or possibly not have become conscious of at all.

A BATTLE OF SOUNDS

The young film industry of Italy uses very fine, interesting dramaturgical sound effects, showing thereby once more that it is in the first rank of those who are now striving to re-create the film as an art. In Luigi Zampa's excellent anti-Fascist film *Vivere in pace*, the great central scene is built upon purely acoustic effects. A German corporal comes to the house of the Italian peasant who is harboring a wounded American Negro soldier. The soldier must be hidden away quickly. In their hurry, the peasant family can find no better place than the wine cellar. The German is feeling very comfortable, however, and stays on and on and cannot be induced to go. He asks for food and drink. He wants to have a good time. The Italian peasant and his family sit silent and yawning, trying to get rid of the German through boredom. But suddenly funny noises are heard from the wine cellar. The soldier, tired of being shut up in the cold and the dark, has broached a cask of wine and got drunk. The German pricks up his ears. Just as suddenly, the Italian peasants break into noisy cheerfulness, to drown out the dangerous noise. The drunken soldier smashes up everything in the cellar. The gentle, sober old peasant and his elderly wife begin to shout songs, yell, and dance and drag the German into a noisy debauch. Desperately they compete with the noises from the cellar. What follows is a battle between noises, a diabolical scene that grows all the more exciting as the soldier, who has run amok in the cellar, tries to get out, kicking and battering at the door. The shadow of death falls on the breathless, feverish merriment. Finally the soldier breaks down the door and the revelry, as if cut in two, freezes into mute, stiff immobility.

Even more moving is Vergano's sound scene in the film *Il Sole Sorge Ancora*. A priest, a member of the Resistance who has been condemned to death, is being taken to the place of execution by the Germans. A crowd collects along the road. The crowd grows larger, the ring surrounding the priest denser. The priest begins to pray, first softly, then more loudly, as he walks along. The camera follows with a tracking shot. The priest is visible all the time, but of the crowd no more than two or three faces are seen, as the priest and the camera pass them. The priest is reciting the litany. Two or three of the crowd whisper the response: "Ora pro nobis." The priest walks on and on, and the response grows louder. We see no more than two or three people, but we hear ever more and more, in an ominous crescendo. The scene remains a close-up, and no crowd is shown, but more and more voices answer "Ora pro nobis." We hear the swelling of sound like the roaring of a torrent. It is the audible revolt of the people; its menacing power and emotion turns into a formidable acoustic symbol, precisely because we cannot see the crowd. If we saw the crowd, then the storm of voices would be explained, for the voices of so many people could scarcely be less loud. But then the sound would lose its particular significance. The film could never show a crowd of such size as we are made to experience in that isolated, symbolic sound not contained by any real space. This is the voice of the nation and yet we hear it in a close-up of the martyr-priest, as an answer to the mute play of his features.

I do not say that such a decisive dramaturgical role for sound is indispensable in every sound film. As the silent film has ceased to exist, the sound film must operate with many different kinds of stories. The sound film today is not a specific kind of film but the whole of what there is of the film, and hence the specific style of one sort of film cannot be obligatory for it. It must present everything that comes along. Still, it is a pity that the sound film has almost completely dropped the cultivation of sound effects.

PROBLEM OF THE SOUND PLAY

This is a good opportunity to discuss the form problem of the sound play in general. Wireless plays are impossible without verbal explanations and descriptions of the scene. We cannot understand even words in their exact sense if we cannot see the facial expression and gestures of those who speak. For the spoken word contains only a fragment of human expression. People talk not just with their mouths. The glance, a twitching of a muscle in the face, movements of the hands speak at the same time, and all of them together add up to the exact shade of meaning intended. The word is merely one of the tones in a rich chord, so we do not understand even the word in its precise meaning if we cannot see who said it and when, in what circumstances and in what connection. As for the sounds of nature, we know them so little that we often fail to recognize them unless we see what is emitting them. A farmhouse may in a pinch be represented by voices of animals. But even then the listener will not be able to say whether the mooing of cows, neighing of horses, crowing of cocks, cackling of hens, barking of dogs represent some bucolic farm or a livestock market. Even recognizable sounds merely indicate the generality of the things they stand for. But the life of all image-art is in the concrete, exact presentation of the individuality of things.

The rustling of a forest or the noise of the sea cannot always be distinguished—in fact, the rustling of paper and the dragging of a sack along a stone floor are deceptively similar to them. Our ear is not yet sufficiently sensitive. It is the sound film that will train it, just as the silent film trained our eye. A hunter would recognize sounds in the forest which the city dweller would not. But, on the whole, most of us would not even find our way about in our own homes if we had to rely on our ears alone.

For this reason, radio plays always explain in one way or another what we are supposed to "see," and the sounds in a radio presentation are merely acoustic illustrations of a narrated scene or a scene made intelligible by words.

THE PICTURE FORMS THE SOUND

In a sound film there is no need to explain the sounds. We apprehend together with the word the glance, the smile, the gesture, the whole chord of expression, the exact nuance. Together with the sounds and voices of things, we see their physiognomy. The noise of a machine has a different coloring for us if we see the whirling machinery at the same time that we hear it. The sound of a wave is different if we see the wave's movement. Just as the shade and value of a color changes according to what other colors are next to it in a painting, so the timbre of a sound changes in accordance with the physiognomy or gesture of the visible source of the sound, experienced along with the sound itself in a sound film in which acoustic and optical impressions are linked into a whole.

In a radio play, the stage has to be described in words, because sound alone does not create space.

SILENCE

Silence, too, is an acoustic effect, but only where sounds can be heard. Silence is one of the most specific dramatic effects of the sound film. No other art can reproduce silence; neither painting nor sculpture, neither literature nor the silent film can do so. Even on the stage, silence occurs only rarely as a dramatic effect, and then only for short moments. Radio plays cannot make us feel the depths of silence at all, because when no sounds come from our set, the whole performance has ceased, as we cannot see any silent continuation of the action. The sole material of the wireless play being sound, the result of the cessation of sound is not silence but just nothing.

SILENCE AND SPACE

Things that we see as being different from each other appear even more different when they emit sounds. They all *sound* different, but they are all silent in the same way. There are thousands of different sounds and voices, but the substance of silence appears one and the same for all. That is, at first hearing. Sound differentiates visible things; silence brings them closer to each other and makes them less dissimilar. Every painting shows this happy harmony, the hidden common language of mute things conversing with each other, recognizing each other's shapes and entering into relations with each other in a composition common to them all. This was a great advantage the silent film had over the sound film. For its silence was not mute; it was given a voice in the background music, and landscapes and men and the objects surrounding them were shown on the screen against this common musical background. This made them speak a common silent language and we could feel their irrational conversation in the music that was common to them all.

But the silent film could reproduce silence only by roundabout means. On the theatrical stage, cessation of the dialogue does not touch off the great emotional experience of silence, because the space of the stage is too small for that, and the experience of silence is essentially a space experience.

How do we perceive silence? By hearing nothing? That is a mere negative. Yet man has few experiences more positive than the experience of silence. Deaf people do not know what it is. But if a morning breeze blows the sound of a cock crowing over to us from the neighboring village; if from the top of a high mountain we hear the tapping of a woodcutter's ax far below in the valley; if we can hear the crack of a whip a mile away—then we are hearing the silence around us. We feel the silence when we can hear the most distant sound or the slightest rustle near us. Silence is when the buzzing of a fly on the windowpane fills the whole room with sound, and the ticking of a clock smashes time into fragments with sledge-hammer blows. The silence is greatest when we can hear very distant sounds in a very large space. The widest space is our own if we can hear right across it and the noise of the alien world reaches us from beyond its boundaries. A completely sound-less space on the contrary never appears quite concrete or quite real to our perception; we feel it to be weightless and unsubstan-tial, for what we merely see is only a vision. We accept seen space as real only when it contains sounds as well, for these give it the dimension of depth.

On the stage, a silence which is the reverse of speech may have a dramaturgical function, as for instance if a noisy company sud-denly falls silent when a new character appears. But such a silence cannot last longer than a few seconds; otherwise it curdles, as it were, and seems to stop the performance. On the stage, the effect of silence cannot be drawn out or made to last.

In the film, silence can be extremely vivid and varied, for al-though it has no voice, it has very many expressions and gestures. A silent glance can speak volumes; its soundlessness makes it more expressive because the facial movements of a silent figure may ex-plain the reason for the silence, make us feel its weight, its men-ace, its tension. In the film, silence does not halt action even for an instant, and silent action gives even silence a living face.

The physiognomy of men is more intense when they are silent. More than that, in silence even things drop their masks and seem to look at you with wide-open eyes. If a sound film shows us any object surrounded by the noises of everyday life and then suddenly cuts out all sound and brings the object up to us in isolated close-up, then the physiognomy of that object takes on a significance and tension that seems to provoke and invite the event which is to follow.

DRAMATURGICAL FUNCTION OF SOUND IN THE SHOT

If dramaturgy is the teaching of the laws of dramatic action, is it possible to speak about dramaturgy in connection with a single shot? Does not the most energetic action manifest itself only in the sequence, in the interrelation of varying conditions following each other? Well, the film has nothing to do with the classic prob-lem of the ancient Greek philosophers who asked whether move-

ment consisted of a series of distinct conditions and whether a series of static conditions could ever become motion. For although
each frame of the film is a snapshot of a separate motionless condition, our eye does not perceive it so. What we see is motion. The
motion picture is what it is because even the shortest shot shows
movement. The smallest particle of action, be it internal or external action, is always action, the optical manifestation of which is
movement—even within one and the same shot. This is how it
strikes our senses and our consciousness, and this is what matters
in art. The specific task of the film is to seize on and localize by
means of close-ups the very instants when the decisive, initiating,
or direction-changing impulses enter the action.

However extensive an event is, however vast its scale, there has
somewhere been some small spark which was the immediate cause
of the explosion; a pebble must have loosened somewhere and
started the landslide. These dramaturgically decisive particles of
time can be presented by the film in a single shot. It can show the
one man on whom it all turned, at the very instant which matters:
that last-but-one second of hesitation in a glance of the eye, the
one gesture in which the final resolve manifests itself. All this the
film can separate by a close-up from the more general picture of
the scene in which the causal course of the whole process is shown
from beginning to end. In such fatal, decisive close-ups, sound too
can play a cardinal dramaturgical part.

Moments when a man is alerted by a slight noise, or hears a
word, may be of fatal significance. The close-up will show the face
and let us hear the sound too. It will show the drama enacted on
the face and at the same time let us hear its cause and explanation. This is done in two planes, with counterpointed effects.

SOUND-EXPLAINING PICTURES

Not only the microdramatics expressed in the microphysiog-
nomy of the face can be made intelligible by the sound which
causes it. Such a close-up-plus-sound can have the inverse effect.
The close-up of a listener's face can explain the sound he hears.
We might perhaps not notice the significance of some sound or
noise if we did not see its effect in the mirror of a human face.
For instance, we hear the screaming of a siren. Such a sound does

not acquire a dramatic significance unless we can see from the expression on a human face that it is a danger signal, or a call to revolt. We may hear the sound of sobbing, but how deep its meaning is will become evident only from the expression of sympathy and understanding appearing on some human face. Further, the acoustic character of a sound we understand is different too. We hear the sound of a siren differently if we know that it is a warning of deadly peril.

The face of a man listening to music may also show two kinds of things. The reflected effect of the music may throw light into the human soul; it may also throw light on the music itself and suggest by means of the listener's facial expression some experience touched off by this musical effect. If the director shows us a close-up of the conductor while an invisible orchestra is playing, not only can the character of the music be made clear by the dumb-show of the conductor; his facial expression may also give an interpretation of the sounds and convey it to us. And the emotion produced in a human being by music and demonstrated by a close-up of a face can enhance the power of a piece of music in our eyes far more than any added decibels.

ASYNCHRONOUS SOUND

In a close-up in which the surroundings are not visible, a sound that seeps into the shot sometimes impresses us as mysterious, simply because we cannot see its source. It produces the tension arising from curiosity and expectation. Sometimes the audience does not know what the sound is they hear, but the character in the film can hear it, turn his face toward the sound, and see its source before the audience does. This handling of picture and sound provides rich opportunities for effects of tension and surprise.

Asynchronous sound (that is, in which there is a discrepancy between the things heard and the things seen in the film) can acquire considerable importance. If the sound or voice is not tied up with a picture of its source, it may grow beyond the dimensions of the latter. Then it is no longer the voice or sound of some chance thing, but appears as a pronouncement of universal validity. Earlier I mentioned the "Ora pro nobis," in the fine Italian film, which grows into such a storm of popular protest and indignation in the close-ups that a picture of even the most vast crowd that

could be photographed would only diminish the effect. The surest
way a director can convey the pathos or symbolical significance of
sound or voice is asynchronously.

INTIMACY OF SOUND

Acoustic close-ups make us perceive sounds which are part of
the accustomed noise of day-to-day life but which we never hear as
individual sounds because they are drowned in the general din.
Possibly they even have an effect on us, but this effect never becomes conscious. If a close-up picks out such a sound and thereby
makes us aware of its effect, then at the same time its influence on
the action will have been made manifest.

On the stage, such things are impossible. If a theatrical producer
wanted to direct the attention of the audience to a scarcely audible sigh, because that sigh expresses a turning point in the action,
then all the other actors in that scene would have to be very quiet,
or else the actor who is to sigh would have to be brought forward
to the footlights. All this, however, would cause the sigh to lose its
essential character, which is that it is shy and retiring and must remain scarcely audible. As in the silent film so in the sound film,
scarcely perceptible, intimate things can be conveyed with all the
secrecy of the unnoticed eavesdropper. Nothing need be silenced
to demonstrate such sounds for all to hear—and yet they can be
kept intimate. The general din can go on; it may even drown completely a sound like the soft piping of a mosquito, but we can get
quite close to the source of the sound with the microphone and
with our ear and hear it nevertheless.

Subtle associations and interrelations of thoughts and emotions
can be conveyed by means of very low, soft sound effects. Such
emotional or intellectual linkages can play a decisive dramaturgical
part. They may be anything—the ticking of a clock in an empty
room, a slow drip from a burst pipe, or the moaning of a little
child in its sleep.

SOUND CANNOT BE ISOLATED

In such close-ups of sound we must be careful, however, to bear
in mind the specific nature of sound, which never permits sound
to be isolated from its acoustic environment as a close-up shot can

be isolated from its surroundings. For what is not within the film frame cannot be seen by us, even if it is immediately beside the things that are seen. Light or shadow can be thrown into the picture from outside and the outline of a shadow can betray to the spectator what is outside the frame but still in the same sector of space, although the picture will show only a shadow. In sound, things are different. An acoustic environment inevitably encroaches on the close-up shot, and what we hear in this case is not a shadow or a beam of light but the sounds themselves, which can always be heard throughout the whole space of the picture, however small a section of that space is included in the close-up. Sounds cannot be blocked out.

Music played in a restaurant cannot be completely cut out if a special close-up of, say, two people softly talking together in a corner is to be shown. The band may not always be seen in the picture, but it will always be heard. Nor is there any need to silence the music altogether in order that we may hear the soft whispering of the two people as if we were sitting in their immediate vicinity. The close-up will contain the whole acoustic atmosphere of the restaurant space. Thus we will hear not only the people talking; we will also hear what relation their talking has to the sounds all around them. We will be able to place their talking in its acoustic environment.

Such sound-pictures are often used in the film for the purpose of creating an atmosphere. Just as the film can show visual landscapes, so it can show acoustic landscapes, a tonal milieu.

EDUCATING THE EAR

Our eye recognizes things even if it has seen them only once or twice. Sounds are much more difficult to recognize. We know far more visual forms than sound forms. We are used to finding our way about the world without the conscious assistance of our hearing. But without sight we are lost. Our ear, however, is no less sensitive; it is only less educated than our eye. Science tells us, in fact, that the ear can distinguish more delicate nuances than the eye. The number of sounds and noises a human ear can distinguish runs into many thousands—far more than the shades of color and degrees of light we can distinguish. There is, however, a considerable difference between perceiving a sound and identifying its source. We may be aware that we are hearing a different sound than before, without knowing to whom or what the sound belongs. We may have more difficulty in perceiving things visually, but we recognize them more easily once we have perceived them. Erdmann's experiments showed that the ear can distinguish innumerable shades and degrees in the noise of a large crowd, yet it could not tell with certainty whether the noise was that of a merry or an angry crowd.

There is a very considerable difference between our visual and our acoustic education. One of the reasons for this is that we so often see without hearing. We see things from afar, through a windowpane, on pictures, on photographs. But we very rarely hear the sounds of nature and of life without seeing something. We are not accustomed, therefore, to draw conclusions about visual things from sounds we hear. This defective education of our hearing makes it possible to create many surprising effects in a sound film. We hear a hiss in the darkness. A snake? A human face on the screen turns in terror toward the sound and the spectators tense in their seats. The camera, too, turns toward the sound. And behold! the hiss is that of a kettle boiling on the gas ring.

Such surprising letdowns may be tragic too. In such a case the slow approach and the slow recognition of the sound may cause a far more terrifying tension than the approach of something seen and therefore instantly recognized. The roar of an oncoming flood or landslide, cries of grief or terror which we discern and distinguish only gradually, impress us with the inevitability of catastrophe in almost irresistible intensity. These great possibilities for dramatic effect stem from the fact that a slow and gradual process of recognition can symbolize the desperate resistance of the consciousness to understand a reality which is audible but which the consciousness is reluctant to accept.

SOUNDS THROW NO SHADOW

Auditive culture can be increased like any other, and the sound film is very suitable to educate our ear. There are, however, definite limits to the possibilities of finding our way about the world purely by sound, without any visual impressions. The reason for this is that sounds throw no shadows—in other words, sounds cannot produce shapes in space. Things which we see we must see side by side; if we do not, one of them covers up the other so that it cannot be seen. Visual impressions do not blend with each other. Sounds are different; if several of them are present at the same time, they merge into one common composite sound. We can see the dimension of space and see a direction in it. But we cannot *hear* either dimension or direction. A quite unusual, rare sensitivity of ear, the so-called absolute, is required to distinguish the several sounds which make up a composite noise. But their place in space, the direction of their source, cannot be discerned even by a perfect ear, if no visual impression is present to help.

It is one of the basic form problems of the radio play that sound alone cannot represent space and hence cannot alone represent a stage.

SOUNDS HAVE NO SIDES

It is difficult to localize sound, and a film director must take this fact into account. If three people are talking together in a film and they are placed so that we cannot see the movements of their mouths, and if they do not accompany their words by gestures, it is almost impossible to know which of them is talking, unless the voices are very different. For sounds cannot be beamed as precisely as light can be directed by a reflector. There are no straight and concentrated sound beams as there are rays of light.

Visible things have shapes with several sides, right side and left side, front and back. Sound has no such aspects; a sound strip will not tell us from which side the shot was made.

SOUND HAS A SPACE COLORING

Every natural sound reproduced by art on the stage or on the platform always takes on a false tone coloring, for it always assumes the coloring of the space in which it is presented to the public and not of the space which it is supposed to reproduce. If we hear a storm, the howling of the wind, a clap of thunder, etc., on the stage, we always hear it in the timbre proper to the stage, not in the timbre proper to the forest, or ocean, or whatnot the scene is supposed to represent. If, say, a choir sings in a church on the stage, we cannot hear the unmistakable resonance of Gothic arches; for every sound bears the stamp of the space in which it is actually produced.

Every sound has a space-bound character of its own. The same sound sounds different in a small room, in a cellar, in a large empty hall, in a street, in a forest, or at sea.

Every sound which is really produced somewhere must of necessity have some space quality, and this is a very important quality indeed if use is to be made of the sensual reproducing power of sound! It is this *timbre local* of sound which is necessarily always falsified on the theatrical stage. One of the most valuable artistic faculties of the microphone is that sounds shot at the point of origin are perpetuated by it and retain their original tonal coloring. A sound recorded in a cellar remains a cellar sound even if it is played back in a motion-picture theater, just as a film shot preserves the viewpoint of the camera, whatever the spectator's viewpoint in the cinema auditorium may be. If the picture was taken from above, the spectators will see the object from above, even if they have to look up to the screen and not down. Just as our eye is identified with the camera lens, so our ear is identified with the microphone and we hear the sounds as the microphone originally heard them, irrespective of where the sound film is being shown and the sound reproduced. In this way, in the sound film, the fixed, immutable, permanent distance between spectator and actor is eliminated not only visually, as already mentioned, but acoustically as well. Not only as spectators, but as listeners too, we are transferred from our seats to the space in which the events depicted on the screen are taking place.

Theory of the Film, 1953

Treatment of Sound in The City

Henwar Rodakiewicz

The conception of the function of sound in film is a very definite one. Whether it be music, narration, or voices treated in a musical pattern, sound is always an integral part of the film. It should be always additive, never merely repetitive. In other words, nowhere during the course of a film do picture and sound say the same thing; rather, they complement each other. Thus the picture seen without sound, or the sound heard without picture, is an incomplete experience, since neither one is intended to be self-sufficient. It is only in the fusion of the two elements that film springs to life and becomes a vital unit.

Such a point of view has been held since the very beginning and is to be found in the development of the shooting script and in the subsequent and eventual cutting of the material itself. To give variety, interest, and greater scope to the work, two distinct types of continuity have been borne in mind consistently: (1) a continuity of picture, accompanied by sound; and (2) a continuity of sound, accompanied by picture.

The first may be described as a series of interconnected events whose logical development is depicted in more or less continuous action—i.e., a self-evident story told in motion pictures: in sequence A, the farmer driving to the blacksmith's in his wagon; in sequence E, the progress of the baseball game.

The second would be a series of visual images, following and expressing the development of a thought continuity, free to move and jump far afield and not concerned with or limited by any sequence of physical action. Such is the conception of that part of sequence E in which the film leaves the rather tightly knit episodes in Greenbelt and enlarges its scope to include the other Greenbelts of the world, both existent and planned for the future, along with their places of work and civic centers, visualized in a framework of decentralization.

A word may be said here concerning the relative proportion of music and narration in the film. An absolute minimum of spoken words is desirable, and the film is so planned, since the story is told both directly and by inference mainly through picture continuity. Totaled—but, at the most, one third of the final cut length of the film will follow voice continuity.

Given such a conception of the use of sound in this film, it is evident that sound here will serve as a theme with variations—as in the case of the special contrapuntal treatment of voice and picture at the end of the film. And these variations in turn require carefully worked-out transitions. Any purely arbitrary shift from one type of sound to another immediately reveals the superficial and unrelated nature of that sound, since its roots must then be sheared from any close relation to the pictured image. In this film, in every case, the emergence of the narrator's voice from a sequence of music, or the re-introduction of a musical accompaniment, is clearly and intimately related to the changing visual images. These transitions therefore spring from the scene itself and for this reason are smooth and natural.

As a simple illustration of this, one might cite an example in the early portion of sequence E. There we have been dealing with the various means of decentralization, in a continuity of the narrator's voice accompanied by swift images of transportation facilities, together with images of the distribution of electrical power. The camera ends on a close shot of the motor of a transport plane just as it is turned over by the starter. As it fires, the magnificent roar quite naturally drowns out the voice, and we take off for Greenbelt, where the new continuity requires only music to give it greater expression.

Such, in general, is the function of sound in this picture. In order to understand it more thoroughly, it might be well to regard each sequence in the picture individually.

SEQUENCE A (NEW ENGLAND)

From the very beginning of the film, with its title cards on New England backgrounds, through the simple theme of the farmer and his son driving to the village, pausing at the ford, then continuing to the smithy, up to the point where the boy runs to read the notice the sexton is tacking on the wall, there is only music. That music sings the counterpart of what the pictures are saying —simple, friendly, green, peaceful, old New England. To use words here would criminally destroy the lyric quality we are attempting to establish and would violate an aspect of our basic concept—which is never to let sound detract from picture continuity. One can say only one thing at a time, and we are saying it here in terms of a simple picture story, but a very important one, since it is of the very essence of the film, the foundation of our thesis, which must reach the audience in a pure and readily acceptable form and touch them deeply.

When the sign is being tacked up, with the boy watching and the sexton turning to smile at him, the music fades and a church bell begins tolling. We cut to a church and then to the interior scene of a town meeting. The sound of the bell fades, or perhaps merely recedes and continues as a curtain-like background, and the narrator's voice begins. It is the first spoken word in the picture and arises quite logically from the fact that a town meeting is in progress. The camera stays with the meeting for a bit and then swings in what might be termed a mild and leisurely montage through various aspects of the New England scene—weaving, scything, basketmaking, the milling of corn, and so on—ending with another shot of a church, which brings the sound of the tolling bell to the fore again as the narrator's voice fades. Thus, this whole episode is very definitely bounded and treated as an interlude in the story continuity of the farmer and his son. The duration of this little exploratory and descriptive survey should not be more than two minutes. This means that approximately 300 words can be spoken comfortably.

Here the question arises: what shall these words be? To give a listing of old barter and trade figures, old regulations and resolutions, would not seem quite in the mood of what the New England sequence has to say. Given adequate space for their recitation, they might perhaps, through indirection, reflect something of the time. But it would seem far more suitable to draw material from such sources as Horace Bushnell's discourse in 1851, or from Samuel Sewall's diary (the American equivalent of Pepys)—using either outright quotations or perhaps transposing and compressing and giving new form to the material. By doing this, one could very well give an interesting and descriptive personal account of, let us say, the events transpiring during the course of several days' time in the life of an early New Englander. Naturally, the incidents would be carefully chosen to heighten the feeling of charm and intimacy and community life, and when spoken against the visual background outlined above would most certainly lend reality to a kind of homespun quality.

Not only is it unnecessary that picture and sound deal literally with identical subject matter; it is highly inadvisable. The continuity here is one of voice, and the film images serve as background, very definitely played to reinforce mood and feeling.

As the voice ends, the sound of the church bell comes back to full volume and almost immediately dissolves, musically speaking, into the ringing of the anvil. This is heard as the camera shifts to the exterior of the blacksmith shop—from which point we gently pick up and carry forward the picture-story continuity. Music is born of the anvil beats—and as the camera moves closer and closer to the red-hot iron, the music becomes the more intense and ringing. At the last, completely blinding flash of sparks, we cut to:

SEQUENCE B (INDUSTRY)

And suddenly we are enveloped in the huge, fiery display of tons of molten metal pouring into a large ladle in a modern steel mill. The music will emphasize the change in scale.

This sequence is so shot and so put together that the pictures tell their own story. Beginning with a brief impression of great dark caverns filled with sputtering steel and smoke against which the shadows of men move in their work, passing through the belching, vomiting, spewing that is the exterior aspect of the steel mills, the sequence quickly moves in a logical progression to the surrounding homes of the workers and to their families. Perched on hillsides, squeezed in congestion, suffocated by smoke, the children play on the railway tracks and the mothers pump their drinking water a few paces from the rows of open privies.

Though not tightly bound together by any specific sequence of action, the continuity of subject matter is very apparent, and was purposely so treated as a direct contrast to the single gentle line followed in New England. Narrative is unnecessary, for the images are brutally vivid. Any words that could be said—whether a cold, matter-of-fact account of the development of the Monongahela Valley and the growing demand for steel, or excerpts from the annual reports of the large steel industries (incredible as they would sound spoken against the pictures), or any words at all—would surely distort the purpose of this sequence, for, because of the juxtaposition and contrast of words and picture, they would inevitably resolve themselves into a cynical and one-sided commentary, which is neither a completely true representation of the scene nor our aim in this sequence. So music is all that is needed on the sound track. The pictures will speak for themselves and tell their story far more vividly and honestly.

SEQUENCE C (METROPOLIS)

Music will form the basis of the sound in this sequence. Natural effects, such as sirens, whistles, bells, elevated trains, also appear. But, in addition to the music and the natural sounds, voices are heard. However, the voices and the distinct words they speak are in no sense narration, as we commonly accept the term. Instead, the voices—perhaps a good half dozen easily distinguishable—are treated as if they were part of the musical score. That is, we think of them as added instruments to the orchestra. They emerge from the background, overlap their themes, and subside again, just as do the oboes or cellos or French horns as they follow the score. They are in no sense superimposed word effects but are a genuine and integral part of the orchestra. We must have the feeling that the speakers are sitting among the players and that their words are written for and interwoven with the music.

As an illustration, we might take the voices' first appearance in this sequence. The camera has been one with the morning crowd streaming from elevated trains, hurrying from ferries, erupting from subways, squeezing into buildings. It enters a building and shows rows of stenographers, flying fingers, darting keys. Voices take up the mad rhythm, speaking the stereotyped closing phrases of business correspondence: "Most sincerely yours—" "We beg to remain—" "Trusting that we may hear—" We hear women's voices and men's voices, the secretaries and the executives, the small fry and the big shots. And as the camera cuts to the outside and rakes down an ever faster series of ascending geometrical patterns of identical windows, the voices build in number and tempo and staggering intensity until the camera reaches a passing elevated train below, whose infernal din drowns them out.

Or, to use another example, when the camera is concentrating on the "congested" signs (instead of showing the actual accident) we hear the rapidly approaching gong of the ambulance. And as we see the intern step off and the injured man being bundled in, we hear voices again: "Calling Dr. Bixby—fractured pelvis—lacerations of the scalp—" "Dr. Buttenheim—internal injuries—" and so on. This undertone of sound, together with the ambulance bell, again gives an ominous meaning and background to the scenes of the children playing in the traffic-jammed streets, and later to the hapless man trying to cross the street in the face of onrushing cars.

And again during the lunch-hour interlude, a voice fugue will be worked out, using the extraordinary appellations given short orders, as counterpoint to the hectic scene. It would seem essential to work in close collaboration with the composer in all these word episodes, for the rhythm of the sounds must be of a piece with the music accompanying them.

The sound transition from the breaking pane of glass to the startled pigeons, and the anticipation of the fire engine by hearing the alarm first, is of course an obvious one, as is the church bell ringing over the deserted downtown streets. But the whole sequence is filled with unusual opportunities for the use of sound both as a link and as a contrast and throughout as an extremely important element in the portrayal of the congestion, hurry, inhumanity, and hazards of the metropolis.

SEQUENCE D (HIGHWAY)

Though occasionally there is need to use natural sound effects such as the screeching of skidding tires, the impact of a collision, the blast of raucous horns, this sequence, as in B, is essentially a musical sequence. Really even more fundamentally so, for, as outlined briefly in the introductory note in the shooting script, its form and pattern rest very definitely on the musical framework. Though the arrangement of shots does follow a rough continuity, the reason for their placement, relation to each other, and duration on the screen arises from the meaning and logic of the music. The fine final cutting will be done to match the score, to portray with precision the musical themes as they are developed. Thus, the basic significance and meaning of the sequence is carried in the unfolding of the music, and the images on the screen are the visual expression thereof, an expression at once ghastly and ludicrous, frenzied and static, spirited and frustrated. From the very beginning, which follows on the heels of the tolling church bell over the deserted city streets—the very first shots of cars suddenly dancing gaily toward the camera, only to stop as abruptly in the traffic jam whose end is never seen—to the frantic roller-coaster episode at the end, over which the stuck automobile horn blares its interminable blasphemy, the sequence is of complete homogeneity of sound and picture.

It is to be noted that though this sequence may seem to be in the nature of comic relief—an interlude—following the insistent pressure the metropolis has brought to bear, it serves a greater function as well. Because of the sudden and unexpected transition to the sequence on the highway, the metropolis scene never really reaches a climax. In fact, it is the purpose of this sequence to serve as climax. It builds steadily and surely and crystallizes all the agony and despair documented in the metropolis sequence, until in utter hopelessness it fades out at the end.

SEQUENCE E (GREENBELT)

It is in this sequence that we have the bulk of the narration to be heard in the picture. Its presence arises as definitely and structurally from the filmic construction as did its absence in other sequences. It is inherent in the treatment of the material—material which deals not only with "what is" but to a much greater extent with "what can be." It looks to the future—and for the sake of clarity and to increase the scope of the conception, it seems wise to follow, in much of the sequence, a narrative continuity. However, visual continuity also has its place (both important and inviolate) in this section of the film.

A point of significance should be mentioned here. It is essential that the narrator be chosen for a certain special quality of fluidness, clarity, and resonance of voice. His voice should be recognizable instantly and never possibly confused with any other voice in the film. Furthermore, his voice will always represent the "good," whether past, present, or future. It will be he who speaks in the New England interlude, and he will not be heard from again until this sequence, which, speaking whenever there is need for narration, he will carry through to the end. Here the previous use of his voice only in terms of the "good" will reach a climax with the ending of the film. For not only will he help to tie New England with Greenbelt, but as the "voice of Greenbelt"—and all the Greenbelts of the world—he will represent and defend them against the verbal assaults of the doubters and attackers.

The last sequence ended with a complete fade-out, of scene and music both. This one fades in with a crescendo of clean fresh music on a quick montage of water spilling over dams, electric switches being thrown, streamlined trains getting under way, and finally a gleaming transport plane taking off. As the plane flies through a cloud, the drone of the engine fades, then the ship emerges again and the narrator's voice begins—the voice of the "good" speaking from the sky. The narration continues while the film makes a quick magic-carpet trip to various "Greenbelts," using the new means of transportation and communication—planes, radio, fast trains, and superhighways. In general outline and feeling, the spoken words should be as follows:

"New trails in the sky—swift, sure, not merely to humble time and conquer space but to change the towns and cities from old to new, to lift them from their drab confines and spread them in the open, where there is air to breathe and trees to grow, where there is life worth living and sun for children to play in.

"New trails for new towns—planned from the beginning, planned with a respect for the present, with a vision for the future. Arranged, composed, drafted, built, to meet the needs of living, the means of livelihood, the quality of ease and rest and recreation.

"New means of communication to link these cities that are never large and monstrous, to link them with each other and with their smaller satellites, to make them one in purpose and effect.

"New fast ways of transportation to make the bond complete. Old industries that cannot move their roots are reached by these —by trails of iron and concrete. By new divided highways; bridges; cloverleafs. Through underpasses, bypasses; along the new divided network; buses cutting time: Greentown to Steeltown, 30 miles; Greentown to Steeltown, 30 minutes."

And as the camera draws close to the spinning tire, its shrill song drowns out the voice. The sound continues as we dissolve to a large water-power dam and becomes subtly the whining of the generators. And as the camera cuts rapidly to banks of shining transformers, high-tension towers, and hurtles along them to a factory, the whine that has become a piercing shriek descends in rapid steps, as does the electricity, until it is a pleasant hum. Again the camera cuts back to the gleaming towers, and this time (and covering the subsequent times the camera repeats this process) the narrator begins to speak again:

"Power—power—new power, instant power, distant power. Power to reach into the land wherever man may wish—far from its source, close to man's needs. Power tapped from threads in the sky, from volts and amperes, from 220,000 to 110—

"Power for industry—spread in the open, near towns in the green. In clean paths through the mountains—flying over fields, striding the valleys, an ever spreading network of light and mastery. Power—controlled, sootless, wasteless, soundless—so split asunder the tight waddings of humanity, spread them, decentralize them, to give them air and light and space, to free them from crushing suffocation—"

The last factory touched upon in this rapid series of journeys is an airplane factory, and as the ship warms up to take off, the roar of its motors drowns out the voice. Once in the air, the drone subsides and, gently, music begins. Almost immediately we are over

Greenbelt, and we plunge into the detailed sequence that is played there. The continuity is strictly visual, and so music is the only element on the sound track and no further comment is needed.

This continues for almost the entire Greenbelt episode. However, as the film reaches the point where the local newspaper is introduced and the man in the press picks up and glances at the news sheet, the narration begins again. With its aid, the camera covers a lot of ground, touching on the question of medical care in planned cities, the cost of homes, the community facilities.

As morning comes—together with the delivery of newspapers— we follow the men leaving for work, by car and by bus, from Greenbelt and other green cities; we follow them over the planned highways to ideal factories. And with the camera and in the narration we show what can be achieved in the way of civic centers, picnic grounds, and recreational developments of all kinds. Returning to the homes, where the wives are making use of the advantages provided by community planning, we pass on to the children in the schools. Here the narration will pause, for the visual images are all that is necessary to tell the story of progressive education in ideal surroundings.

As the camera finally moves up close to a child completing a drawing, and then as the drawing fills the screen—a drawing that is a child's concept of a lovely home in charming surroundings— and then as the camera swings slowly over to another drawing, another child's counterpart of hideous slum dwellings, we reach an important transition in the film. The music announces it as well. With swiftly building quick shots of incredible housing conditions, we land suddenly on a contrasted shot of a planned city. Immediately a savage voice bursts forth in denunciation, and then as the narrator—the voice of the "good"—parries, the camera sees only the ugly side. This important contrapuntal concept is worked out in great detail in the shooting script and cannot be illustrated as well here. But of the utmost significance is the treatment of the voices. As noted in the script, the whole group—of perhaps five or six—is conceived as being all in the same room together, firing volleys of abuse and cynical doubt, often overlapping in their eagerness, while the voice of the narrator breaks in from time to time, never ruffled, always steady and sure. The dialogue as outlined in the script needs only development to make it complete.

The final words of the narrator: "We have in us the ever widening knowledge of the sciences, the power to control our environment, the challenge to overcome disease, diseases of the body, diseases of society. We have the intelligence and the understanding, we have the means whereby, the power and the ability . . ." are indeed meant to stand, and with a final swelling of music the film comes to an end.

From unpublished notes to the film

Music in the Movies

KURT WEILL

The American movie audience is getting music-conscious. Scores of successful pictures are being discussed at cocktail parties almost in the same way that ballet scores were discussed in the salons of Paris in the twenties. The recording firms release albums of music from outstanding pictures; composers write orchestral suites based on their picture scores; symphonic arrangements of themes from their scores are played over the radio. In the street I heard a young man whistling the theme that indicates d.t.'s moving in on poor Ray Milland; and somebody told me about a lady who closes her eyes as soon as she has taken her seat in the movie theater, so that she can listen to the music undisturbed by the pictures which are shown with it. Can it be that the movies, after having given a terrific boost to the art of popular songwriting, are now beginning to popularize the work of contemporary composers?

It would not be the first time in the history of music that a powerful institution became a sponsor for musical creation. The great polyphonic masters of the sixteenth century worked in the service of the Catholic Church; Bach had to write a cantata for the Sunday service in his church every week—and the early symphonic and operatic works of the eighteenth century were commissioned by European princes and aristocratic landowners for the entertainment of their guests. Today, in a more democratic world, music has become a powerful medium in the hands of those who provide entertainment for the masses. The men who make our movies are well aware of this. In their projection rooms they have seen many pictures without music, and they know how much the score helps to "warm up" the action of the picture, to heighten the emotional impact, to cover up weaknesses in the plot development or in the acting of certain scenes, and to hold together episodes which would seem quite disconnected without a musical bridge. They know that a scene which is slow and dragging can be made exciting with the proper musical treatment. They know that a good melody will move an audience when the words or the acting don't succeed.

As a clear indication of the importance which they attach to music, the Hollywood studios have built up large and very efficient musical departments. There are staffs of first-rate conductors, vocal coaches, arrangers and orchestrators, sound experts and technicians, with choral groups who have been especially trained for microphone singing, and orchestra musicians who can read anything at sight. I have been very much impressed in Hollywood with the amount of work, the craftsmanship, which goes into the recording of a score. I think that nowhere in the world is music rehearsed and prepared with such care, with such minute study of the musical problem at hand, as in the Hollywood sound-recording studios. The method that is being used here is the same one they use in every phase of the making of a picture, in the preparation of the script, in the actual shooting, and in the cutting. It is the method of detail. A picture is a mosaic of numerous small sequences, sometimes not longer than ten seconds, rarely more than two minutes. Each of these sequences is treated as a unit in itself and is prepared with the utmost care. The same is true for the musical treatment. A small piece of music is rehearsed at length until the orchestra is ready for a perfect rendition. The conductor has long discussions with the producer, the director, the sound man, the cutter, sometimes even with the composer, to determine what effect is needed and then the best way to achieve it. And many times there are changes, rewriting, rerecording.

From the standpoint of the composer, this urgent demand for music in the motion-picture industry means, of course, a great deal. There are not many markets for contemporary music, apart from so-called "popular music," in this country. There is practically no outlet for the American composer's operatic ambition, unless we succeed in creating such an outlet away from the opera houses. The radio offers very limited opportunities for original musical creation. The few available markets (concert, ballet, schools, theater) have too small a capacity to take care of an abundance of creative talent in this country. It is no wonder that many composers look to the movies as a possible solution of their problems. There is hardly any doubt that some day the motion picture will take its place beside the musical theater as a free, unrestricted outlet for a composer's imagination. This will be possible only when a formula for a truly musical picture is found and developed. But even today, in the limited field of background music for pictures, a considerable number of good composers find a welcome opportunity to write music (sometimes a great deal of it), to improve their technique by hearing their own music, to have large audiences become familiar with their style—and to make a good living. The position of music in general and of the contemporary composer in particular is rather encouraging if we consider the fact that the whole development of music in the movies is only about forty years old and that the whole field of "musical pictures" has hardly been scratched.

It all started with the pianist in the early movie theaters. He has become a part of history, often quoted, imitated, laughed at, and parodied. To most people of my age, the sound of the piano in the nickelodeons is a cherished childhood memory, and many times when we see one of those standard situations in a movie— the villain triumphing over his innocent victim; the daughter being expelled from her father's house; the mother being separated from her child—we are longing to hear again that tinny old worn-out piano, playing "The March of the Gladiators," "The Virgin's Prayer," or the *William Tell* overture. The fact remains that the silent movie needed music as a dry cereal needs cream.

In the years that followed, as the silent picture grew up into a full-fledged form of theatrical entertainment, its musical treatment became an important branch of the music industry. The large motion-picture theaters which sprang up in cities all over the world employed large orchestras, and wherever a good musician was in charge of these orchestras, he tried to arrange a clean, carefully

worked-out musical continuity for the picture, using the entire repertory of symphonic and operatic music. The leading theaters in
large cities had very good orchestras of symphonic size and a staff
of arrangers working overtime to have a complete score ready for
each picture.

Men like Hugo Riesenfeld and Erno Rapee created a technique
for the "underscoring" of a picture. They had the same basic aesthetic problem which our modern film composers are faced with:
should the music follow the dramatic action or emphasize the
emotional development of the picture? They chose a sort of mid-
dle-of-the-road solution with strong inclination toward the emotional development, which is still, basically, the way the problem
is solved in our musical departments. The larger studios provided
the theaters with lists of suggested musical numbers for their pictures. They also prepared stock repertories of short musical pieces
to be used for certain effects—train, thunderstorm, chase, revolution, etc. Some Hollywood studios sent out complete musical
scores with their pictures. Chaplin was especially interested in his
scores and spent a lot of time with his musical assistants to achieve
a musical mood in complete conformity with the mood of the picture. (I will never forget the haunting, bittersweet melody at the
end of *The Circus* when Chaplin disappears in the distance, a dis-
illusioned man, ready to face life.) In some cases young composers
wrote entire original scores for silent pictures. A score for the Russian picture *Potemkin*, by Meisel, created a sensation in Europe.
The International Music Festival in Baden-Baden in 1928 was ded-
icated to film music.

But, shortly after, the birth of the talking picture changed the
situation entirely. It is significant that the first talkie of world rep-
utation, *The Jazz Singer*, was a musical picture. Overnight, the
popular song had become an important ingredient of picture making. Hollywood studios bought entire song catalogues from music
publishers. Song writers, conductors, arrangers, dance directors
moved from Broadway to Hollywood.

At the same time, the producers and directors of dramatic, non-
musical pictures realized that a good underscoring job contributed
a great deal to the success of a picture and that the right sound-
track mixture of spoken dialogue, music, and sound effects was an
integral part of its production. This opened a new field for the

composer, and soon the big movie centers of the world created a new species of musician, the motion-picture composer. A number of young composers who showed a special talent for this kind of work have developed, with great skill, a sort of standard technique for the underscoring of pictures. A man like Alfred Newman, who must have scored hundreds of pictures, is a master in his field. Other excellent craftsmen whose names are familiar to the movie audiences are Steiner, Korngold, Rosza, Stothart, Young, and Waxman, to name only a few.

These men know, from years of experience, the requirements and the limitations of their work. They know that a good score, according to the producers, is one which you don't hear but which you would miss if it were not there. They know that there seems never to be enough time left for the scoring of a picture; that they never get more than four weeks, in most cases not more than two weeks, to do the job. They also know that their music will be mixed with dialogue and sound effects and that, since this proceeding is out of their control, many fine "effects" which they have worked on in their sleepless nights will be inaudible. Most of them write in the idiom of the early twentieth century, in the style of Richard Strauss, Debussy, Ravel, and Scriabin—partly because that is the musical language they have been brought up in, partly because the producers have accepted it as the "safest" kind of music. All of them prefer pictures with a lot of silent scenes where their music is "in the clear," undisturbed by dialogue. Sometimes they take too great advantage of those moments of freedom—in these cases their overpowering, voluptuous sounds are out of proportion to the action of the film. There seems to be a general tendency toward over-orchestrating in Hollywood pictures, and at times it is very disturbing to try to hear a quiet dialogue between two people fighting against an orchestra of sixty, with the brass going full blast over agitated figurations in the violins.

In addition to these "professional" scoring experts, the picture industry is using from time to time, and not nearly enough, the services of outstanding contemporary composers. Just as an important playwright or novelist adds originality and a certain freshness of approach to a movie script, an "outside" composer who loves the medium and is willing to accept its limitations can make important contributions in the field of film music. The French industry of the pre-war period, working for a small market, with a small budget, and therefore more inclined toward experiments, commissioned leading composers like Milhaud, Honegger, Auric. The result was an exceptionally high standard of music in French pictures and such outstanding scores as Honegger's *Mayerling*, Auric's *A Nous La Liberté*, Milhaud's *La Grande Illusion*. The great contribution which these French composers made was the underscoring of the scene with a musical composition of clearly definable form. Their music had a rather objective attitude toward the action of the picture, and sometimes they created a sort of contrapuntal effect by writing music in a mood opposite to the mood of the scene.

Hollywood also has used outside composers to great advantage. Aaron Copland's scores for *Of Mice and Men* and *Our Town* are perfect examples of creative music-writing for the movies. Other well-known composers who have had a stimulating influence on film music in Hollywood are George Antheil (*The Scoundrel, Angels over Broadway*, etc.), Werner Janssen (*The General Died at Dawn*), Bernard Herrmann (*All That Money Can Buy, Citizen Kane*), Alexander Tansman (*Flesh and Fantasy*), and Ernst Toch (*Peter Ibbetson*).

Yet one cannot help feeling that all the enthusiasm, all the hard work, all the ingenuity that goes into the making of these film scores, is, from the standpoint of the creative musician, more or less wasted, as long as the composer's task is not more than to provide a musical background for a picture which is completely finished at the time when he starts working. There cannot be any doubt that there are much more interesting, more ambitious, more genuinely creative opportunities awaiting the film composer. The motion picture is a perfect medium for an original musico-dramatic creation on the same level as the different forms of the musical theater: musical comedy, operetta, musical play, and opera. If we want to develop an art form (or a form of entertainment) in which music has an integral part, we have to allow the composer to collaborate in the musical theater.

There are three categories of motion pictures which already offer the composer a more active, more imaginative participation. The documentary films, which have been pioneers for new forms and techniques, have used music as an equal partner with picture and narration. They are in a position to do this because they are to a great extent silent pictures which leave room for music to express emotions, to set the tempo, to "speak." They allow the composer to use his own musical language, to employ different orchestra combinations, to write with the same originality and integrity as if he were writing for the concert or the theater. Louis Gruenberg's score for *The Fight for Life* is a masterwork in this category, a completely integrated piece of film dramatic music. In the same class belong works by Copland (*The City*), Virgil Thomson (*The River*), Marc Blitzstein (*Night Shift, Valley Town*), Hanns Eisler (*Forgotten Village*), and some excellent scores by young American composers for the O.W.I. film division.

Another important stepping stone toward a truly musical film is the animated cartoon. Here the music is actually written first and the characters are "animated" to the rhythm and accent of the music. The cartoon is the "ballet" among the different forms of movie entertainment, and some of the scores written for Disney's pictures are fine examples of popular ballet music.

Finally, in the field of the film musical itself, which is generally identified with a sort of glorified amplification of the musical-comedy format, there have been quite a number of very successful attempts at interweaving music and action into a satisfying unity. In René Clair's early pictures (*A Nous La Liberté, Le Million*), music and song grow out of the action to such an extent that we are never aware of a "number" starting or ending. Ernst Lubitsch followed a similar pattern in his early musicals, and Rouben Mamoulian, with the help of Rodgers and Hart, created in *Love Me Tonight* a really intelligent, uncompromising musical picture which has become a kind of classic of its genre. Many producers and directors realize today the enormous possibilities of a higher form of musical pictures, and the song writers are becoming more and more instrumental in the conception and preparation of these pictures. I am trying myself, whenever I have a chance, to develop certain elements of this genre. In my *Dreigroschenoper* film, I tried to translate the form of the musical play into the medium of motion picture. In the Fritz Lang film *You and Me*, I tried out a new technique by using songs as a part of the background music, expressing the "inner voice" of the characters (Milestone used this technique lately in *Walk in the Sun*), and in the picture *Where*

Do We Go from Here, Ira Gershwin and I wrote a regular little comic opera for the scene on Columbus's ship. It is a pretty safe bet that eventually something like a "film opera" will grow out of all this, and it is quite possible that the much-talked-about "American opera" will come out of the most popular American form of entertainment—the motion picture.

Harper's Bazaar, September 1946

PART FOUR

The Plastic Structure

"I make a picture, and proceed to destroy it. But in the end nothing is lost; the red I have removed from one part shows up in another."

PABLO PICASSO

Dynamic Composition

ALEXANDER BAKSHY

*I*nsofar as visual images constitute the basic material of the motion picture, the problem of cinematic composition is nothing else than the organization of these images in a sequential order. It is clear that there is more than one way of carrying out such an organization. The simplest and most obvious way is to arrange the images in an order in which they become so many connected links in the chain of representations that forms the narrative. In this case the actual form of images plays a subordinate part, being at best—as in close-up, for instance—only a function of their representational content.

The motion picture as a storytelling art has been principally concerned with supplying the spectator with such visual *information* as would ensure the desired intellectual and emotional reaction. At first, when the plots were simple and the technique still elementary, a straightforward stringing together of a series of scenes was all that was considered necessary for unfolding the story. Later the more complicated stories and the greater detailedness of images helped to bring into use the flashback and parallel action, the two cutting devices that introduced the method of intermittent composition. In this way the content of images became for the first time a formal element of cinematic composition. This formal character of the treatment of images, be it noted, had nothing to do with their visual form; it was merely a means of organizing content—a means which unquestionably has its origin in the peculiar mechanical structure of the motion picture but which also has its analogues in other non-visual arts, as for example in fiction and poetry.

During the last few years, some very interesting attempts have been made in various countries to develop other methods of formal composition on the basis of image content. The problem has been attacked from two different sides. On the one hand, experiments have been tried to establish a primary cinematic unit in the form of a group of images constructed somewhat on the lines of a grammatical sentence. Examples of this method are found in Eisenstein's *Ten Days That Shook the World*, in which the use of symbols in the construction of various "figures of speech" deserves special notice. On the other hand, attempts have been made to base the composition of the film as a whole on such methods of formalized treatment of the image content as the arrangement of "rhymed" sequences with certain images recurring at definite intervals, or of whole cycles of sequences on the lines of a repeating pattern somewhat after the manner of certain verse forms. Dziga Vertov is regarded in Russia as the head of this school of cinematic composition.

Side by side with the line of development just described, which is based on the assumption that *the form of cinematic composition is the function of the sum total of its image content*, the history of the motion picture shows another line of development, which sometimes crosses the former and sometimes follows an independent course, and which proceeds from the assumption that *the content matter of a film is the function of its organized visual form.*

Ever since the first motion pictures were made, it has been universally recognized that the cinematic visual image has one fundamental characteristic which distinguishes it from the visual images in other arts. This characteristic is movement. Although the term, particularly in its solemn guise of "dynamic quality," has acquired a sort of mystic halo, it is well to remember that it is essentially pragmatic in its origin and represents strictly definable properties of the motion-picture mechanism. The men who made movies when the art was still new and unexplored were not theorists. All they were concerned with was to give their pictures a semblance of life, and it took them only a short time to discover that a motion-less object on the screen was as good as dead. Hence the orgy of recorded motion which distinguished the early movies.

It was at a comparatively early stage, too, that the necessity of movement, not only in the characters and objects but in entire scenes in relation to one another, was realized. Two factors dictated this necessity. In the first place, there was the concentrated technique of cutting, arising from the fragmentary nature of the film record, which had the dual effect of speeding up movement and compressing time. In certain situations this compressing effect was found to conflict rather too harshly with the sequence of events in *real* time. For instance, a scene showing a man in front of a street door, followed immediately by a scene showing the same man inside the house, is likely to produce the impression of something unreal. An interval of time is clearly demanded between the two scenes, and this is supplied by an interpolated third scene, which may be a close-up of the man or the view of the room he is about to enter, or some other related subject. The method of parallel action is an extended application of the same principle and achieves a similar effect of expanded time, which sometimes, as in the climaxes of Griffith's pictures, is deliberately prolonged beyond even the realistic implications of the subject, for a specific emotional effect.

The other and perhaps even more important reason for changing scenes, and thus introducing a greater mobility of visual images, is found in the very character of realistic acting when it is used on the screen. In real life or on the stage, speech itself constitutes action. A conversation between two persons may encompass a series of events pregnant with dramatic significance, although the person speaking may engage in very little physical movement. On the screen the situation is different. While the stage actor who uses speech can sustain a situation without a change in the setting for the length of a whole act, the screen actor finds his resources of expression exhausted within as short a time as a minute. It was to relieve the screen actor of this predicament, and at the same time to give greater emphasis and variety to the means of expression, that long situations were reduced to a series of fragmentary scenes with long and medium shots, close-ups, and "angles" thrown in for the sake of variety and emphasis. It is instructive to note that, with the advent of talkies, long scenes depending entirely on dialogue and showing very little movement made their appearance on the screen. The fact that the later talkies returned to the technique of the silent picture, with its short and fragmentary scenes, only goes to prove that the handling of dialogue on the screen is now more efficient and that the old "dynamic" form of composition still wields a superior power of emotional appeal.

If the movement involved in the change from one scene to another brought to the fore the immediate significance of the form of the visual image, the movement resulting from a series of such changes, organized in a manner conforming to a certain rhythmic scheme, placed the visual form in the position of the dominant factor in the building of cinematic composition. At this instance it is unnecessary to go into a description of the various methods of rhythmic organization of images, beyond pointing to the work of Abel Gance, Leger and Murphy, Murnau, Eisenstein, and Dovzhenko.

The important fact to be borne in mind is that cinematic rhythm is a form of visual composition which is itself charged with powerful emotional appeal and at the same time, while remaining independent of the image content, conveys and shapes the latter's appeal as well.

The effect of rhythm is to organize sequences of visible beats and accents. It establishes a visual continuity of intermittent images as a function of time. It leaves untouched, however, the problem of spatial continuity, of the spatial relationship of images to one another as elements of the visual cinematic composition. No pictures known to the writer have so far suggested a satisfactory solution of this problem. And yet, so long as this problem remains unsolved, the motion picture as a medium of dynamic visual art will never reach complete maturity. The continuity of visual form implies a dynamic composition of which the only existing illustration in other visual arts is found in the moving composition of ballet. Just as in the latter, the cinematic visual form has to be built in time, and its elements of composition should be not static images but lines of forces or movements in definite directions. It goes without saying that movement in this sense includes not only moving objects, or movement of images in time only, but also their movement in space over the entire surface of the screen. The technical obstacles which stood in the way of such dynamic composition have been removed by the various devices for multi-screen and multi-image projection. In them, therefore, lies the promise of the mature cinema whose intellectual and emotional appeal will be the function of its dynamic composition.

Experimental Cinema No. 1, 1931

The Sense of Form in Cinema

ARTHUR LENNIG

The cinema is as rich, broad, complicated, and simple as life itself. Of its many aspects I should like to discuss its attempts at achieving form. There is always the danger of distortion and oversimplification with such a subject, yet hopefully a few basic outlines can be established.

In any discussion of the history of film, we might say that there are basically two major approaches or attitudes toward artistic expression. One could be called formal, a means by which some kind of order is imposed on material; and the other could be called organic, in which the form derives from what has been pictured. Such a distinction is clear in the abstract but is far more opaque in individual cases, and the two cannot easily be separated. For valid form cannot exist without a correlative content, nor can content (no matter how interesting) exist without some measure of form.

Form can dominate, can be so pervasive (as, for instance, in Egyptian art), that only a few artists could move freely enough within the standardization and stylization to achieve any kind of individual expression. Form limits, but it can also enhance. For example, Bach, in the St. Matthew Passion, although working within a very tight orthodox fugal framework, powerfully caught the shrill emotions of "Crucify Him." Here, as most listeners would admit, is created an almost perfect rendering of the emotions of the crowd; and yet Bach remains within classical, formal bounds.

In the best of such works the artist struggles and succeeds within strongly imposed limitations. But, as Wordsworth said, "Nuns fret not at their convent's narrow room"; and neither does the artist, within the limitations he chooses for himself. Thus the poet willingly orders his content, shapes his ideas, and adjusts his phrasing and rhyme to the confines of the sonnet form.

In more intuitive methods of expression, there is no strict adherence to or even concern with form per se. Of course a work must have form if it is to exist, but in such cases the form grows from the material rather than being imposed on it. Thus the poet writes as much as he wants and in any rhyme scheme. Fourteen lines are not his limit. Yet, as Eliot once said, free verse is not free to the artist who uses it.

In the art of the film we have these same broad divisions. In one, experience is rendered "as is" (with of course some selection); in the other, experience is ordered by form. There are dangers in both methods. By ignoring preconceived, controlling form, the intuitive or organic filmmaker tends to be shapeless and chaotic, giving in to impulses that perhaps could be checked for better clarity, while the formal and theory-ridden filmmaker tends to be so rigorous in the application of his methods, so monomaniacal in his concern for order, that he lets the very essence of life fade from his work. Naturally, there are dangers as well as satisfactions to both approaches; but both in their own ways have resulted in masterpieces. Renoir's *La Grande Illusion* is a great film, an organic work in which the shots grow out of the settings and actors without ever the faintest sense of preconceived order. Its lack of overt form is not a drawback, for the film is sustained by its deep humanity and sensitivity, and so, in a sense, achieves a proper balance of content and style. Eisenstein's *The General Line* (*The Old and the New*), with its episodic story, could be meritless if handled by a so-called intuitive director. The one thing that redeems the film is Eisenstein's methods: here is a mind wrestling with chaos and trying to order it. All too often, however, films are formless—disciplines can easily be evaded—and the content not of sufficient worth to make the work cohere.

Content, like a man's philosophy, is what holds the disparate aspects of existence together. When the content is essentially of value, it may create even in an intuitive treatment a fine film.

Flaherty's *Nanook of the North* succeeds because the subject matter fuses with the filmmaker's obvious sincerity and enthusiasm,
despite his utter disregard for form. Flaherty's other films were less
successful; with weak material, his intuitive method collapsed. The
content could not sustain the helter-skelter shooting. His later
films, like *Moana,* become mere tropical-island photography and
self-indulgent episodes, neither building nor heading to anything.
With directors more aware of form, even if the content were less
than encouraging, their very way of seeing sustained the work. At
least there is something to look at; at least the mind can see a man
struggling with a kind of order, even though the balance between
what he is saying and how well it is being said is uneven.

In the early films, the camera was a mere recording device, a
means by which action could be photographed. Whatever interest
there was in these films came not from the form—which was nonexistent—but from the subject matter. Griffith was the first to
develop the camera's potentialities. In his desire to tell a story
well, to render rather than merely to record, he developed the
basic grammar of cinema. He made use of the close-up, of cross-
cutting, of reflecting the intensity of action in the swiftness of the
editing, and in the careful use of composition and movement
within the frame. Film was no longer a conglomeration of long
scenes, a pictorial run-on sentence. His *Intolerance* was perhaps
the first film to suit the story and the action to a preconceived formal idea of counterpoint, an effort in which form and content
were completely indivisible. That the overall idea of the film did
not entirely work was not due to Griffith's cinematic methods but
rather to his limitations as a thinker. In *The Birth of a Nation* and
Intolerance, he had an almost perfect blend of stylization in setting, creative use of space, and exciting and visually oriented stories blended with an imaginative use of camera placement and editing. This wholeness of form and content would break down later,
not only with Griffith but also with subsequent directors. Other
men would explore both areas (what the camera was photographing and how shots were edited) and develop both far beyond him.
But nobody seems to have blended these areas together as success-
fully as Griffith; and for that reason, not just for his innovations,
he remains one of the major artists of the cinema.

The areas that Griffith explored were to be picked up and improved in Germany (1919–27) and Soviet Russia (1924–30). The films of these countries were by far the most form-conscious. The German films concentrated on what the camera photographed (settings, lighting, angles, actors), while the Russians concentrated more on how shots were put together. Thus form took two related but still divergent paths:

1. *Abstract or stylized visual content.* The Germans were not particularly concerned with the relationship of shot to shot. They were entranced instead with the world of artifice that the cinema could create. They employed the devices of the theater—the use of sets, professional actors, and carefully arranged lighting—while the Russians did just the opposite, dismissing such a "created" world. The Russians did not want to construct reality in a studio by stressing its essential outlines and basic character, by reducing unnecessary details or other kinds of ephemera into clarified outlines, but instead they went outside the studio into the real world; and there, by means of camera angle, but mostly by cutting, they attempted to stylize reality, to organize it into an exciting and dynamic mode. Some theoreticians have therefore come to the conclusion that a derived world is basically superior to a created world of artificial elements. It is not better; it is different.

To render actuality more precisely, some of the German film artists chose distortion and stylization (a milder form of it) in order to transcend mere surface naturalism so that they could get to the essence. Griffith had begun this trend in *Intolerance*, in which a shot shows Jenkins, the boss, sitting alone in a giant room, a means by which Griffith stressed the man's isolation and indifference to humanity. The Germans went beyond the sheer manipulation of space. There was a further wish to abstract. The most important film of this genre was *The Cabinet of Dr. Caligari*. Its expressionistic sets, stylized make-up, and patterned movement presented a world that no longer could be confused with actuality. It depicted essence, the truth beyond the real, just as the Greek mask was a distillation of emotion. *Caligari* was essentially a set designer's film. The camera recorded more than it rendered.

The wish to stylize continued in *The Golem* (1920; Wegener), *Warning Shadows* (1922; Robison), *The Street* (1923; Grune), *The Chronicle of the Grey House* (1923; Gerlach), *The Treasure* (1924; Pabst), *Waxworks* (1924; Leni), *The Last Laugh* (1925;

Murnau), and especially the films of Fritz Lang. In *Destiny, Dr. Mabuse der Spieler, Das Nibelungenlied, Metropolis, Spione,* and *M* (though to a lesser extent), we can see in varying degrees the German emphasis on abstraction. In many of these films, almost all the shots were made at the studio. To the Germans, the real world was too complicated, too cluttered. A real forest did not look good enough, did not capture that mythic sense of what a forest *ought* to be, so the filmmakers built one as in *Siegfried*. In *The Last Laugh*, streets were built and apartment houses constructed to order, to reflect more purely the effects the director was striving for.

Lang's filmic sense was basically architectural, a characteristic that betrays his early schooling. He concerns himself with visuals: but visuals as forms, not textures. He is not painting with light like von Sternberg, but sculpting with it. He does not amass crowds like Griffith to lend realism to scenes. Lang's crowds exist merely to form pleasing designs; the viewer seldom cares what happens to them. In Arthur Robison's little-known film, *Warning Shadows*, the emphasis is not on the sets but on the use of light. Shadows are not used just for ornamental or melodramatic effect but are actually the thematic substance of the film, the means by which Robison explores illusion and reality.

What the Germans stressed was what the camera could photograph; therefore sets, acting, lighting, and camera movement became their superb contribution, but it was only one aspect of form in cinema. What they never really examined were the aesthetics of shot manipulation, of montage. That field lay comparatively untouched.

2. *Form achieved with editing.* For years Griffith's *Intolerance* was the high point of the art of editing. Even the great director himself would not approach the complexity or the sheer nervous tension and intensity of that film. Later, another intuitive worker, Abel Gance, would make use of rapid cutting in *La Roue* (1922) and *Napoleon* (1926), but it remained for Eisenstein to explore the medium more fully. If Griffith was its first grammarian (though an intuitive rather than a cerebral one), Eisenstein became its first aesthetician. The young Russian director went far beyond Griffith's usage. He consciously examined and discovered the laws of form that govern film.

Both Eisenstein and his fellow Russian, Pudovkin, believed that a film was built from various pieces and that shots were linked together to form a whole. Of course this mode of seeing, stated by Kuleshov, came in turn from a close study of *Intolerance*. However, the methods that Griffith used were complex enough to offer different things to different people. Pudovkin borrowed Griffith's story development, his building of character, his psychological insights, his humanizing of history, and his use of setting lighting, and of course his methods of cutting to make the plight of his characters real and effective. Eisenstein chose Griffith's broader sweep of history and modeled his films after the exciting moments of Griffith's concluding reels. Eisenstein tended to see shots as visual abstractions; Pudovkin saw them more as means to personal revelations.

Basic to Eisenstein's method was the individual shot—an entity spliced between others—which had these important qualities:

Narrative—the subject of the shot; the factual or literal content.

Formal—the length of the shot; the placement in the edited whole.

Emotional—the "feeling" one gets from looking at the shot, based not only on subject matter but also on lighting, texture, angle, etc.

To Eisenstein, a film was more than just scenes which were linked to match action and to tell a story. What was *process* (the mechanical joining of shot to shot) became *subject* to him. By careful manipulation of shots, he transcended the film's usual prosaic and direct statements in such a way as to achieve a richer means of expression, akin in its clashes of ideas and suggestive overtones to some kinds of poetry. He increased the vocabulary of the cinema by making ingenious use of rhythm, space, and time. Juxtaposition was raised from an occasional trick to an essential aspect of the art; and editing, which had been mere device, a means, became matter itself. This process of juxtaposing one shot (A) to another (B) frequently formed not only a visual conflict or collision but also an intellectual concept, an idea born from the mating of shots which perhaps mean little in themselves. This manipulation of the content and length of shots extended the language of cinema. But, to control this language properly, it was necessary for the director to do his own editing, since the placement of the individual shots now became the most creative aspect of the film.

Hamlet says: "Suit the word to the action," and Alexander Pope advises: "The sound must seem an echo to the sense." On occasion, Eisenstein achieved this. In the Cossack dance sequence from *October*, he reveals his interest in pure form and in rhythmic cutting. He captured the swift action, the jumps, the smiles, the quick turns—the very spirit of the dance. Having a number of cameras at his disposal, he simultaneously photographed the dancer from various angles. As the pace of the dance increases, the editing becomes more rapid. Each shot is trimmed to its shortest expressive length. Sometimes "takes" of five or six frames flash and disappear. As the dance approaches its climax, the cutting becomes more agitated: four frames, three frames, two frames, and finally a series of one-frame shots. His attempt, no matter how hard on the eyes, is perhaps the cinema's most creative interpretation of dancing.

The German films, on the other hand, did not attempt to echo the "sense" in quite this way. In Fritz Lang's *Metropolis*, for example, the director tried to demonstrate what the mechanized city of the future would be like. The film shows vast gangs of workers moving in lock step, gigantic dials of machines, and various other kinds of futuristic trappings. This world, however, is the studio craftsman's. Lang shows man to be the slave of the machine by superimposing a Gargantuan image of Moloch, into whose jaws the workers advance. This is brilliant theater and effective cinema as well, but Lang does not attempt to capture in the cutting the feeling of the mechanization. Instead of realizing that a machine would have a pulse or rhythm, and by this means intercutting various shots of machines and workers into a complex rhythmic pattern, he relies on the set maker.

Montage has often been misinterpreted. Frequently critics and audiences recognize it only in its more flamboyant moments. It is not, however, something *inserted*, but something *inherent* to the medium itself. It is a clear-cut way of rendering action. Just as Bach can give us both joy and deepest sorrow within form, so can the montage method be unobtrusive and reflect any mood, be it revolutionary or funereal. Eisenstein's striving for collisions often created too nervous and fragmented a reality to be enjoyed before it wearied the eye and the mind. He did not learn to shift speed, to alternate presto with largo; by making everything presto, he lost one very important aspect of drama: contrast.

Eisenstein began *Ivan the Terrible* in the early 1940's. Prevented by the government from using his montage method, he modified it. Instead of contrasting areas and movements, he attempted to break up scenes in terms of small areas of space, so that a man walking into a room would be followed by a medium shot of the body starting to sit down in the chair, then a close-up as the face moved into the repose of the man thinking. Ideological conflict and manipulation of crowds vanished, but space broken into small, frozen units remained. Indeed, *Ivan the Terrible* is perhaps the most formal of all films. The cutting is unobtrusive, perhaps even unnoticed by the careless eye, but each shot is governed by a kind of classical, formalized vision. In *Ivan* there is not only a tight control of the composition, placement, and editing of shots, but also a stylization of movement, lighting, gesture, and make-up. In combining his sense of the camera with the German concern for the abstract, Eisenstein achieved the cinema's most formal work. Indeed, although Eisenstein years before disapproved of films such as *Caligari* and *Siegfried*, his *Ivan* is much closer to them than he would have cared to admit.

Although many of Griffith's devices, some of Eisenstein's theories, and some of the staging techniques of the Germans have become common film practice, most directors have not concerned themselves with form. In the 1940's and 1950's in particular, directors presented their stories in a semi-natural way (that is, no method was imposed upon what was being shot, nor were sets anything but realistic), and film seemed to be nothing more than clearly photographed scenes. The popularity of the wide screen further discouraged cutting, so that film retrogressed until in many ways it became aesthetically pre-Griffith. Moving cameras, deep-focus lenses, and panning took the emphasis off the manipulation of shot to shot; this tendency, plus the use of the voice to carry most of the plot, made the film visually quite dull. Even the thirties, which had seemed such a barren period at the time, appeared as a Golden Age of editing in comparison. Certainly the vitality of Griffith and the Russians disappeared. In the 1960's, however, a resurgence of cutting occurred, influenced mostly by the TV commercial, which attempts to pack into sixty seconds as many shots as possible. The cinema, as a result, has become more visually exciting than ever, picking up from the late twenties where the Russians left off. But this rapid cutting often has little sense of form and frequently is an indulgence of directors who luxuriate in swift cutting as if it were a C. B. De Mille milk bath.

Perhaps it could be said that both the Germans and the Russians had a narrow sense of form and that now the medium has grown up past their boldly experimental excursions. To an extent this is true. But some directors, such as Lester, Godard, and even Bergman (in something like *Hour of the Wolf*), seem to throw in everything around them and hope somehow that raw material will be digested by the audience. This style (or lack of it) is a betrayal of the present age's preoccupation with action—fast driving, frenetic dancing, a kind of insane wish for activity, for *doing things*, though the things themselves add up to be mere experience without meaning. Whereas the Russians made rapid cuts to create ideas, today's cuts are often just something to look at, more clatter than matter. Swift editing is not a virtue in itself. There is really no more genius in making four cuts where, five years before and in a different fashion, only one would have been made. Nor does rapid cutting itself make a work more profound. Indeed, some filmmakers have switched the burden of storytelling or meaning from themselves to the audience. To a point this is good, but it can easily seduce a filmmaker into evading and abrogating his own duties. Cinema, like any art, is not a grab bag (or at least shouldn't be), and some of the films now raved about by the "in" critics will fade all too soon.

Despite a content and style that appeal to current fashion, there is no substitute for an acute mind seeking a definitive way of expressing itself. Mirroring life is not enough; it must be refracted: and form, of course, is the refraction, the one means by which chaos sifts down into order, by which the anomalies and sheer extravagance of life, in all its vacuous and ridiculous and bumbling details, crystallize into something finer.

Revised from *Film Notes*, 1960

The Other Direction

JONAS MEKAS

*W*hat do we mean when we say films are *avant-garde, experimental, underground, personal?* What we mean, what it is, is that every art has two extremes, two ends. On one end, man expresses himself by telling stories, by retelling myths. He reenacts certain situations, experiences through characters—protagonists—and then goes to the other end of himself, where it becomes vaguer and vaguer, more abstract, where man can express himself only very indirectly, by suggestions, where he doesn't exactly *know* really how to express things. It all becomes very intuitive and very indirect—symbols, metaphors. Here we enter the area of non-narrative poems, poetry. Then we come to the extreme end, where it becomes totally abstract. Take storytelling painting and take Mondrian; take Faulkner, and then go to the real extreme of poetry, that is, to Concrete Poetry.

In cinema we were—and still are as far as I can see—only at the narrative end; that is, one end, one part of man. This part of man expresses itself in cinema through narrative forms. We are interested in only one part of man. But this is a complete misdirection of our attitude toward cinema, a misdirected conception of cinema that we have, and we take this as normal. What about the other part, which expresses itself through non-narrative forms, through poetry? That seems to us like just fooling around. The experimental film, the avant-garde film—that isn't cinema, that's only fooling

313

around. Imagine a man who is teaching literature and is only teaching the novel, only the narrative forms of literature, and ignoring poetry, ignoring Ezra Pound, ignoring Blake, ignoring almost every poet who ever existed unless he wrote epic poems in which there are characters. That's okay. That we should teach in schools and universities. That is literature. But Blake, haiku—three lines, a few syllables—that's not serious. Yet that's exactly our attitude in cinema, and we take it as normal. In literature, it would be ridiculous; in music, it would be ridiculous; in painting, it would be ridiculous. In cinema—normal.

What the avant-garde is and what the avant-garde did during the last ten years developed those non-narrative forms. I say ten years because those ten years were really a concentrated period of attention in that direction. The roots always go much further, to the twenties, to the very beginning of the cinema. But the vocabulary, the forms, and the technology of the non-narrative cinema, of the poetic cinema, have been worked out during the last ten years.

When we go to see a narrative film (and I am not now talking about journalistic or all other forms of film), we expect certain plots, certain excitement, certain suspense to hold our interest. We are dealing with a very strange area of entertainment when we consider the reasons why we go to the cinema. We go to a gallery to see paintings for reasons which are not always very clear, but it isn't always for entertainment. We see something, deduce something from those paintings, those colors, those forms. Something attracts us. We keep coming back to certain paintings, certain artists, for reasons that we don't even know. They do something to us that makes us feel we should see them again. In music, there are certain compositions we want to listen to again and again.

In cinema, we feel that if it really holds us there for those ninety or a hundred minutes with climaxes, constant suspense, then it is okay. But if we have to put some effort of our own into the viewing, that is already bad. Take our newspapers, our reviewers—I can imagine Bosley Crowther or somebody sitting there as if behind a steel wall. He protects himself totally from what is there. And we have to work very hard to get him. But he wouldn't put himself into that film. Now when we come to poetry, to the avant-garde film—films which are there—there are no obvious cli-

maxes, no suspense, no excitement, no thrill on the surface that
would really "grab" you. They don't attack you. They're very simple, inoffensive, unobtrusive. They don't want to impose anything
on you. To get anything from these films, in the first place, you
have to get yourself in a certain attitude. You have to put yourself
into it, open yourself completely so that something, whatever it is,
in that work, will begin to float, talk, come in to you. There will
be contact between that film and you. If you can get yourself into
that very open, receptive attitude, you can abandon your precon-
ceptions and expectations and just see whatever there is on the
screen.

Cinema has so many ends, directions, so many uses—like words
and literature. You can write a poem, you can write a short story,
you can write haiku, or a journalistic piece about a bridge that has
just been built or about the war in Vietnam—any subject you
want. You can write a textbook. So we have cinema put to all
these uses. Bruce Baillie's *All My Life,* for instance, is like a haiku.
Just one simple image. There are many filmmakers who are concerned today with this form of very short film—one image, one idea.
(I say haiku as the easiest of references.) Taking any subject, any
object, and making it the center of the work. Against those who say
that film needs a big subject, a big theme, we say that anything
could be a subject of a film, of a poem. A scent, a flower—like Andy
Warhol making a film on a man eating a mushroom for forty minutes or Michael Snow with water dripping into an enamel plate
for ten minutes. But as you watch it, it becomes a meditation on
that subject. One feels the subject is invested with great love, that
whatever is around you is worth that attention and that love. Not
only those happenings and situations in which there is action, plot,
and climax, but *anything* under the sun—perhaps even having
nothing to do with life, with human beings. But how can we love
human beings if we don't love water drips or a fence surrounded
with roses? These films, their subjects, their themes, are very small.
Just maybe a feeling, a mood. When we go to a commercial film,
a theatrical narrative or art film, and when we ask what is the subject of that film, we usually have many obvious, "important"
themes we can point out. But these other films are very unpreten-
tious. They don't want to change you by force. They don't work,
they do not plot, to undermine you so you will be this or that.

One mood, one feeling—but it's a mood or a feeling that the artist who made the film had and considers important. The artist believes it is important that man has these moods, that they survive, that man doesn't become too simple, too mechanized. He believes that there are certain areas which the narrative film with its melodrama and its action, plot and suspense, does not descend to, and that it's up to the non-narrative forms—to poetry, to certain forms of painting or of music—to express these feelings or emotions, thoughts or movements, that are on some deeper levels of our existence. And these films are there to register them on film for us.

When one cannot express something directly and clearly, one uses indirect means. The rhythm, the movement of a film is one of those means whereby man can express certain things that he doesn't really know how to express. Pacing and rhythm become very important in film. There are rhythms and speeds of excitement, there are rhythms and speeds of meditation, of loving, of gentle feelings. There are certain rhythms you respond to immediately without knowing what it is all about. You respond to the movement, to the rhythm, and it does something—you may not even be able to describe it clearly. The same thing happens when you are standing in front of certain paintings. There are loud, crying paintings that work on some very entertaining level, and there are also others in which certain shapes, lines, nuances, colors touch something on certain levels in you, which begin to wake up in you areas that are not too clear but that are there, crying to be developed.

Any comparison—as when I say that in avant-garde film there is a parallel to poetry and literature—cannot be taken literally, because these are different media. But there was a time when cinema was much younger, when filmmakers were afraid to be in the same room with any other art. They wanted to be independent; they stressed their independence from all other arts. But today that is not necessary. Cinema has established itself and doesn't have to have that kind of inhibition. We know that all the arts are expressions of man expressing different aspects of our being, so that somewhere and at some point each of the arts touches. They come to some one center from which it can be said that the same idea, or the same feeling, the same thought, can be expressed through *any* other art. But, you see, one must descend into the very seed where that thought or feeling begins and man wants to express it. It is then directed to that area where man is most capable, the area he has mastered—movement, sound, cinema, or words. And already that depends on the path of one's life.

The basis of all creation is the restructuring of reality. Restructured reality becomes different depending on which art you use. There are large areas; there are traditions. There are materials; there is technology. There are all the past works. Then we come to the theories, the aesthetics, the practices. And then we begin to find out really what it is that "grabs" you. Something can grab you even if you are not ready—certain colors, certain surface things that stand out. Later you come back and you find out that that was not the essence of the particular work, that there is something more subtle, much deeper there.

We know that there is poetry and there are poets, and we find that some people are interested in poetry, some not. Some react to a poet; some do not. Or I find nothing in this poem or in this film or in this painting, and then someone else comes and says this poem or film or painting is the greatest, it changed my life. So it always comes back to you, to where you yourself are, what stage of your life you are in. For instance, there are certain composers that one prefers, and others one just doesn't get anything from and yet may come to later in life when one's life direction has changed. A number of things are involved. It always depends on the viewer.

One could say it is like a pyramid. At the top there are those who are most developed in sensitivities, in intelligence and experiences—both quantitative and qualitative—and then on the very bottom those who are like minerals and vegetables. Each of the levels has a different kind of art, different kind of food, different kind of people, and these change as one grows. For that growth— and I believe that we should constantly develop and grow, or, rather, that we have no choice, for those are the laws of life—for that growth one always goes through stages, abandons certain art which for somebody else will be of value but which to you is no longer of value as you look forward to more and more subtle forms, as you grow. Of course it is possible that you are "growing" backwards. Hollywood has tried to influence growth by its insistence on certain kinds of film. For a long time Hollywood had control of all the theaters across the country—four or five thousand—and there was no choice. Man was reduced to one kind of visual or cinematic food. Again, we know the laws of life. If one is exposed for too long to the same primitive kind of "underground" cinema—because that's what Hollywood is, a true underground cinema which gives primitive, gross reality simplified emotions and feelings—one will be dragged down to the ground and under the ground.

Today we have certain art theaters and we have the universities, so we have a certain choice. We don't have to show only the lowest kind of film. We can begin to show Bergman. And eventually come to Brakhage, because before we come to Brakhage we have to go through all kinds of other stages.

We usually think only in extremes, and the usual attitude is that the avant-garde film ignores other cinema. The avant-garde has never opposed the other cinema. It's the newspapers that distorted what the avant-garde really is all about, our attitudes. We are not against Hollywood. Hollywood is there. We are not against narrative cinema. We are doing different things. Poetry is not opposed to narrative. A short piece of music is not opposed to a symphony. There is no opposition; each does a different thing. A cow is one thing, a horse another, and a sheep another. They are not opposed, but each of them *is* a different animal. So it's important to remember that when we are speaking of this cinema, we don't mean to cut out the rest. We take cinema as a whole. Each film, each area, each rung does its job in a different field of experience.

There are poems that are needed to make certain moral points. There are occasional poems which can be read and presented to a wide public and read in a loud voice. But then there are poems which you read only by yourself, at home, in the evening, when you don't want any disturbance. You read and deal with just that poem because it concerns more private, more personal, more subtle areas of experience. One area the avant-garde film deals with is the private, personal area. You will not always react to these films. They may look like nothing to you. You may be open to them, find something in them, only if you are watching by yourself or with two or three friends in your own home, or perhaps on seeing the film for the third, fourth, fifth, or even tenth time. We are looking forward to the days when you will be able to have your own private libraries—when the technology of cinema will allow it. That will change your understanding of what the avant-garde is all about, what film poetry is all about, what non-narrative film is all about, and what narrative film is all about—because that will change too. You will discover that many of the narrative films you preferred, found great, that grabbed you, will fall to pieces on the second or third viewing. They will not give you anything any more. But you will also turn to some other narrative films (like Dreyer's) which give you, no matter how many times you look at them, something else each time.

I keep talking about small films, films that do not force anything upon you. As the cinema progresses, the latest preoccupation of some filmmakers in the vanguard of film is with very limited subjects—the window, the flower, the fence. Sort of Minimal Film. Some filmmakers are going into great detail; some are dealing just with patterns. They don't even show the pot or the window, they just stick to the flower. In a sense, the farther man jumps into space, the more he also goes to the other extreme (and really one needs the other). He becomes more and more private. He finds joy in details. He invests every detail with love and attention. There is no end to how small that detail can be. This personal approach to everything, this feeling that everything can be beautiful and important, that no matter how small or insignificant it is, it can be a subject for a work of art—this direction inwards then bounces back to the other extreme. I would say that our flight to the moon is only a crystallized opposite. The spiritual direction that is transformed into matter. The farther we want to fly into space, the deeper we have to go inward. That's how it happened. It's no coincidence that we are landing on the moon just when the interest in bio-chemical and mystical explorations is at its highest in this country and around the world; besides the very stagnant, very mechanical attitudes and systems of today, there is this opposite pole, this other direction.

New Cinema Review, September 1969. *Transcription of a talk made at the Seventh Annual Fordham Film Study Conference, July 25, 1969. Tape by Bob Parent; transcription by Margo Breier*

Notes on the Contributors

ALEXANDER BAKSHY, author of several books on the theater and film, was the film critic for *The Nation* from 1927 to 1933.

BELA BELAZS, a screenwriter and the author of children's books in Hungary, is rated among the most important contributors to the theory of film art.

NICOLA CHIAROMONTE is co-director, with Ignazio Silone, of the distinguished Italian cultural journal *Tempo Presente*.

MAYA DEREN, who died in 1961, was an avant-garde filmmaker who lectured and wrote widely on film aesthetics.

CARL DREYER, the Danish director, is best known for his pictures *The Passion of Joan of Arc, Ordet*, and *Day of Wrath*.

SERGEI EISENSTEIN first achieved world fame with his film *Potemkin* in 1925. Although he completed only seven films, he is considered one of the world's most influential filmmakers.

ROBERT GESSNER, who died in 1968, was the founding president of The Society of Cinematologists, the first American to teach cinema as a liberal art, and the author of eight books. His last book was *The Moving Image*.

ARTHUR GOLDSMITH is editor and head of instruction at the Famous Photographers School.

EZRA GOODMAN is the author of *The Fifty Year Decline and Fall of Hollywood*. He has written many feature articles on movies for magazines and newspapers. In 1950 he became film critic for *Time* magazine and then Hollywood correspondent for the same publication.

HILARY HARRIS is a documentary and experimental filmmaker who has won awards for his pictures at festivals at Brussels, Locarno, Montreal, Venice, Cork, and Belgrade.

WILLIAM JOHNSON has been engaged in film criticism for a number of years. At present he is on the staff of *Scholastic Magazine*.

JOHN HOWARD LAWSON is a distinguished playwright and screen writer and the author of *Theory and Technique of Playwrighting and Screen Writing, Film in the Battle of Ideas*, and *Film: The Creative Process*.

ARTHUR LENNIG teaches filmmaking at The State University of New York. He is the author of *The Silent Voice: A Text* and editor of *Film Notes* and *Classics of the Film*. At present he is at work on a biography of D. W. Griffith.

HERBERT A. LIGHTMAN is editor of *American Cinematographer* and an authority on motion-picture photography and production techniques.

JONAS MEKAS, filmmaker and poet, is the guiding spirit behind the underground film movement. He is also the editor of *Film Culture* and film columnist for *The Village Voice*.

IVOR MONTAGU has had a long career in film. He was the first film critic for *The* (London) *Observer* and *New Statesman*, worked with Hitchcock in England and with Eisenstein in Hollywood, and was the original translator of Pudovkin's *Film Technique*.

IRVING PICHEL was an actor and director on Broadway and in Hollywood in the forties and fifties, and wrote extensively about both the theater and motion pictures.

HENWAR RODAKIEWICZ is a distinguished writer and director of documentary films. At present he is directing independent features and television documentaries.

STANLEY J. SOLOMON teaches English at Iona College.

GREGG TOLAND, who died in 1948, was considered one of Hollywood's greatest cameramen. He was director of photography for *Citizen Kane*,

Wuthering Heights, Grapes of Wrath, The Long Voyage Home, and *The Little Foxes.*

KURT WEILL, who died in 1950, was a composer of operas, ballets, and musical comedies. He is perhaps best known for his collaborations with Bertholt Brecht, particularly *The Threepenny Opera.*

Selected Bibliography

AGEE, JAMES, *Agee on Film*. Boston: Beacon Press, 1964.
ALPERT, HOLLIS, *The Dreams and the Dreamers*. N.Y.: Macmillan, 1962.
ALTON, JOHN, *Painting with Light*. N.Y.: Macmillan, 1962.
ARMES, ROY, *The Cinema of Alain Resnais*. N.J.: A. S. Barnes, 1968.
ARNHEIM, RUDOLPH, *Art & Visual Perception*. Berkeley: University of California Press, 1954.
———, *Film as Art*. Berkeley: University of California Press, 1958.
BAKSHY, ALEXANDER, *Path of the Modern Russian Stage*. London: Cecil Palmer & Hayward, 1916.
BARNES, ALBERT C., *The Art in Painting*. Merion, Penna.: The Barnes Foundation Press, 1925.
BARR, ALFRED H., JR., *What Is Modern Painting?* N.Y.: Museum of Modern Art, 1952.
BARRY, IRIS, *Let's Go to the Movies*. London: Payson & Clarke, 1926.
———, *D. W. Griffith: American Film Master*. N.Y.: Museum of Modern Art, 1965.
BATTOCK, GREGORY, *The New American Cinema*. N.Y.: Dutton, 1967.
BAZIN, ANDRÉ, *What Is Cinema?* (ed. Hugh Gray). Berkeley: University of California Press, 1967.
BELAZS, BELA, *Theory of the Film*. London: Dennis Dobson, 1952.
BENOÎT-LÉVY, JEAN, *The Art of the Motion Picture*. N.Y.: Coward-McCann, 1946.

BETTS, ERNEST, *Heraclitus, or the Future of the Movies*. N.Y.: Dutton, 1928.

BLOEM, WALTER S., *The Soul of the Moving Picture*. N.Y.: Dutton, 1924.

BLUESTONE, GEORGE, *Novels into Film*. Berkeley: University of California Press, 1961.

BOWEN, DALLAS, *Plan For Cinema*. London: Dent, 1936.

BRUNUEL, ADRIAN, *Filmcraft*. London: George Newnes, 1935.

BRYHER, W., *Film Problems of Soviet Russia*. Switzerland: Territet, 1929.

BUCKLE, GERARD FORT, *The Mind of the Film*. London: Routledge, 1926.

CARTER, HUNTLEY, *The New Spirit in Cinema*. London: Harold Shaylor, 1930.

————, *The New Theatre & Cinema of Soviet Russia*. N.Y.: International Publishers, 1925.

COCTEAU, JEAN, *On the Film*. New York: Roy Publishers, 1954.

COWIE, PETER, *Antonioni, Bergman, Resnais*. N.Y.: Yoseloff, 1964.

————, *The Cinema of Orson Welles*. N.J.: A. S. Barnes, 1965.

DAVY, CHARLES, ed., *Footnotes to Film*. N.Y.: Oxford University Press, 1937.

DEREN, MAYA, *An Anagram of Ideas on Art, Form, and Film*. Yonkers, N.Y.: Alicat Book Shop, 1946.

DEWEY, JOHN, *Art as Experience*. N.Y.: Milton, Balch, 1934.

DICKINSON, THOROLD, *Soviet Cinema*. London: Falcon Press, 1948.

DONNER, JORN, *The Personal Vision of Ingmar Bergman*. Bloomington: Indiana University Press, 1964.

DURGNAT, RAYMOND, *Nouvelle Vague: The First Decade*. Loughton, Essex: Motion Publications, 1963.

EISENSTEIN, S. M., *Film Form and Film Sense*. N.Y.: World Publishing Co., 1949.

————, *Notes of a Film Director*. Moscow: Foreign Language Publishing House, 1958.

EISLER, HANS, *Composing for the Films*. N.Y.: Oxford University Press, 1947.

EVERSON, WILLIAM K., *The American Movie*. N.Y.: Atheneum, 1963.

FAURE, ELIE, *The Art of Cineplastics* (trans. Walter Pach). Boston: Four Seas Press Co., 1923.

FELDMAN, JOSEPH and HARRY, *Dynamics of the Film*. N.Y.: Hermitage House, 1952.

FREEBURG, VICTOR OSCAR, *Pictorial Beauty on the Screen*. N.Y.: Macmillan, 1923.

————, *Art of Photoplay Making*. N.Y.: Macmillan, 1918.
FULTON, ALBERT R., *Motion Pictures*. Norman: University of Oklahoma Press, 1960.
FRY, ROGER, *Vision and Design*. London: Penguin Books, 1940.
GEDULD, HARRY M., *Film Makers on Film Making*. Bloomington: Indiana University Press, 1968.
GOMBRICH, E. H., *Art and Illusion*. N.Y.: Phaidon Press, 1962.
HACKER, LEONARD, *Cinematic Design*. Boston: American Photography Publishing Co., 1931.
HALAS, JOHN and ROGER MANVELL, *Technique of Film Animation*. N.Y.: Hastings House, 1959.
————, *Design in Motion*. N.Y.: Hastings House, 1962.
HOUSTON, PENELOPE, *The Contemporary Cinema*. Baltimore: Penguin Books, 1964.
HUNTER, SAM, *Modern American Painting and Sculpture*. N.Y.: Dell, 1959.
HUNTER, WILLIAM, *Scrutiny of Cinema*. London: Wishart, 1942.
HUSS, ROY and NORMAN SILVERSTEIN, *The Film Experience*. N.Y.: Harper & Row, 1968.
JACOBS, LEWIS, *Emergence of Film Art*. N.Y.: Hopkinson & Blake, 1969.
————, *Rise of the American Film*. N.Y.: Teachers College Press, 1968.
————, *Introduction to the Art of Movies*. N.Y.: Farrar, Straus and Giroux, 1960.
KAEL, PAULINE, *Kiss Kiss Bang Bang*. Boston: Little, Brown, 1968.
————, *I Lost It at the Movies*. Boston: Little, Brown, 1965.
KAUFFMANN, STANLEY, *A World on Film*. N.Y.: Harper & Row, 1966.
KEPES, GYORGY, *Language of Vision*. Chicago: Paul Theobold, 1945.
————, *The Nature of Art and Motion*. N.Y.: Braziller, 1964.
KNIGHT, ARTHUR, *The Liveliest Art*. N.Y.: New American Library, 1959.
KOSTELANETZ, RICHARD, ed., *The New American Arts*. N.Y.: Collier Books, 1967.
KRACAUER, SIEGFRIED, *Theory of Film*. N.Y.: Oxford University Press, 1960.
————, *From Caligari to Hitler*. N.Y.: Noonday, 1959.
KYROU, ALDO, *Luis Buñuel*. N.Y.: Simon and Schuster, 1963.
LANGER, S. K., *Problems of Art*. N.Y.: Scribner's, 1957.
LAWSON, JOHN HOWARD, *Film: The Creative Process*. N.Y.: Hill & Wang, 1964.

————, *Theory and Technique of Playwrighting and Screenwriting.* N.Y.: Putnam's, 1949.

LEYDA, JAY, *Kino: History of the Russian and Soviet Film.* N.Y.: Macmillan, 1960.

LINDGREN, ERNEST, *The Art of the Film.* N.Y.: Macmillan, 1962.

LONDON, KURT, *Film Music.* London: Faber and Faber, 1936.

McCANN, RICHARD D., *Film: A Montage of Theories.* N.Y.: Dutton, 1966.

MACDONALD, DWIGHT, *On Movies.* N.Y.: Prentice Hall, 1969.

MANVELL, ROGER, *New Cinema in the U.S.A.* N.Y. and London: Dutton-Vista, 1968.

————, *New Cinema in Europe.* N.Y. and London: Dutton-Vista, 1966.

————, *Film.* London: Penguin Books, 1950.

————, *Experiment in Film.* London: Grey Walls Press, 1949.

MOHOLY-NAGY, LADISLAUS, *Vision in Motion.* Chicago: Theobold, 1947.

MONRO, THOMAS, *The Arts and Their Interrelations.* Cleveland: The Press of Western Reserve University, 1967.

————, *Toward Science in Esthetics.* N.Y.: The Liberal Arts Press, 1956.

MONTAGU, IVOR, *Film World.* Baltimore: Penguin Books, 1960.

MUENSTERBERG, HUGO, *The Photoplay.* N.Y.: Appleton, 1916.

MUSSMAN, TOBY, ed., *Jean-Luc Godard: A Critical Anthology.* N.Y.: Dutton, 1968.

NEEGAARD, EBBE, *Carl Dreyer: A Film Director's Work.* London: British Film Institute, 1950.

NICOLL, ALLARDYCE, *Film and Theatre.* N.Y.: Crowell, 1936.

NILSSEN, VLADIMIR, *The Cinema as a Graphic Art.* N.Y.: Hill & Wang, 1959.

NIZHNY, VLADIMIR, *Lessons with Eisenstein* (trans. and ed. Ivor Montagu and Jay Leyda). N.Y.: Hill & Wang, 1962.

PEARSON, RALPH, *Experiencing Pictures.* N.Y.: Brewer, Warren & Putman, 1932.

PERRY, GEORGE S., *Films of Alfred Hitchcock.* N.Y. and London: Dutton-Vista, 1965.

PUDOVKIN, V. I., *Film Technique* (trans. Ivor Montagu). London: George Newnes, 1933.

READ, HERBERT, *Concise History of Modern Painting.* N.Y.: Praeger, 1959.

————, *The Philosophy of Modern Art.* N.Y.: Meridian, 1952.

————, *The Meaning of Art.* London: Faber and Faber, 1956.

REISZ, KAREL, *The Technique of Film Editing*. London: Focal Press, 1952.

RENAN, SHELDON, *An Introduction to the American Underground Film*. N.Y.: Dutton, 1967.

RHODE, ERIC, *Tower of Babel*. Philadelphia: Chilton Books, 1967.

RICHIE, DONALD, *The Films of Akira Kurosawa*. Berkeley: University of California Press, 1966.

RICHTER, HANS, *Film Goers of Today, Film Friends of Tomorrow*. Berlin: Herman Reckendorf, 1929.

RODMAN, SELDON, *Conversations with Artists*. N.Y.: Capricorn, 1961.

ROTHA, PAUL and RICHARD GRIFFITH, *Film Till Now*. N.Y.: Twayne, 1960.

——, *Rotha on Film*. London: Faber and Faber, 1958.

——, *Movie Parade*. N.Y.: Studio Publications, 1936.

——, *Celluloid: The Film Today*. N.Y.: Longmans Green, 1931.

SARRIS, ANDREW, *The American Cinema*. N.Y.: Dutton, 1969.

——, ed., *Interviews with Film Directors*. N.Y.: Bobbs-Merrill, 1967.

SETON, MARIE, *Sergei M. Eisenstein*. N.Y.: Grove Press, 1960.

SIMON, JOHN, *Private Screenings*. N.Y.: Macmillan, 1967.

——, *Acid Test*. N.Y.: Stein & Day, 1963.

SMITH, RALPH, ed., *Esthetics and Criticism in Art Education*. Chicago: Rand McNally, 1966.

SONTAG, SUSAN, *Against Interpretation*. N.Y.: Farrar, Straus and Giroux, 1966.

SPOTTISWOODE, RAYMOND, *Grammar of the Film*. Berkeley: University of California Press, 1959.

——, *Film and Its Techniques*. Berkeley: University of California Press, 1957.

STEENE, BIRGITTA, *Ingmar Bergman*. N.Y.: Twayne, 1968.

STEPHENSON, RALPH and J. R. DEBRIX, *The Cinema as Art*. Baltimore: Penguin Books, 1965.

TALBOT, DANIEL, *Film: An Anthology*. N.Y.: Simon and Schuster, 1959.

TAYLOR, JOHN RUSSELL, *Cinema Eye, Cinema Ear*. N.Y.: Hill & Wang, 1964.

TRUFFAUT, FRANÇOIS (with HELEN G. SCOTT), *Hitchcock*. N.Y.: Simon and Schuster, 1967.

TYLER, PARKER, *Classics of the Foreign Film*. N.Y.: Citadel, 1962.

——, *Underground Film*. N.Y.: Grove Press, 1969.

——, *The Three Faces of the Film*. N.Y.: Yoseloff, 1960.

——, *Magic and Myth of the Movies*. N.Y.: Holt, 1947.

WARD, JOHN, *Alain Resnais, or the Theme of Time*. London: Secker & Warburg, 1968.

WARD, ROBIN, *Hitchcock's Films*. N.J.: A. S. Barnes, 1965.

WARSHAW, ROBERT, *The Immediate Experience*. N.Y.: Doubleday, 1962.

WEINBERG, HERMAN, *The Lubitsch Touch*. N.Y.: Dutton, 1968.

———, *Josef von Sternberg*. N.Y.: Dutton, 1967.

ZEVI, BRUNO, *Architecture as Space*. N.Y.: Horizon Press, 1957.

Index